The Importance of Milton Ernest

Village History and Heritage Trail

David Newman

First published 2006

Text © David Newman

ISBN 0-9552927-0-0

ISBN (From 2007) 978-0-9552927-0-5

Published by

11 Arkwright Road
Milton Ernest
Bedford
Bedfordshire
MK44 1SE
01234 822322
thenewmanrace@talk21.com

Printed by

Cromwell Press
Trowbridge
Wiltshire

Front cover illustration: Radwell Road, Milton Ernest, painted in 1999
by David Green of Wilden Gallery, Chequers Hill, Wilden, Bedfordshire.

Researched, Written & Designed by David Newman of Milton Ernest Parish Council.

With thanks to....

Milton Ernest Parish Council, especially Pauline Berry and Deborah Inskip.

P3 (Parish Paths Partnership) – Carrie-Anne Rowley and Ed Burnett.

Bedford Borough Council, Bedfordshire County Council Parish Paths Partnership and the Local Heritage Initiative for the generous grants which funded this book.

Bedfordshire & Luton Archives & Records Service, especially James Collett-White and Trevor Cunnick. Also Pamela Birch, Laura Johnson and Nigel Lutt.

Stephen Coleman and Adrian Fett at Bedfordshire County Council.

The following Milton Ernest Villagers (and ex-Villagers) for their help, photographs and memories:
Rachel Atkinson; Monica Boielle (a former head teacher of Milton Ernest School); Maureen Catlin (Milton Ernest Garden Centre); Bill Dunham; Jane Green; Roger Harris; Clifton Ibbett; Janet Ingle (Milton Ernest Lower School); Kate Jones (Great Grand-Daughter of George Barnett, a former head teacher of Milton Ernest School); Tony Marsh; Bev Plumbley (Queen's Head Hotel); David Purser; Connie Richards; Rob and Kathy Robson; Susan Sail; Peter and Pamela Smith; Harvey Starey; John Starey; Prue and John Harris Watson; George Willars; and Kathleen Willars.

Charles Shepherd for his help in researching the war records of John Michael Bryan.

Roger Pratap of Majesticare and Jan Dobrzanski, for agreeing to the permissive path at Milton Ernest Hall.

Sally Siddons of The Book Castle, 12 Church Street, Dunstable, Beds, LU5 4RU.

And finally to my family, Susan, Amelia and Dylan for supporting me during my quest to produce this book.

Local Heritage *initiative*

Contents

Fig 1 – Children on Bedford Road, which is now the busy A6. Note that the child to the right has a walking stick.

Introduction from the Author

In 1992 I moved to Milton Ernest with my wife Susan. Our home, the middle section of what was originally West Manor Farmhouse, dated back to 1640 and I had the urge to research its history. My early visits to the Records Office in Bedford gave me so much information about the village that I was swamped. Individual pieces of information didn't satisfy my curiosity and I found myself wanting to know more and more about Milton Ernest. Unfortunately, I soon discovered that no-one had written a book on the history of the village, so I couldn't satisfy my thirst for information. Our children, Amelia and Dylan, were then born and the time for research diminished.

By 1999 my thoughts had returned to researching the history of Milton Ernest. I wanted to write a book to be published for the start of the Millennium. However, I underestimated the amount of research involved and probably wasn't helped by my characteristic of wanting to know every last detail! A chance meeting with Jane Green from Milton Ernest, who was also researching the village history, helped spur me on and together we interviewed long standing residents from the village. But two years later I still hadn't finished gathering the data.

In 2001 we moved house within the village, this time to 11 Arkwright Road, and the momentum was lost. However, being elected to Milton Ernest Parish Council in 2003 became the catalyst to completing the research, as I volunteered to be part of a sub-committee which aimed to produce walks in and around the village. A simple heritage walk soon turned into a book, as I had such a vast amount of information at my fingertips from the years of research I had already undertaken. Six final months of gathering data and I was ready to put the information into words. This took longer than expected!

The narrative commenced on 8th March 2004 and just over two years later on 16th April 2006 the book was complete. People who know me are aware of my love for stats, so here goes! According to Microsoft Word's statistics, excluding the considerable time spent on research, this book took me 504 hours to write and edit, which is the equivalent of exactly twenty-one days (three weeks!) of non-stop work. It consists of 82,045 words and 391,193 characters excluding spaces. If you don't believe me, count them for yourself!

Unfortunately writing the book was one thing, getting permission from the illustration copyright owners was another! With 278 figures in the book this was never going to be an easy task, particularly as many of the photographs came from books whose publishers no longer exist. The name of the original photographer or even source of some photographs have been lost in time, which isn't surprising considering some are almost one hundred years old. Thankfully everyone who I managed to contact was more than willing to allow their photograph to be included. Thanks to each and every one of you. In some instances where I have not been able to discover who holds the copyright for the picture, and it hasn't been through the want of trying, I have decided to publish anyway. My view is that it's better for a photograph to be seen and enjoyed than sit and gather dust. My apologies go out to any original owners who come forward after the publication. If you contact me I'll be more than happy to acknowledge you in any future re-issues.

Included with this book is a heritage walk map with a summary of the history of each building. This was the original intention of our P3 (Parish Paths Partnership) group before I got carried away with the project! Hopefully, I have produced the best of both worlds – a detailed history and an abridged version with an easy to follow map which will be easier to use for those people who undertake the heritage trail.

Fourteen years after my initial idea to research the history of my house, here it is, 'The Importance of Milton Ernest', the book I wish I'd had available to me at that time. I hope you enjoy learning about this important village and see the heritage for yourself as you follow the trail around Milton Ernest.

DAVID NEWMAN
2006

In the Village of Milton Ernest.

Fig 2 – Radwell Road looking towards the A6. Note the 'Barracks' on the left and the 'Old Forge Hall' in the distance, both now demolished. The cottage which is now the 'Strawberry Tree' has a complete stone wall which has since been altered to give access to the car park.

2

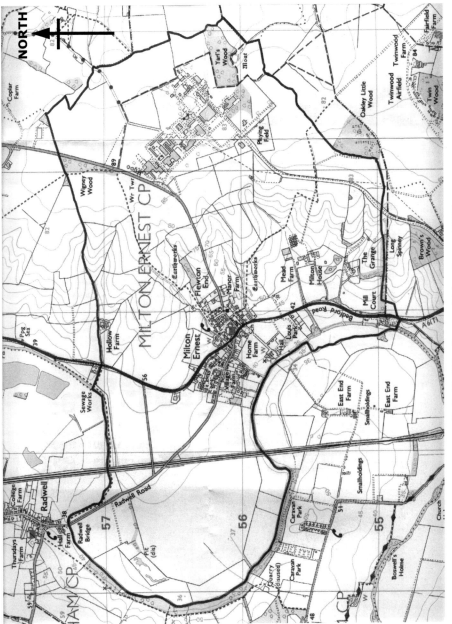

Fig 3 – The Milton Ernest parish boundary as at 2006.

3

The Importance of Milton Ernest

Section One: Four Thousand Years of History

6

The Importance of Milton Ernest Parish History

'The Importance of Milton Ernest' is not just a play on words based on an Oscar Wilde play, but also recognises the events over the last four thousand years which have shaped the village into what it is today. The heritage trail, within this book, gives details of the old buildings that still exist today and even some that have not survived to the twenty first century. What it cannot convey is the importance of the village and its people throughout history. This part of the book is devoted to doing just that, giving the walker a thorough understanding of past times before setting out to see the sites.

Milton Ernest village lies some five miles upstream from Bedford, on the eastern side of the River Great Ouse. The parish has a total area of 1,581 acres and contains the nucleated village and some scattered settlement. The southern and eastern portions of the parish are on high ground (85 metres above sea level) whilst the west is flat and low (35 metres above sea level) and is frequently flooded by the Ouse.

Milton Ernest parish, which is situated in the hundred of Stodden, has a greatest length of 1.3 miles north to south and a greatest breadth east to west of 2.3 miles. It is surrounded by the adjoining parishes of Bletsoe, Thurleigh, Clapham, Oakley, Pavenham and Felmersham.

There are no finds recorded in the parish for the prehistoric period, so the earliest known evidence of settlement in Milton Ernest is the Bronze Age (2500BC to 700BC). A number of ploughed out round barrows have been identified, most of which are situated on the flood plain of the River Great Ouse just above the level of the water table. At this time the countryside was mainly woodland so near to the river would have been an ideal place to settle. The river would have been their 'road' in and out of the settlement.

Iron Age (700BC to 55BC) settlement evidence has been discovered on the highest ground in the east of the parish. Two dark areas with large burnt pebbles, typical of sites of this period, and pottery were found. One site (south west of Yarl's Wood) was isolated, with the other (south of Wigney Wood) being on the edge of a large iron slag patch. These patches were formed as a by-product of an iron smelting process. As there is no iron ore in the district, their presence indicates that the ore was brought to the higher land of Milton Ernest because it was once abundant in woodland. Here there was enough fuel to make the fire to create the iron.

The next evidence of occupation is of the Romano-British period (55BC to 410AD). There is evidence of two such sites, both isolated, in the parish, one of which is next to a small quarry (north of New Road to the east of the railway line) while the other is just south of Yarl's Wood. Also at the bottom of River Lane it is thought that the Romans built a ford to cross the river. Certainly there is no doubt that there was a ford, as it is marked on historic maps, and the Roman theory has some credence, as when the river was dredged in the twentieth century a number of Roman coins and paving slabs were brought up from the river bed.

Other Roman artefacts include coins presented to Benjamin Helps Starey in 1862. These had been found during digging work at Milton Ernest Hall and included one of Constantine the Great (274AD to 337AD). Five years earlier the Reverend Charles Colyear Beaty-Pownall gave an account of Roman remains found during the construction of the railway through the parish. He also found a Roman quern of puddingstone in the grounds of the vicarage. A quern is a small stone device for hand grinding grain to make flour for bread making, while puddingstone is formed from a number of small rocks solidified together in naturally occurring cement.

In 1937 a dense scatter of pottery was found in the garden of Chestnut Cottage on Bedford Road, which suggested that a Roman potter may have been based there. And in 1961 during an excavation at Yarl's Wood, Roman pottery was found and evidence of Roman occupation. All of this evidence suggests that the Romans settled in Milton Ernest.

After the Roman period, the next suggestion of settlement comes from the name Yarl's Wood which is probably of Scandinavian origin.

By the start of the medieval period (1066 to 1485) the Domesday Book of 1086 shows that the settlement was then known as Mildentone or Middeltone, meaning 'Middle Farm'. The name was probably derived as the village is midway between Clapham and Sharnbrook as you travel up the Ouse. This would suggest that the name Middeltone originated after the surrounding area was occupied.

The Domesday Book recorded the disposition of wealth and power in England twenty years after the Norman Conquest. Size of the land was measured, for tax purposes, in hides (approximately 120 acres) and virgates of which there were four to the hide. The four main Milton Ernest landowners listed in the Domesday Book were: Adeliza, wife of Hugh de Grandmesnil (3 hides 1 virgate) with Ivo, steward of Hugh de Grandmesnil, as tenant; Nigel d'Aubigny (2 hides 3 virgates) who had a tenant called Turgis; Walter the Fleming (2 hides), his tenant being Reginald; and Hugh de Beauchamp (1 hide 3.5 virgates) with William Basset as tenant.

These estates of the landowners were later known as manors. The Manor of Middeltone (Adeliza's land) was centred on the present site of East Manor Farm, and the Manor of Bassets is where Milton Ernest Hall is sited. There was a further Manor known as Babs which wasn't mentioned until 1544. Babs Manor was probably sited on the earthworks to the south of East Manor Farm (Thurleigh Road), as old maps denote a Babs Lane and a Babs Close in this area. However, just to confuse matters, Thomas Fisher, Ellis Shipley and Samuel Wyatt sold West Manor Farm (Radwell Road) in 1804 to Serjeant Vaughan under the name 'Manor of Babs'. Appendix 2 which denotes the owners and tenants of each manor in Milton Ernest records that William Babyngton owned the Manor of Bassets in 1414. Could Babs Manor have once been part of Bassets Manor and the name been derived from Babyngton or is this just a coincidence? Unless some documentary evidence is discovered the exact whereabouts of Babs Manor will remain a mystery.

Fig 4 - The Erneys Family Coat of Arms.

The Manor of Bassets was held by the local Basset family until 1372 while during the period from the thirteenth century to the early part of the sixteenth century the Manor of Middeltone was owned by the de Grey family. The chief tenants of the de Greys were the family of Erneys or Hernis. The first mention of them occurs in 1221, when it is recorded that John de Hertewell owed 'half a mark for having brought a suit against Robert son of Ernis for land in Middelton'. It seems that the Hertewell family had acquired the land which belonged to Nigel d'Aubigny at Domesday, before seeing it be absorbed into the land owned by the Erneys family.

It was through the Erneys family that the village took its distinctive name – from Middeltone to Middleton Ernys (thirteenth century) to Milton Herneys (fourteenth century) to Mylton Harneys (fifteenth century) to Milton Harnes (sixteenth century) to Milton Ernesse (seventeenth century) before arriving at Milton Ernest.

A manor for which no name has been recorded but which belonged to Walter the Fleming in 1086 became part of the barony of Wahull until at least 1537. Known tenants were William de Lega (1279) and Peter Hulier (1371).

In 1227 there is reference to a hermitage owned by Newnham Priory. This was located on the outskirts of the parish just south of Yarl's Wood. The name hermitage refers to the home of a religious individual or group seeking solitude and isolation. As the priory became richer this religious retreat grew and developed into a manor house surrounded by a moat for protection.

Fig 5 – The hermitage entrance uncovered during the 1961 archaeological excavation.

Fig 6 – The heraldic pendant shield discovered during the dig at the hermitage.

On 18th July 1271 records show that Simon Langhoe, "....namely a cottager and clerk of the chapel, took a stoup in his hand, intending to go and milk the cow in the court-yard of the priory barn in the hermitage and as he came to the middle of the court-yard he had an illness called 'Mal de flaunke' (*a kick in the ribs*) fell down and immediately died by misadventure....".

In 1961 the hermitage site was excavated revealing a small stone building with two rooms and outhouses. Pottery and other artefacts, including a heraldic pendant shield circa 1350, indicate occupation from the twelfth to the sixteenth century. This fits in with the archives which record that a disastrous fire swept through the whole establishment in the late sixteenth century, destroying the hermitage.

By the early part of the fourteenth century, probably between 1300 and 1320, the population of Milton Ernest had reached a maximum and every available acre of land was cultivated right up to the parish boundary. The size of the village itself has since greatly shrunk and is still only about half of its fourteenth century area. This decrease in size originated with the overpopulation of the land and the consequent under nourishment of the villagers. Under Section 1 of the Ancient Monuments and Archaeological Areas Act, 1979, two sites in the village have been registered as a monument under the title 'Shrunken Medieval Village at Milton Ernest'. The areas of importance are the earthworks which run north-east for 420 metres from Flewton End, and a 320 metres long field to the south of East Manor Farm. These earthworks give an indication as to the extent of the medieval village boundary and contain banks and ditches which define tracks, plot and field boundaries. There is also evidence of house platforms alongside the tracks. Although over three thousand shrunken medieval villages are recorded nationally, Milton Ernest is important as it is particularly well preserved.

Fig 7 – A painting of Milton Ernest Church, the Vicarage and Thurleigh Road by Thomas Fisher circa 1820.

The population of the village did not completely recover due to ensuing epidemics and because of the increase in the profitability of sheep farming in the fifteenth century and the consequent need for less labour.

Bubonic Plague was said to have visited Milton Ernest in 1557. The burial register for the village does support this view, as between 1557 and 1559 there were 60 deaths, an average of twenty per year. In the twenty years before this period and the twenty years after, there was an average of fewer than five deaths per year. This Black Death was spread by rat fleas. Once bitten people would develop flu like symptoms and usually died within days.

On the death of Walter Erneys in the mid sixteenth century, probably through the plague, the Erneys male line failed and the Manor of Milton Ernest was divided amongst his daughters. One of these married Christopher Turnor from Haverhill, Suffolk, another married William Strange and a third daughter gave her share of the manor to Edmund

Turnor, son of the aforementioned Christopher. This meant that the Turnor family owned the Manor of Milton Ernest.

Meanwhile by 1578 Thomas Rolt had bought the Manor of Bassets, the third share in the Manor of Milton Ernest from William Strange and the land which once belonged to the nameless manor recorded in the Domesday Book. The FitzGeffrey family had owned this manor from 1511. A widow, Judith FitzGeffrey married John Rolt, Thomas' son, which helped him attain the land. The three areas of land purchased by Thomas Rolt were amalgamated under the title of the Manor of Bassets.

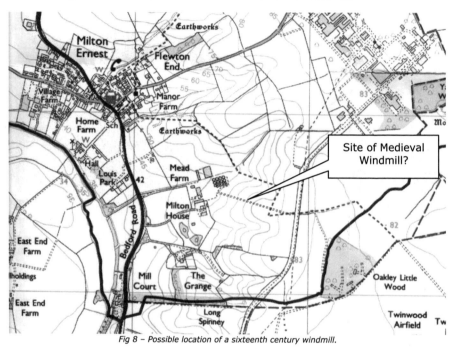

Fig 8 – Possible location of a sixteenth century windmill.

With the nameless manor being absorbed and the ownership of the Manor of Babs changing hands on a regular basis, the principal land owners in Milton Ernest for almost two hundred years were the Turnor and Rolt families. By the nineteenth century the manors of Milton Ernest and Bassets would be sold on a frequent basis and never remained in the hands of any one family for long, while the Manor of Babs disappeared from the records.

At the time of the dissolution of the monasteries (1536) several mills were owned by Warden Abbey. It is thought that one of these may have been a windmill located on the west facing slope to the south of the village (on the track just to the east of Milton House).

In 1576 a tragedy occurred in the village as the parish burial registers hold the following entry "Upon the second day of July 76 were buries these men that were drowned in the water by misadventure". The men in question were George Newcom, Richard Emerye, Nicholas Kinge and Arian Aprupe. There are no records as to what exactly happened but it must have been a time of great shock and sadness for such a small village to lose four of its men folk in such circumstances.

Two years later, in 1578, records for 'Milton Harnes' mention that "there is a suspicion of whoredom betweene William Swyngland and John Fletchers wyfe".

Fig 9 – The Manor of Milton Ernest, later called East Manor Farm, now known as The Manor House. This snowy scene, circa 1940, was taken from fields near Thurleigh Road looking westwards towards Milton Ernest. The picture gives a feeling of how the area would have looked four hundred years ago.

In 1584 a bishop visited Milton Ernest and the villagers informed on their vicar, Robert Sutton, for quarrelling with his neighbours and for being in the alehouse at unlawful times of the night!

On 20th June 1603 Jane Howe was baptised. She was the daughter of Mary Howe who was recorded in the parish register as a harlot! Although the term refers to a prostitute, it has also been used to describe a common woman servant or a woman tramp. Therefore it is difficult to conclude as to whether the oldest profession was being worked in Milton Ernest in the early seventeenth century!

In a 1605 will, John Smith, yeoman (a farmer who farmed his own lands), left his wife, Elizabeth, "a swarm of bees"!

Times were hard in the early seventeenth century as can be seen from the records of the Archdeacon's Courts. These were regularly held and disciplined people for every conceivable offence against morals and ecclesiastical discipline. Three parishioners of 'Milton Ernys' are known to have come under the lash of the court. They were Leonard Willimot for carting on St. Luke's Day; James Hailey for winnowing corn on Easter Tuesday; and Walter Griffin for "putting upp netts and catching larks on a holliday". Griffin was sentenced under the Archdeacon of Bedford's Administration Act at Ampthill in February 1616.

On 18th May 1619 Richard Fisher, a yeoman of Milton Ernest, was buried at All Saints' Church. Shortly after his death an inventory was produced, dated 25th May 1619, which gives a fascinating insight into his house and belongings. The inventory is reproduced below with the original spellings.

His weringe apparrell, his Bibell, his sword & fowling peece, £5.

In the hall

ij formes, ij chares, ij stowles, ij lininge wheeles, one cheese presse, one kneading troughe, 6s. 8d.

one barrell, one pouldringe tubbe, one tabel, one littell cofer, 3s 4d.

one mashing fatt, one tubbe, one stoupe, one paile, one mustard querne, one boule, one sothing dishe, 9 chesfatts, 10s.

one brasse pan, one copper, iij kettels, ij brasse potts, one posnete, one warminge pan, ij spicemorters, ij chafingdishes, 50s.

one dripping pan, ij cobirons, ij andirons, ij spitts, one gridiron, one fireshovle, one pare of tonges, ij pare of pott hookes, one racke, one fring pan, 10s.

In the parlor

one table, one cubbard, one cheste, one chare, one buffetstoule, one drinkestalle, 40s.

iiij drinke barrills, one salteing troughe, one cherme, ij tubbs, 5 boules, one wodden traye, one meale barrell, one tunnell, trenchers one dussine, ij bordes & other implements there, 30s xx puter dishes, viij porringers, vj fruite dishes, one quarte pott, v tunes, one puter boule, ij salts, ij puter candelsticks, ij lathine candels, spounes ij dussine, 53s. 4d.

one pare of ballances, one breadgraite, one leaden weight, one pare of bellowes, 2s. 6d.

In the chamber over the hall

one pare of flexen sheets, v pare of hempe teare sheets, vj tabel napkings, one flexen towell, iij flexen cubbard clothes, ij flexen tabelclothes, one harden tabelclothe, iij flexen pillowbeeres, & iij hand towells, £3.

In the chamber over the parlor

one borded bedsteade, iij coofers, ij bords, one truncke, one wollen wheele, ij hechells, 18s.

one fetherbeed, one boulster, ij pillowes, one matteris, ij coverlidds, iij blankets, 50s.

ij fishe netts & died woll, 28s.

flex & ij pare of fullers sheeres, 40s.

one pare of stockecards & ij pare of wollcards, 2s. 6d.

cheese & bacon, 30s.

one tenor saw, one hande sawe, one axe, one addes, iiij augers, one chissell, one drawing knife, 5s.

one pychpan, one sheepe brand & other ould iron, 6s.

In the servants chamber

One borded bedsteade, one boulster, one coveringe, one blancket, 3s. 4d.

In the pasture and yearde

viij kyne, one horse, £30.

one pare of tentors, fullinge earth & wood to burne, 36s.

ij stockes of bees, 10s.

ij swine hodges, 26s. 8d.

one ladder & pullin, 4s. 10d.

one pare of cartgeeres, one cart saddell, one pare of cartroopes, iiij mullinge halters, a shoodd carte, £3. 6s. 8d.

In 1633 the Manor of Milton Ernest was confiscated from Christopher Turnor (born 1607) when he was charged with delinquency. However, the charge wasn't proven and the estate was returned, but not until 1647, some fourteen years later! Christopher was immediately knighted and created third baron of the Exchequer. In 1664 he sat on the commission which condemned to death those Puritans implicated in the Northern Plot. Christopher Turnor was also a member of the special court created to adjudicate between owners and occupiers of property ravaged by the Great Fire of London in 1666. When he died in 1675 having outlived his son and grandson, the manor was purchased by his younger brother Edmund who built six almshouses in the village in 1695. These were endowed with thirty one acres of land and were to provide a refuge for the aged.

Fig 10 – A painting by Thomas Fisher, circa 1820, of the Almshouses at Milton Ernest.

The Manor of Milton Ernest was owned by the Turnor family until 1715, a total of 165 years.

Meanwhile the Manor of Bassets continued to be held by the Rolt family until 1746, giving them 184 years of ownership. The most famous person of the family being Samuel Rolt, a member of Parliament, who died in 1717. In 1729 Thomas Rolt erected an unusual bread box in the church which was designed to hold twelve loaves for distribution to the poor every Sunday. This was in memory of his wife, Susanna, who died in 1726 and made the provision in her will.

The population of Milton Ernest in the mid seventeenth century can be estimated at 200 based on the Hearth Tax returns of 1671.

The earliest recorded industrial activity apart from milling is weaving. Thomas Jackson left his daughter Elizabeth, "my three loomes in my shopp" in his Will dated 1605. How long textile manufacture lasted in Milton Ernest is unknown, but there is no mention in the nineteenth century trade directories. The village also had a victualler (either a food

16

shop keeper or inn keeper who provided meals) called Robert Stratton in 1615 and even a printer named Underhill Robinson at the start of the eighteenth century. John Chapman was described as a 'lace buyer' in 1641, the first known lace dealer in the Ouse Valley. Two Stone Masons are recorded in 1744.

In the seventeenth century barges came up the Ouse from Pavenham carrying stone from the quarries which was used to build cottages in the village.

A charge of bastardy was brought against John Williamson of Milton Ernest and Anne Grange of Bletsoe in April 1725. An act of 1576 allowed Justices to imprison the parents of an illegitimate child. The records do not show the outcome of this particular case.

On 11th September 1729 a warrant for regimental transport was issued to the constables of Milton Ernest. The constables were ordered to carry the baggage of the Duke of Bolton's Regiment from the Castle Inn, Bedford, to Northampton on the following day.

The earliest records for The Queen's Head and The Swan public houses date back to 1733 and 1785 respectively, although pubs were in the village a lot earlier than these dates. For example, in 1584, Robert Sutton, the vicar, was accused of "being in the alehouse at unlawful times of the night"! Other earlier records of pubs are in the wills of Godfrey Moore (1671) and Richard Teedon (1712) who are both recorded as being an 'inn holder' and also by the marriage entry of Essex Archer, who was a Milton Ernest inn keeper in 1698. Whether these three men, and the aforementioned Robert Stratton, were the host of the Queen's Head or The Swan or a different establishment altogether cannot be determined.

John Peck (1736-1776), who was a relative of the Peck clockmakers of Bolnhurst, is known to have made clocks in Milton Ernest from 1759 to 1776. The family must have continued the trade in the village, as silver watches dated 1840 and 1842 exist with the inscription 'John Peck of Milton', and Reginald Parrott, recalls, in his memoirs, that his family owned a grandfather clock with a beautiful brass dial bearing the name 'John Peck, Milton'. The Pecks lived and worked in a cottage facing 'The Green'. By 1974 all that was left standing of this cottage, where Reginald Parrott was born, was one gable end with a date stone inscribed 1749. It has since been demolished.

Fig 11 – A grandfather clock which was made in Milton Ernest by John Peck.

Fig 12 – A close up of the clock with the inscription, John Peck MILTON

On 3rd November 1740, Abraham Robinson was buried in the churchyard having 'perish't in ye snow'. He was fifty-two. Sadly, the next person to be buried at Milton Ernest was his son, also called Abraham, who drowned aged just ten. Heartbreaking times for Mary Robinson, the wife and mother.

At the Elders Conference of the Moravian Church, held in Bedford on 15th April 1758, the following was recorded: "We are at a loss with Widow Sturges in Milton. She is an old pious dry woman that came by mistake among us; we therefore asked our Saviour, whether we should entirely leave her to her own way?" The answer was no.

The Archdeaconry Courts of Bedford on 22nd April 1776 issued orders of penance against Ann Cox and James Brown who were found guilty of adultery. On 16th February 1778 Elizabeth Grigg was also issued with an order of penance, this time for fornication. A penance being a punishment that someone willingly suffers to show that they regret something wrong that they have done.

In 1779, Lawrence Sparks, a blacksmith of Milton Ernest, appeared at the Bedfordshire Quarter Sessions and was found guilty of keeping a gun when not qualified. He was fined £5.

The year 1784 saw an epidemic of "fever" in the village which claimed ten of the fourteen people who were buried in All Saints'. The fever claimed the lives of the following villagers: James Little (aged 54), Hannah Asku (39), Henry Asku (15 months), John Walker (47), John Asku (39), Elizabeth Swain (17 months), John Waldick (18), Ann Brown (26), Abraham Little (60) and John Tabert (46). The Asku family were the worst affected with John and Hannah, who had married on 11th October 1764, and their son, Henry, all losing their lives. John's father Stephen Asku had also died from the fever some five months earlier.

Over time roads through Milton Ernest have disappeared. Two of them used to go to Thurleigh, one of which went through the earthworks to the north of the village. The other was a continuation of the present Thurleigh Road and went on a direct north eastern route to Thurleigh rather than the current north detour, built after the Second World War, to Wigney Wood. Other roads, now gone, included one to the Hermitage; Babs Lane, which ran through the earthworks to the south of East Manor Farm; one from Milton Ernest to Ravensden; and Ashtree Field Road, which started at Green Farm and headed north.

At the time of the 1803 Enclosure Act, when communal large open fields were divided up into hedged or fenced privately owned fields, the village was nucleated around the church and the green with some linear development along the road towards Radwell. At this time there were two sites for quarrying, the Radwell and Thurleigh Roads were established and the parish had three woods covering 53 acres – Lawn, Yarl's, and Wigney. Lawn Wood was joined to the north of Yarl's Wood but is now arable land. The woods would have been banked for animal keeping.

Fig 13 – Rushden Road in the early twentieth century.

Bedfordshire Quarter Sessions Rolls record what is described as a "riot" at Milton Ernest in 1821. Thomas Hine, a farmer and constable in Milton Ernest, gave evidence. He was called out of his bed between twelve and one o'clock on a Sunday morning and was told that if he did not get up immediately and go into the street opposite the Queen's Head (*presumably Thurleigh Road*) "murder would ensue". When Thomas Hine arrived on the scene everyone had gone back into the Queen's Head. He went inside and ordered them to leave the premises and "they went out pretty quiet". Hine charged them to go home but some went into the Swan. Again he ordered them to go home but they "proceeded up the street making a great noise" and threw several stones at him. Henry Hart and Joseph Parrott then began to fight. Thomas Hine got hold of Hart to take him into custody but John Solesbury then struck Hine with the intention of liberating Hart. Hine let go of Hart and seized Solesbury instead. He was leading Solesbury away when he was suddenly surrounded by 20 to 30 men. "The mob cried out put them in the pond (*it would seem there was a pond in Radwell Road at this time*) and we were driven twenty yards until we were on the brink of it". Then after "much pulling me and my assistants about rescued the prisoner". One of the assistants, John Sturges, senior, a labourer of Milton Ernest, also gave evidence. He had hold of Solesbury by the collar on the edge of the pond but he was "pulled away from me with such violence that he left his shirt collar in my hand". Sturges also stated that "Henry Hart was one of the persons who struck at me with his fist. Edward Hart shoved and pulled me about. I heard the voice of William Brown swearing in the mob. Thomas Griggs was shoving me and Mr Hine about". Eventually the situation must have been resolved. Unfortunately, the records do not show the outcome of the case nor of any punishments which might have been issued.

Fig 14 – Milton Ernest's local policeman in conversation with George Robinson on Thurleigh Road, circa 1940.

Fig 15 – The Police House, Milton Ernest, 1965.

Fig 16 – PC 187 outside the Police House, 1965.

As the 1821 incident highlights, Milton Ernest used to have its own policeman. A purpose built police house was built on Rushden Road. This was located on the right hand side of what is now the A6 as you head north. Maps show that there has been a building on this site for at least two hundred years. Whether it was always the site of the police house is unknown. Certainly in 1965 a modern looking police house was sited there. At that time the policeman's beat was Milton Ernest, Felmersham, Radwell and Pavenham, all visited by bicycle. Today the 'Old Police House' has been significantly changed and converted into a residential property.

In the mid nineteenth century there were three abortive schemes to build railways northwards from Bedford which involved Milton Ernest. In 1845, the Leicester & Bedford Railway plotted a line which in Bedfordshire would have gone through Sharnbrook, Milton Ernest, and then slightly to the east of the present mainline railway station in Bedford. The company's bill was rejected in the Lords and their assets were purchased by the Midland Railway Company.

The Southern Midland Railway also attempted to build a line close to Bletsoe and Milton Ernest in 1845. The route was surveyed by Robert Stephenson (1803-1859, son of George Stephenson whom he helped build 'The Locomotive' and 'The Rocket' steam locomotives) and it would have run to St John's Station in Bedford. Again it was rejected in Parliament and again the Midland stepped in and purchased the assets.

The London & Nottingham Railway plotted a line through Bletsoe and Milton Grange to Clapham Road, Bedford but the company was wound up. Eventually the Midland Railway was commenced in 1855, opened in 1857 and widened in 1871. The workers lived in huts built by the side of the newly-constructed railway line. Many people will have since glanced out of their train carriage and seen the small settlement of Milton Ernest. Amongst them could have been Charles Dickens who wrote to a Bedford paper complaining about the speed of the train journey between Leicester and Bedford!

In 1834 the Oakley Hunt built kennels in Milton Ernest and these remained until 1972.

A brickyard at the north end of the village was known to be in operation at least between 1847 and 1869, but the site was presumably no longer used in 1882 as it was shown as the 'Old clay pits' on a map from that year.

Census data taken in Victorian times gives an interesting insight into the constitution of Milton Ernest. For example the number of homes rose from 92 in 1841 to 113 in 1891. In the same period the population decreased from 446 to 413. Incredibly, 279 (63%) of the villagers in 1851 were actually born in Milton Ernest. A further 23% were born in Bedfordshire, leaving just 14% of the village population being born outside of the county. It certainly was a local community in those days.

The census also shows the occupations of the villagers. Employment dropped from 60% (267 people) of the population in 1841 to just 40% (167 people) in 1891. This seems to be mainly due to the decline of the local lace trade. In 1841 there were 96 lace makers, some as young as six years old. By 1891 this total had fallen to just 13. These numbers represented a fall from 36% of the working population to just 8%. The reason for the down turn in the fortunes of the hand made lace makers can be attributed to the increase in machine made lace, which although not of the same quality was acceptable to the popular market.

Fig 17 – Milton Mill.

The other main occupation for the villagers was agricultural labourer, with a consistent third of those people employed listing this as their profession in the censuses between 1841 and 1891.

Victorian trade directories show Milton Ernest as being a self contained village. In addition to lace makers and agricultural labourers there were around thirty different trades, including baker (2 in the village), beer retailer, blacksmith (2), brewer, brick maker, builder, butcher (2), carpenter (2), carrier (2), coal dealer, draining pipe manufacturer, draper, farmer (5), general dealer, grocer, huntsman, innkeeper (2), maltster, miller, post office, shepherd, school master and mistress, shoemaker, shopkeeper (2), tailor, thatcher, vicar and wheelwright.

In the mid nineteenth century the noted church architect William Butterfield was active in the village, designing Milton Ernest Hall. He also built Milton Mill in 1857 and Meadow End House in 1867, both of which lie to the south of the village.

Milton Mill cost £1,500 to build and was occupied by Frederick Newbery and his family from the day it opened until at least 1903. Newbery employed five men and four boys at the Mill. He also farmed 100 acres and employed a further five men and two boys for this purpose. After Newbery, Harry Curtis and then Charles Quenby, who fought in the Boer War, were the village millers.

Earlier records show that Milton Ernest had one mill at the time of the Domesday Book. This was owned by the wife of Hugh de Grandmesnil. In 1279 the Abbott of Warden rented a mill worth seven shillings from John Ernys. William Ireland, a miller, was buried in Milton Ernest in 1555. Other archives record four mills in 1639 and five in 1735.

Even in a time without cars the roads were not safe as this report from the Saturday 3rd July 1875 edition of the Bedfordshire Times proves: "A fatal accident occurred at this village on Thursday week, when a child named William Farrer was run over by a cart, whilst playing in the road. He only breathed once after being picked up. An inquest was held on the next day at the Queen's Head. Accidental death". The burial register records that William Henry Farrer died on 24th June 1875 at the age of just one year and seven months.

In 1891 there was an "incident of amusing character" in Milton Ernest. Bedford Mercury reported that on Thursday 16th April "two men, strangers and foreigners, visited this village with bagpipes and a performing monkey. The men stopped to take refreshment chaining, their performer outside to the scraper; not liking his position Jacko very soon managed to break loose and made off to a neighbouring farm. He soon scaled the water pipe, on reaching the roof ran up the tiles and placed himself upon the ridge of the farm house to the astonishment of all. After some considerable time he was coaxed down with milk in a basin, when his masters felt making sure of him but failed. Not being satisfied he made the second attempt and ran across a cow yard into a shed, when several, with the masters, went in to him. After a diligent search he was found hidden under a machine and was soon captured. When made secure he had a beating for his trouble. His chain was soon mended and then began his performances to the bagpipes".

The Local Government Act of 1894 established parish councils. The Act specified that such bodies should be elected in rural areas with a population of over 300. Milton Ernest had a population of 413 at the time and therefore a parish council was a requirement of the Act. A poll was held on 17th December and those elected met in the village schoolroom at 6.30pm on 31st December 1894 for the first meeting of Milton Ernest Parish Council.

At the inaugural meeting Hugh Andrew, who had polled the most votes, took temporary chairmanship and proposed that there should be an 'outside' chairman and put forward the Reverend John James Burton who hadn't been elected through the poll. The decision was unanimously accepted and the vicar ran the rest of the meeting. Thomas Street, the farmer from East Manor Farm, decided not to take up office and his position was taken by William Musgrove at the second meeting on 29th January 1895. The first ever Milton Ernest Parish Councillors were as follows, with the votes received in the 17th December 1894 poll in brackets:

Chairman John James Burton (n/a) – Vicar – Vicarage.
Vice Chairman Hugh Andrew (44) – Farmer – West Manor Farm – Age 39.
Clerk Frederick Newbery (43) – Miller & Farmer – Milton Mill – Age 63.
Councillor Stephen Hooker (39) – Machinist – Radwell Road – Age 31.
Councillor George Parrott (38) – Thatcher – River Lane – Age 61.
Councillor Alfred Chapman (36) – Justice of the Peace – Milton Ernest Hall.
Councillor William Horne (31) – Agricultural Labourer – River Lane – Age 33.
William Musgrove (22) – Gardener – Bedford Road – Age 54.

Two further decisions were made at that first meeting on New Years Eve 1894. It was decided that Milton Ernest Parish Council would hold bi-monthly meetings and meet on the last Tuesday of the months of January, March, May, July, September and October. There would also be an Annual General Meeting in April. The other decision related to the appointment of the Clerk. An extract taken from the minutes of the meeting are transcribed below:

'The Chairman stated that under the provisions of the Act, the Council was not free to appoint whoever they might choose, as a salaried Clerk. In a parish where there is an Assistant Overseer nominated by the Vestry, and appointed by the Justices, such Assistant Overseer "will be the Clerk" unless the Council appoint one of their number to act as Clerk without salary. Mrs Emma Mole being the Assistant Overseer appointed in this manner, the office would necessarily devolve upon her, if none of the Councillors would take it without salary. After full discussion it was unanimously resolved, that considering the difficulties in the way of a woman holding this office, one of the Councillors should be Clerk without salary'.

How times change. In 1894 Emma Mole wasn't given the position of Clerk as she was a woman. In 2005 Milton Ernest Parish Council not only has a woman Clerk but also a woman Chair and two women Councillors. It can only be wondered what the 1894 parish council would have thought of that!

Chair	From	Period as Chair of MEPC	
		Years	Months
Reverend John Burton	31 Dec 1894	1	11
Mr Hugh Andrew	24 Nov 1896	1	5
Mr George Barnett	19 Apr 1898	4	6
Mr Frederick Newbery	28 Oct 1902	0	10
Mr Stephen Hooker	11 Aug 1903	1	5
Mr Samuel Marsh	31 Jan 1905	3	2
Lord Ampthill	13 Mar 1908	6	4
Mr Samuel Marsh (Second term)	31 Jul 1914	7	9
Mr William Rowlatt	19 Apr 1922	12	0
Mr John Underwood	16 Apr 1934	2	11
Captain Stephen Starey	15 Mar 1937	12	3
Mr Ernest Page	7 Jun 1949	17	2
Brigadier H. Hutchinson	4 Aug 1966	1	4
Mr J. Ritson	5 Dec 1967	1	4
Mr Neil Winter	24 Mar 1969	6	1
Mr G. Tucker	29 Apr 1975	4	2
Mr Brian Lewis	5 Jun 1979	1	11
Mr C. Izzard	5 May 1981	2	0
Mr Neil Winter (Second term)	17 May 1983	2	0
Mr Robert Lincoln	7 May 1985	4	0
Mr Neil Winter (Third term)	23 May 1989	2	0
Mr Anthony Wittering	2 May 1991	5	2
Mrs Mary Jackson	4 Jul 1996	4	10
Mr Richard Ward	3 May 2001	3	0
Mrs Deborah Inskip	6 May 2004		

Fig 18 – The Chairs of Milton Ernest Parish Council. 22 different people have chaired the Council in 110 years, an average of 5 years each. Ernest Page, Stephen Starey, William Rowlatt, Samuel Marsh and Neil Winter all chaired the Council for over ten years.

An old Milton Ernest tradition used to take place on Plough Monday. This involved the boys of the village blackening their faces and walking around the village carrying sticks and twigs. They would sing traditional songs and beg for money.

Between 1910 and 1913 there are records of a racehorse, owned by Hugh Peel, called 'Milton Ernest'. Any connection with the village is unknown. 'Milton Ernest' the racehorse had a bright start, coming fourth in its first race when fifteen horses didn't finish, and then winning at Wolverhampton on 31st March 1910. However in the next three races 'Milton Ernest' came last, fell and was last again. The surviving records show 'Milton Ernest' as competing in eleven races, winning just the once and being placed in the top four on four other occasions.

In 1914, at the start of the First World War, army officers of the Veterinary Corps, an off-shoot of the 51st Highland Division, arrived in the village. They commandeered all available stabling including most of the kennels of the Oakley Hunt. New sheds sprang up in suitable fields and these formed part of the hospital for the sick and wounded horses. At the time horses had an important role to play in war as they were the main means of transport for hauling the guns, carriages and wagons. Route marches took place through Milton Ernest with kilted soldiers marching four deep, with each company headed with its band of bagpipes and drums. By 1915 the village filled up with men to look after the horses. Not just soldiers though, as men from farms in neighbouring villages came to work as civilians attracted by a wage higher than they would have got on the farm. One army drummer boy set up a barber's shop in Milton Ernest, hiring a room in a house, and by all accounts did a roaring trade.

Fig 19 – A German Zeppelin over Milton Ernest. Photograph taken by George Barnett, Headmaster of Milton Ernest School, circa WWI. The photograph has seen better days but its inclusion is warranted as it is unique.

Soon after the outbreak of WWI, King George V and Queen Mary evacuated some of their family from Buckingham Palace. Two of the young princes stayed with Lady Ampthill at Milton Ernest Hall for safety and were watched over day and night by two detectives. They later became King Edward VIII and King George VI.

Displayed in All Saints' Church is the Milton Ernest Roll of Honour which lists seventy three people from the village who took part in the First World

War. The majority went to either the Western Front or Egypt. The Horne family from Milton Ernest were well represented with six of the men volunteering to fight for their country. They were Albert Horne, who served on HMS Neptune (which was at the Battle of Jutland in 1916) and witnessed the sinking of HMS Vanguard with the loss of over 800 lives on 9th July 1917 at Scapa Flow; Daniel Horne; Ernest Horne, who fought at the Somme; George Horne; Thomas Horne, who was seriously wounded twice before being killed in action; and William Horne, who was wounded at Gallipoli.

In all ten soldiers from the village lost their lives in the Great War. Three more were to die in World War Two.

Fig 20 – Milton Ernest Women's Institute tea party at Mill House, 1923.

Stephen Hooker, whose headed note paper advertised him as a "Motor and Cycle Engineer" with "motor cycles and cycles in stock", applied for planning permission on March 31st 1930 for a garage and petrol filling station. The application was successful and the petrol station stood for many years on what is now the A6 just before the bend as you head towards Rushden. Stephen's son, Wesley Hooker, was the manager of the garage. The business eventually moved to Bedford and became the well known company, "Hooker & Roberts".

In 1937 Stephen Starey, of Milton Ernest Hall, submitted plans for a smallpox hospital. These were approved on 19th June and the isolation hospital was built in a field off Thurleigh Road. It was about a mile from the village and the only access from the road was via a rough grass track. This wooden hospital stood in a compound of about an acre and was enclosed by a wooden fence. The building, which was unmanned when there were no patients, had two sections. One for nurses and staff, the other for those with smallpox consisted of two wards, one for men and one for women. After the hospital was no longer required it was sold to a private owner for use as a domestic residence. It has since been demolished.

Fig 21 – Thurleigh Road, 1939, as you head out of Milton Ernest. Note the narrowness of the road.

In the Second World War, Milton Ernest thankfully wasn't troubled significantly by air raids. Records from the Home Farm ARP (Air Raid Precautions) post at Milton Ernest have the following entries where German bombers came close to the village:

Saturday 3rd August 1940 – Bomb explosion heard 22:15 about three miles away.

Tuesday 24th September 1940 – Heard repeated machines over for some time 01:40.

Thursday 3rd October 1940 – Bomb rattled front door. Plane overhead approx 20:35. 20:45 area control reported a bomb has been dropped on the outskirts of our parish. It has not been possible to locate it. It is unlikely to have caused any damage except possibly to livestock.

Sunday 13th October 1940 – 2 Bombs 00:10.

Saturday 19th October 1940 – Machines overhead 00:59.

Saturday 14th June 1941 – 5 bombs near enough to shake 01:07.

Sunday 29th June 1941 – 4 bombs heard 01:47.

The ARP wardens at Milton Ernest were Captain and Mrs Starey, Mr Barratt, John Ames and C. R. Haycock. Also available "if at home" were H. Godwin and F. Woodson. Milton Ernest also had a Home Guard led by Captain S. H. Starey and Sergeant C. R. Haycock. Records for 1941 show that there were twenty men in the Milton Ernest Home Guard of which twelve men had rifles and eleven men had uniform.

Incredibly, George Willars remembers standing on Radwell Road and seeing the glow from the Blitz on London. Due to the enforced blackout everything was dark except for an orange glow on the horizon. The intensity of the Blitz must have been something to be visible some fifty miles away.

The USAF Eighth Air Force 306th Group were based at nearby Thurleigh Airfield. From there B-17 bombers went on 342 missions, flew 9,600 sorties and dropped 22,500 tons of bombs. From their garden in Radwell Road, George Willars and his family used to count the bombers out and count them back in again. Such was the frequency of the missions that this would be a daily event. They would know exactly how many were missing as well as witnessing the damage incurred by the B-17s during the conflict. The bombers would often return with parts of their wings missing. Official records show that between 7th September 1942 and 19th April 1945, 171 aircraft of 306th Group were lost in action.

Not only were aircraft lost in action but they also crashed in the Milton Ernest vicinity. Planes used to fly above the village on most days to get into formation and Monica Boielle remembers that on one occasion three planes collided whilst circling over the village and the school shaking when they came down in nearby fields. In fact the impact was so strong that a crack appeared in the school house wall. Nat Peck, who played trombone in Glenn Millers orchestra, recalls looking out of a window at Milton Ernest Hall, "...we saw a plane – it was a B-17 – badly battered. It had obviously had problems over Germany and it crashed right in front of our eyes".

George Willars states that his brother also witnessed a plane crashing into a field to the north east of Milton Ernest.

Milton Ernest Hall was commandeered by the United States Army. One benefit for the children of the village was that the American soldiers taught them how to play baseball.

As mentioned earlier, three soldiers from the village were killed in WWII and there were other indirect casualties as well. A further soldier, Arthur Priddon, drowned while swimming in the River Great Ouse in 1942 and Edith Parrott, a villager, was killed by an United States Army motor lorry on 26th February 1943. The inquest was held at the Queen's Head and gave the verdict of "death caused by a fracture of the skull having been accidentally run down by a motor lorry".

In 1942 the Women's Land Army (WLA) opened a hostel on the northern outskirts of the village. An industrial unit has since been built on the Rushden Road site and is currently occupied by Protech Food Systems Limited. Forty Land Girls were housed in the hostel under the watchful eye of Miss Taylor, the warden. These women volunteers were needed on local farms to help grow and harvest cereals, potatoes and fodder beat as well as helping to maintain levels of meat, milk, eggs and fresh vegetables. There was also thatching, dredging, ditching and other sundry tasks to be undertaken including rat catching.

Property	1928	1931	1936	1940
East Manor Farm	-	-	-	Oakley 288
Gables	Bedford 2405	-	-	-
Garage	-	Sharnbrook 49X	Oakley 50	Oakley 250
Grange	-	-	Oakley 24	Oakley 203
Grocer (Haycock)	-	-	-	Oakley 325
Home Farm	-	Sharnbrook 60	Oakley 60	Oakley 260
Kennels	Sharnbrook 15	-	Oakley 66	Oakley 266
Mill House	-	Bedford 2455	Oakley 65	Oakley 265
Milton Ernest Hall	Sharnbrook 13	-	Oakley 31	Oakley 331
Milton Ernest House	-	-	Oakley 90	Oakley 209
Motor Haulage (Marsh)	-	-	Oakley 59	Oakley 259
Post Office	-	-	Oakley 38	Oakley 238
Vicarage	-	-	Oakley 52	Oakley 252
West Manor Farm	Sharnbrook 32	Sharnbrook 50Y	Oakley 61	-

Fig 22 – Early telephone numbers from Kelly's Directories.

Between the wars the telephone was introduced to the village. Figure 22 illustrates how the number of houses with a telephone increased from just four in 1928 to twelve by 1940. It is interesting to note that Milton Ernest was originally served by Sharnbrook telephone exchange before switching to Oakley which still provides the service today. In fact progress has seen the original two digit telephone numbers increase to the six digit numbers that we recognise today.

As major landowners the families of Erneys, Basset, Turnor and Rolt lived in the village for centuries. Since parish records began in 1538, the most popular surnames in the village have been Hart (144 different people with that surname), Brown (126), Solesbery (124), Church (79), Payne (78), Robinson (74), Foster (64), Farrer (57), Parrott (57) and Smith (53).

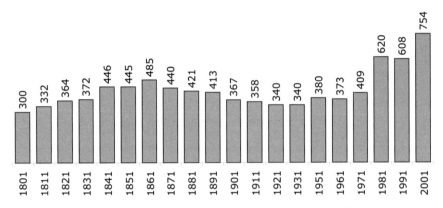

Fig 23 – Milton Ernest population 1801-2001 derived from Census data.

There are no records of any Milton Ernest inhabitants reaching the grand old age of 100 but the following came close and must have seen a great number of changes to the village in their lifetimes: Emma Mole (born Emma Halgarth in Leicestershire, first record in Milton Ernest as a 23 year old cook at the Vicarage in 1851, married William Mole in 1874, became post mistress on his death, and died in 1940 aged 95); George Solesbury (born 1829 in Milton Ernest, married Ann, was a 'plowman' on Village Farm, then a horse keeper, died in 1926 aged 96); Annie Woods (died 1956 aged 96); and the oldest on record, Mary Clarke (died 1980) who at 99 was in her hundredth year when she died.

The population of the village has grown significantly in recent years from an average of 367 between 1901 and 1971; this had almost doubled to 620 by 1981, as a result of the Huntsmans Way and Arkwright Road housing estates. Further development (Riverside View) meant that by 2001 the population had risen to 754.

In 1788 there were 57 houses in the village housing 283 people, an average of 4.96 people per house. Today the population of 754 live in 318 houses, an average of 2.37 people per home. Therefore in two hundred years the number of people living in each house has halved and no doubt the houses are much bigger then they used to be as well!

Street	Properties	% of Village
Radwell Road	57	18%
Huntsmans Way	45	14%
Riverside View	41	13%
Arkwright Road	25	8%
Bedford Road	22	7%
London End	18	6%
Thurleigh Road	18	6%
Church Close	16	5%
Marsh Lane	16	5%
Butterfield Court	11	3%
Rushden Road	11	3%
Church Green	10	3%
River Lane	10	3%
Parkside	9	3%
Starey Close	6	2%
Flewton End	3	1%
TOTAL	318	100%

Fig 24 – Table depicting the properties in Milton Ernest by street in 2006. Bedford Road includes 18 properties which are South of the village sign i.e. between Milton Ernest Hall and Milton Court on the A6. Hollow Farm is included within the Rushden Road total.

Amenities came to Milton Ernest in the second half of the twentieth century. Electricity came to the village in 1931 but it was not installed in many homes as the occupants were too poor to afford it. In 1947 a red telephone box appeared in Rushden Road. Three years later, in 1950, the first electric street lamps were erected in the village. There were only two to begin with; one near the Church at Thurleigh Road and the other was at the junction of River Lane and Radwell Road.

Fig 25 –A Milton Ernest public water tap.

33

In 1954 the water mains arrived. Previously people had got water from old pumps, wells in their gardens or the public water taps which were placed in convenient locations around the village. Sewage pipes were introduced in 1963. In 1972 street lamps were installed in the remainder of the village, with the exception of the A6. Gas supply wasn't available until it was connected between December 1979 and February 1980. Street lights were finally installed along the A6 in 1980 while the post box next to the A6 bus stop was provided in 1994.

Fig 26 – The Coronation Parade reaches Bedford Road, 1953.

Towards the end of the twentieth century the parish of Milton Ernest was best known for a local company called Bedfordia; for the location of the Royal Aerospace Establishment (RAE), Bedford; for the home of Sir Trevor Skeet; and for Yarl's Wood Immigration Detention Centre.

Bedfordia has been run by the Ibbett family for three generations. Claude Valentine Ibbett launched the business; Claude's son Clifton then followed in his footsteps; and since 2000, Claude's grandson, John has been Chief Executive. The Ibbett family connection with Milton Ernest began in 1939 when Claude leased Village Farm.

Claude Valentine Ibbett made his living building five to six houses per year. At the start of the Second World War he was just too old to join the armed forces and instead he helped the war effort at home by building air raid shelters. During construction work at Twinwoods Airfield, Clapham,

Claude was made aware of the need for gravel. The nearest location was Willington which was a fair distance for transporting gravel in those days.

So in 1939 Claude struck a deal with Mr Cross to lease Village Farm with the aim of extracting gravel from the land. However there was insufficient gravel at Village Farm and in the end Claude dug out the gravel from an area just north of nearby Felmersham. This is now Felmersham Nature Reserve.

Village Farm was underachieving and with pressure being applied by the War Agricultural Committee for all farms to be more productive Claude took over the running of the farm from Mr Cross. Being a businessman and not a farmer, Claude Ibbett struck a partnership with Colin McKie which was to last for seventeen years. Ibbett ran the business with McKie taking care of the farming. They were so successful that by the end of the War they were able to purchase Village Farm.

By 1949 the business had extended across the road to West Manor Farm where Ibbett and McKie took on the tenancy. Their partnership prospered due to Colin McKie being a brilliant farmer and Claude Ibbett a successful businessman. By the early 1960s they were able to purchase West Manor Farm. During this period they were renowned for their herds of high-yielding British Friesian cows (Village Farm) and Ayrshire cows (West Manor Farm).

Colin McKie also kept Clydesdale horses at the farms. For many years these won the Clydesdale Horse of the Year award at the Royal Agricultural Show. At one such show in Scotland, McKie became the first English person to win the Scottish Cawdor Cup, although the organisers wouldn't allow him to take it out of the country!

Clifton Ibbett took over from his father and founded Bedfordia Farms. Village Farm, which become a pig farm, was the centre of the business which Clifton grew from the original 200 acres to 5,500 acres by the end of the century. He also diversified the company into car dealerships, property investment and development, and plant hire amongst others. In 1987, Clifton proposed a railway station and country park, to be known as Milton Glebe. The plan, however, never came to fruition.

The Royal Aerospace Establishment, Bedford, dates back to a similar period as Bedfordia. As World War Two came to a close, plans were made for a programme of advanced research and development into post-war civil and military aircraft designs. Many of the projects were influenced by the discovery of advanced designs found in Germany. The Royal Aircraft Establishment, at Farnborough, needed to expand to undertake more of this increasingly complex work but it was decided that the site was inadequate and would not be able to accommodate the required expansion. The idea was to create an entirely new National Aeronautical Establishment (NAE) as an offshoot of Farnborough.

Various sites for the NAE were considered before the surveying team chose the airfields at Little Staughton, Thurleigh and Twinwood Farm, which had closed on 14th June 1945. The following year, 1946, saw the commencement of building at both the tunnel and airfield sites. However, the huge grandiose plan for the NAE never materialised, but the Royal Aircraft Establishment, Bedford, later the Royal Aerospace Establishment (RAE), did.

Fig 27 – First Outing of Milton Ernest Good Companions Club, 1956. Back row left to right: Miss Mabel Halgarth, Miss Alice Wilsher, Miss Ethel Stanton. Middle row left to right: Mrs G Ibbett, Mrs Denton, Mrs Annie Clarke, Miss Freda Starey, Mr Robinson, Mrs Woodson, Mrs P Clarke, Mr Ernest Page, Mrs Ada Stanton. Front row left to right: Mrs Page, Mrs Purser, Mr George Bull (The Baker), Mrs Pink, Mrs Sedge Stanton.

The RAE, Bedford, opened in 1954 and had four wind tunnels and a two mile long runway, which was the third longest built in the UK.

For forty years, RAE, Bedford, which was sited in the far eastern part of Milton Ernest parish, undertook supersonic flight tests on its runways and used wind tunnels to provide the aeronautical knowledge essential to the successful design of both aircraft and missiles.

Research at the site led to huge technological breakthroughs in both military and civilian aviation, the biggest advancements being safety related, particularly automatic landing systems, flight control and air traffic management. Work was undertaken on the Concorde project as well as the steep and vertical take off of Harrier jets which enabled ocean aircraft carriers to take on board higher performance heavier aircraft.

At its peak in the 1960s and 1970s there were 1,500 people employed at the RAE site. But by 1994 all flying had ceased and the research and development work was transferred to Boscombe Down. Two years later the site was sold to a development company and became a Business Park.

Sir Trevor Skeet was the Conservative Member of Parliament for Bedford from 1970 to 1983 and then Bedfordshire North until 1997. A total of 27 years representing the people of this area. In 1971 Sir Trevor and Lady Skeet moved into 'The Gables', a house on the southern outskirts of the village.

At the 1970 election, Sir Trevor Skeet, a former MP of Willesden East, overturned a narrow Labour majority in Bedford to take the seat. In the seventies he campaigned against plans to turn Thurleigh Airfield into a third London airport. Stansted was selected instead. When you consider that plans, announced in 2003, to extend Stansted Airport mean that some villages will need to make way for the progress, Sir Trevor's campaign may have saved the actual existence of Milton Ernest. Even if the village had not been under threat, life would certainly have been very different living under the shadow of a major airport the size of Stansted.

New Zealand born, Sir Trevor Skeet was re-elected six times as their MP by the Bedford people, including the new North Bedfordshire seat with a majority of 14,000 votes in 1983. He retired from the House of Commons in 1997 and passed away, aged 86, in 2004.

Yarl's is the name given to a small wood in the far east of Milton Ernest parish. Yarl's Wood is now a nationally known name, as it was given to the immigration detention centre built next to the wood on part of the site of the former RAE, Bedford. Originally to be called Twinwoods, Clifton Ibbett suggested the alternative name of Yarl's Wood and this was agreed at the inaugural meeting of interested persons from Milton Ernest, Thurleigh and Bletsoe. As the Yarl's Wood Detention Centre was built on Ministry of Defence land, the government did not have to comply with the normal planning procedures and so was able to quickly construct the centre with minimal consultation with the local community.

Yarl's Wood became operational on 19th November 2001 and was officially opened in January of the following year. It is thought to have cost £100 million to build and is the largest removal centre of its kind in Europe. Yarl's Wood, which can house 900 detainees, is designed to be the last stop before failed asylum-seekers return home.

Yarl's Wood Detention Centre was quickly in the news for the high standards of its healthcare, religious and recreational facilities. There were also civil liberty protests held outside its gates. But this was nothing compared with the international news that the site made in 2002.

Fig 28 – Aerial photo, taken on 15th February 2002, of the smouldering Yarl's Wood Detention Centre.

On 14th February 2002, there was a riot in Yarl's Wood Detention Centre which was triggered by an incident in which a resident was allegedly manhandled by staff. Whether the riot was premeditated or not is unknown, what is known is that during the rioting a number of fires were started. As the wooden framed building was not fitted with a sprinkler system the fire quickly spread and was soon out of control. The fire went on to destroy half of the centre, causing an estimated £38 million of damage.

On that fateful St. Valentine's Day there were 385 men, women and children detainees in Yarl's Wood. Of these it is thought about 40 took their chance to escape and Milton Ernest villagers were awoken by the sound of the police helicopter helping to hunt for those that had absconded. Many were found hiding in outbuildings in local villages including Milton Ernest.

Six months after the fire, and after sifting through 140 tonnes of rubble and ash, forensic archaeologists declared that no-one had died in the

Yarl's Wood blaze. However, fourteen detainees were still unaccounted for and believed to be still at large within the United Kingdom.

Fig 29 – Close up aerial photo, taken on 15th February 2002, of the smouldering Yarl's Wood Detention Centre.

Today Milton Ernest lies astride the busy A6 road (a traffic census on 9th March 2004 recorded 15,493 traffic movements), its function now, after four thousand years, being predominately that of a commuter village for Bedford. For centuries almost everyone worked on the land and nobody commuted anywhere, now almost nobody works on the land and almost everyone commutes somewhere! It might no longer be a self sufficient village but Milton Ernest is still as important as ever to the people who live there.

Information derived and extracts taken from 'Milton Ernest Parish Registers', 1538 to present day; 'Pigotts Directory', 1839; 'Kellys Directory', 1847 to 1940; 'Bedfordshire Notes & Queries', Volume III, edited by Frederick Augustus Blaydes, 1893; 'A History of the County of Bedford', edited by William Page, 1912; 'John Bunyan, his Life, times and work' by John Brown, 1928; 'Jacobean Household Inventories', F. G. Emmison, Bedfordshire Historical Record Society, Volume 20, 1938; 'A Regional Survey of Milton Ernest' by Beatrice Gillam, Bedfordshire and Luton Archives and Records Service (Reference Z1057/2), 1939; 'Milton Ernest' by Eric Rayner, Bedfordshire Magazine, Autumn 1961; 'Milton Ernest – A Field Study' by J. B. Hutchings, Beds Archaeological Journal, Volume 4, 1969; 'Villages of the Ouse' by Peter Grey, 1980; 'Milton Ernest Parish Survey' by John Margham, May 1982; 'Next to a Letter From Home' by Geoffrey Butcher, 1986; Scheduled Monument, SM13613, 1991; 'Domesday Book – A complete translation' by the Alecto Domesday Editorial Board, 1992; 'Bedfordshire's Yesteryears, Volume 4, War Times and Civil Matters' by Brenda Fraser-Newstead, Nov 1996; 'Memories of Bedford' 1999; 'A Short Illustrated History of the Royal Aerospace Establishment Bedford' by Arthur Pearcy, 1999; 'From Humble Beginnings. The Bedfordia Story' Bedfordshire Country Life Magazine, Summer 2001; 'Milton Ernest' by Dennis Bidwell, Bedfordshire County Life Magazine, Summer 2003; Paul Castle Consultancy traffic census Tuesday 9th March 2004 06:00 to 22:00; 'Look, no hands!' Bedfordshire Times & Citizen article, 29th October 2004, based on 'Wings Over Thurleigh' by Michael Dobson, 2004.

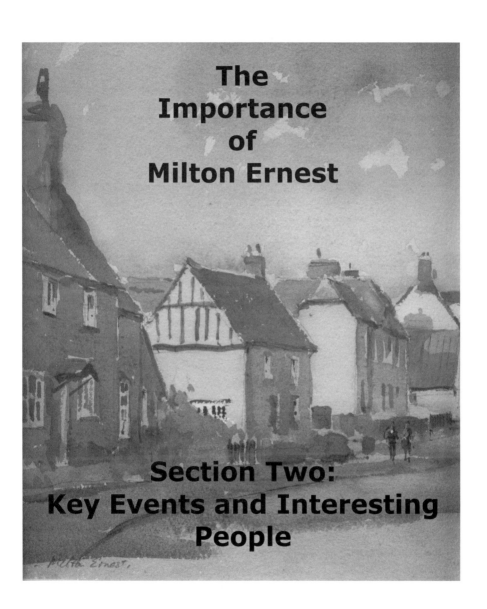

The
Importance
of
Milton Ernest

Section Two:
Key Events and Interesting
People

Mother and Mary Sutton, Witches of Milton Ernest, Executed in 1612

In 1603 James I became King, succeeding Elizabeth I. Within a year he had passed a new Act against witches. To invoke, covenant with, entertain, employ, feed or reward any evil spirit, for any purpose, merited the death penalty. The 1604 Act was far more severe than Elizabeth I's Act of 1563 where causing death by witchcraft was a capital offence but minor offences, unless repeated, were punished moderately. The toughness of the new Act was to have dire consequences for a Milton Ernest family.

Mother Sutton was a poor elderly Milton Ernest widow who was chosen to be hog-keeper by the villagers, a duty she performed faithfully. Mary Sutton and her three illegitimate children lived with her mother in the village.

The Sutton family, like many others, were dependent on the charity of their neighbours. In their case, Master Enger of Milton Mill often gave them food and clothing. But this was to cease when a quarrel occurred between the Suttons and Enger. Soon after, the miller began to lose a lot of livestock - £200 worth in less than two years. Horses would be left well in the stable at night only to be found dead the next morning. Some were found strangled; some had beaten their brains out against the stable walls. Many pigs also died in mysterious circumstances and the locals believed the Suttons to be responsible.

Events came to a head in 1612 when Henry Sutton, one of Mary's children, disobeyed a servant of Enger. The boy refused to stop throwing things into the water around the mill dam for which the servant gave him a blow or two to the ear. Henry ran home crying to his mother. The next day, the servant with another of Enger's men went to Bedford market with a load of corn. Both on the way to Bedford and on the way home the horses pulling the cart bolted. Their behaviour seemed to be triggered by a large black sow, which followed the men from Milton Ernest in the morning and met up with them again on the return journey. Later the sow was seen to enter Mother Sutton's cottage.

A few days after the market day dramas the servant was gossiping about Mary Sutton; he suspected her of having been the black sow or at least the cause of its unusual behaviour, when he was struck on the breast by a beetle. His mind and body at once became paralysed. One night as he lay on his sick bed, he "espied Mary Sutton...in a moonshine night come in at the window...with her knitting work in her hands – and sitting down at his bed's feet, sometimes working and knitting with her needles and sometimes gazing and staring him in the face." At last, Mary Sutton came to him and said "if he would content she should come to bed to him, he should be restored." He had been powerless to move or speak before but God gave him strength: he refused her and she went away.

Fig 30 – The site where the swimming test was undertaken. There would have been a different Mill building at the time of the Sutton's.

When Mr Enger heard about the vision of Mary Sutton, he had the woman brought by force to the elderly servant's sick bed. Mary denied everything but Enger told his servant to prick and draw blood from her. Once this was done the servant began to recover. Mary Sutton, however, managed to touch him before she left and he fell into a worse fit.

One day soon after, Mr Enger's seven year old son saw Mother Sutton taking corn for grinding to the mill. He flung stones at the old woman and called her a witch. This incensed the old lady and she went home to consult with her daughter. Henry Sutton would later testify that he saw his mother and grandmother call up their spirits, Dick and Iude, and let them suck at the teats that the two women had on their thighs. The spirits were then charged to strike Enger's son and drive him to torment. For five long days Enger's boy was gripped by an illness and then he died.

The miller believed the Suttons had bewitched his son to death and conducted a swimming test at Milton Mill dam. The test involved three phases. First, the suspect was swum with only her arms tied and a stout rope round her waist to save the innocent from drowning. If she floated, her body was searched for witch marks (teats, blood moles or moist warts) by an honest woman or two. When these were found the subject was floated again, this time cross bound: the thumb of her right hand bound to the big toe of her left foot and vice versa so that she resembled a human cannonball. This procedure satisfied Enger that the Suttons were witches. Henry Sutton told the miller about the witchcraft practices he had seen at home and, when Mary Sutton heard that her son had testified against her, she broke down and confessed.

The case of the Suttons of Milton Ernest achieved fame far from Bedfordshire because of the way their swimming test was conducted by Mr Enger at Milton Mill dam. It was held to be a model procedure and even fifteen years later the case was still being discussed. For example, Richard Bernard of Batcombe, Somerset, wrote in 1627 in his "Guide to Grand Jurymen" – "Some think it lawful to try one suspected by casting him or her into the water…. as Master Enger in Bedfordshire tried upon Mary Sutton…"

Mother and Mary Sutton were tried in Bedford on Monday 30th March 1612, the earliest known cases of Bedfordshire people prosecuted under the terms of James I's Act. They were found guilty and executed, by hanging, the following day, the victims of local witch beliefs.

Information derived and extracts taken from 'The Milton Ernest Witchcraft Delusion of the 17th Century' by Martha Fulton, Life Magazine, October 1986, which used 'Witches Apprehended, Examined and Executed' a 1613 pamphlet, held in the Bodleian Library, Oxford, for reference.

Underhill Robinson, Bedfordshire's First Printer, 1719

It was well into the second half of the eighteenth century when the printing trade began to spread from London and the university towns to the provinces. Before this period local published material was invariably printed in London, including the work of John Bunyan, or occasionally in Cambridge. The earliest reference to a printer in Bedford was Edward Berrington in 1736 although none of his work survives. It was thirty years later before Bartholomew Hyatt, the first regular printer, appeared in the town. In fact the trade was generally confined to the county town until the 1820s. Before that date there are only two known records of Bedfordshire printers based outside of Bedford. They are J W Morris of Dunstable in 1803 and Underhill Robinson of Milton Ernest in 1719.

Underhill Robinson was born in Elstow in 1691, the son of Reverend John Robinson, who had been curate of Elstow since 1686. In 1695 John Robinson became the Rector of Colmworth and the family remained in that village until his death in 1706.

On 1 September 1707, aged 16, Underhill Robinson was sent to London as an apprentice to the printer William Sayes of Aldersgate Street. He completed his apprenticeship in 1714 and on 4th October of that year became a liveryman of the City of London.

Five years later Underhill Robinson printed a book in Milton Ernest. Written by John Hunt, a Nonconformist Minister from Newport Pagnell, the book was entitled *Vindiciae Verae Pietatis or Evangelical Sanctification truly Stated and Vindicated: And the Common Mistakes of Many Detected*. The religious book, which consists of six introductory pages and a text of 168 pages, has the words *Printed at Milton Ernis, near BEDFORD, by U.Robinson* and the date 1719 on the cover.

Quite why Underhill Robinson chose to return to his native Bedfordshire so soon after completing his apprenticeship will remain a mystery. The fact that he printed a book in Milton Ernest almost half a century before the next record of a printed book in Bedfordshire and 84 years ahead of anyone outside of Bedford is simply amazing. Unfortunately Underhill Robinson died soon afterwards, aged 27, and was buried in Milton Ernest churchyard on 4th May 1719, with his only known work giving him the distinction of having been Bedfordshire's first recorded printer.

Information taken from 'Bedfordshire's First Printer' by Chris Pickford, Bedfordshire Magazine, Autumn 1986 and 'Early Bedfordshire Printers', again by Chris Pickford, Bedfordshire Magazine, Summer 1994.

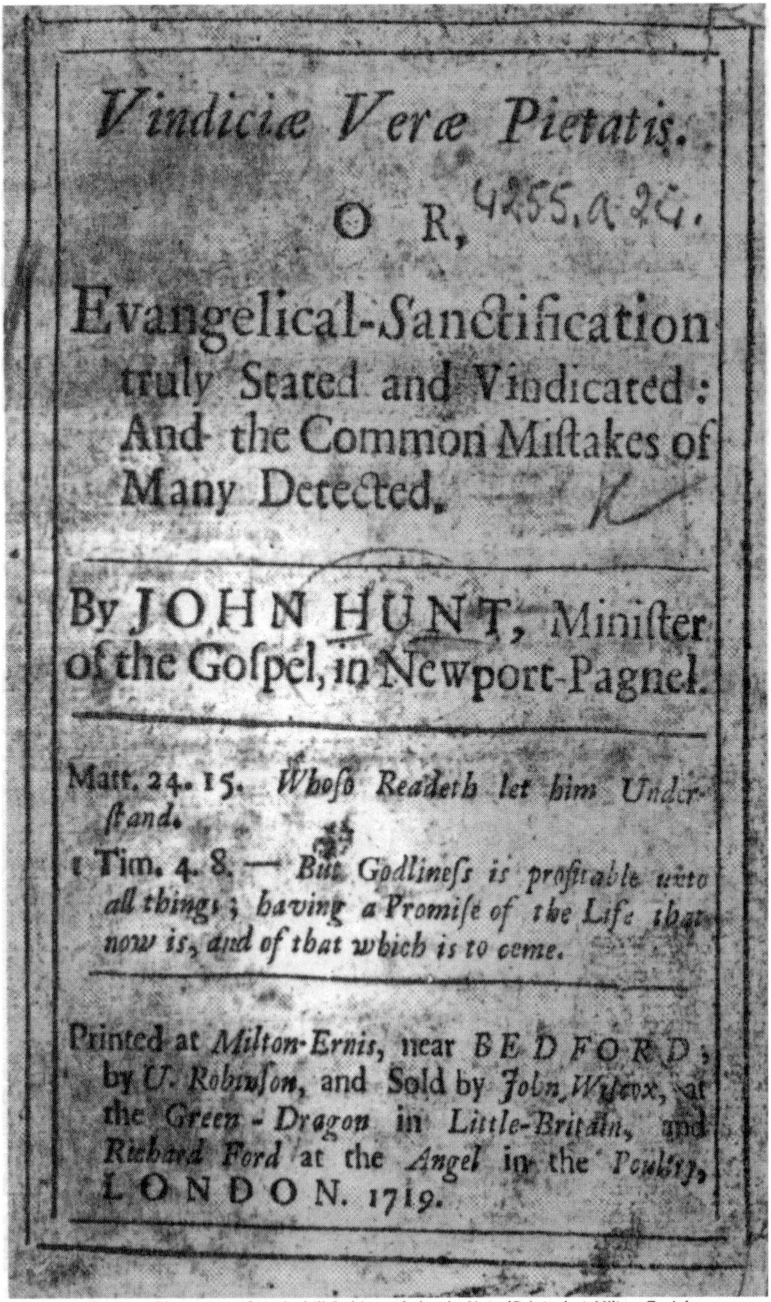

Vindiciæ Veræ Pietatis.

O R, 4255, a 24.

Evangelical-Sanctification
truly Stated and Vindicated :
And the Common Mistakes of
Many Detected.

By JOHN HUNT, Minister
of the Gospel, in Newport-Pagnel.

Matt. 24. 15. *Whoso Readeth let him Understand.*

1 Tim. 4. 8. — *But Godliness is profitable unto
all things ; having a Promise of the Life that
now is, and of that which is to come.*

Printed at *Milton-Ernis*, near B E D F O R D,
by *U. Robinson*, and Sold by *John Wilcox*, at
the *Green - Dragon* in *Little-Britain*, and
Richard Ford at the *Angel* in the *Poultry*,
L O N D O N. 1719.

Fig 31 – The cover of Underhill Robinson's book. Note 'Printed at Milton Ernis'

John Turner's 1834 Milton Ernest Walk

John Turner, a farmer from Bolnhurst, moved to Milton Ernest circa 1815 to what is now known as Home Farm. With him were his wife Anna Maria, and their surviving children Elizabeth, John, Ann and Thomas. The family were no relation to the Turnor family who were major land owners in the village.

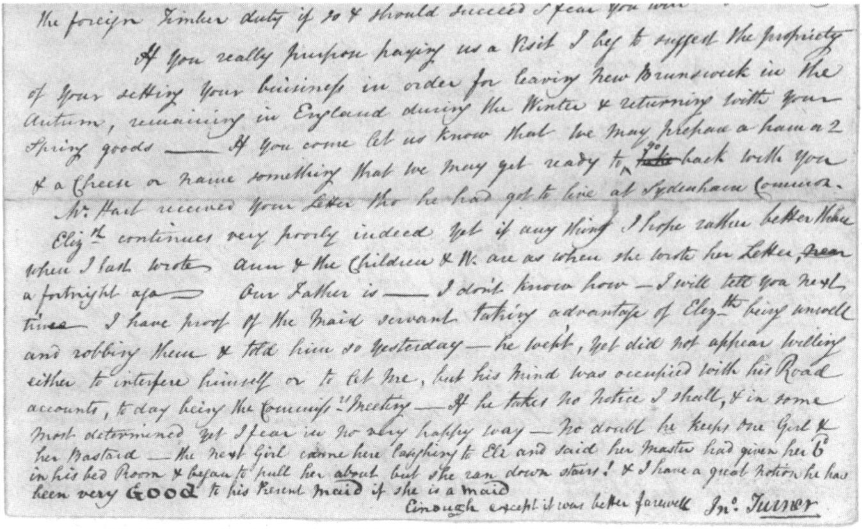
the foreign Timber duty if so & should succeed I fear you will ...
If you really purpose paying us a Visit I beg to suggest the propriety
of your setting your business in order for leaving New Brunswick in the
Autumn, remaining in England during the Winter & returning with your
Spring goods — If you come let us know that we may prepare a ham or 2
& a Cheese or name something that we may get ready to go back with you
Mr Hart received your letter tho he had got to live at Sydenham Common.
Elizth continues very poorly indeed yet if any thing I hope rather better than
when I last wrote Ann & the Children & W. are as when she wrote her Letter, near
a fortnight ago Our Father is — I don't know how — I will tell you next
time — I have proof of the Maid servant taking advantage of Elizth being unwell
and robbing them & told him so yesterday — he wept, yet did not appear willing
either to interfere himself or to let me, but his mind was occupied with his Road
accounts, to day being the Commissrs Meeting — If he takes no notice I shall, & in some
most determined yet I fear in no very happy way — no doubt he keeps one Girl &
her Bastard — the next Girl came here laughing to Eli and said her Master had given her 6d
in his bed Room & began to pull her about but she ran down stairs! & I have a great notion he has
been very GOOD to his Present maid if she is a maid
Enough except it was better farewell Jno Turner

Fig 32 – An extract from one of John Turner's letters showing his handwriting style.

On 12th May 1830, the youngest son, Thomas Turner, aged 34, married Susan Pain, aged 35, of Felmersham, at Milton Ernest All Saints' Church. A year later the newly weds emigrated to St Andrews, New Brunswick in British North America, now known as Canada. Communication was only possible by letter at this time, and fortunately the correspondence written to Thomas by his siblings Ann and John has survived and is held at Bedfordshire & Luton Archives & Records Service. Amongst the sixty Turner documents are twenty four letters, the majority written by John Turner junior to his brother, Thomas. These letters, spanning 1831 to 1845, give a fascinating insight into everyday Milton Ernest life as well as what was happening in Britain during the reigns of King William IV and Queen Victoria.

A number of the letters cover the tragic loss of Susan Turner (nee Pain) who drowned on a journey back home from New Brunswick. Under the heading 'LOSS OF THE BRIG WELLINGTON' in the 1st February 1834 edition of The Times, John Keller, master of the 'Wellington', tells the tale.

It transpires that the brig (a two-mast square-rigged sailing ship which could carry 100 emigrants and cargo to America) set sail from St Andrew's on Monday 23rd December 1833, headed for Cork, Ireland. On 5th January 1834, the Wellington encountered a series of gales with heavy showers of hail and snow. By 9th January the wind was at hurricane strength and the vessel reeled, throwing every individual on deck overboard. The cook, Susan Turner and another crew member met a watery grave. The remaining fourteen crew managed to get back on board. With all of the provisions washed away, the surviving crew ate the ship's drowned cat and made this last eight days. One sailor jumped overboard rather than suffer any further hardship. On 20th January a ship was sighted and a brig named 'Micmac' took the survivors off the wreck of the 'Wellington'. The 'Micmac' arrived safely in Deal, Kent on 28th January 1834. Two days later the storm claimed its fifth victim when a 17 year old sailor died having suffered badly from the frost whilst on the wreck.

Despite pleas from John Turner junior to come home, Thomas remained in New Brunswick and never returned to Milton Ernest. A plaque was erected in Felmersham Church as a memorial to his wife, Susan, who was aged 39 at her death. John Turner senior died on 27th November 1844, aged 86, and is buried in the grounds of Milton Ernest All Saints' Church.

John Turner junior, who had been a baker, took over the running of Home Farm. He died on 16th April 1862, aged 72, and is also buried at Milton Ernest. His sisters Elizabeth Turner and Ann Odell both lived in the almshouses before their deaths in 1863 and 1870 respectively.

Probably of greatest interest to the present day residents of Milton Ernest are two letters written by John Turner junior, which describe in great detail the people and where they lived in the village in 1834. Incredibly, John Turner describes 207 people (56% of the population) and 71 buildings within the text.

The first letter is a circular route, starting and ending at his home, which can be assumed as being the bakery on the corner of Radwell Road and River Lane. The assumption is based on the fact that there were only two bakers in the village at the time and records show that the other baker, William Cook, was based near to the Queen's Head. As the Newell family had yet to move to the village it is fairly certain that John Turner lived at what is now known as the 'Old Bakery'. The second letter picks up on the remainder of the village – River Lane and London End.

<u>Extracts taken from two letters from John Turner of Milton Ernest to his brother Thomas Turner of St Andrews, New Brunswick, British North America, dated Good Friday, March 28th, 1834 and May 2nd, 1834.</u>

Note: Any spelling mistakes have not been corrected. Letters A to P have been inserted to visually depict John Turner's route on a map (see Fig 33) dated 1803, which is the closest to how the village would have been in 1834.

......let us (in our minds) take a walk round this village, perhaps it will cheer you up a bit to call your old neighbours to mind: here's Mr. Neal, his wife & Betty Douglas still living together in the cottage at the end of my garden **(A)** --- Bill Farrer, his wife and 4 children under the same roof --- Tom Griggs from Oakley, carpenter & formerly Whitbreads man & patronised by Susan Askew has a shop in their stable & lives in their kitchen --- Mr. Poole and Lukey are as they were, only one is more feeble & the other more greedy --- Rd Bradsher lives in Freeks Public House **(B)** & sells beer for Mr. Gibbins who has taken the premises & become Wholesale & Retail Brewer --- he has put the place in good repair, hung a new copper, made a store room of the barn & well stocked both that & the cellars with ale. Mr. G. thinks trading is a great thing, but he will soon see that all is not gold that glitters --- Bradsher the other day abused the bakers & said they used poison --- I said he was now a brewer & the kettle should not abuse the pot --- Gibbins blushed! --- Mrs. Pain has no relish for company so we will go to Mr. Lambs **(C)** --- the old gentleman & lady are hearty --- the girls proud & consequently ignorant --- James is an industrious farmer & John is apprenticed with Messrs Trapps of Bedford --- they are all such antinomians in Religion that they have scarce any Charity left for any one, so let us walk up the Close to the brick ended house by the Bletsoe road --- but look on the left, there is poor old John Russell still toiling in his pretty & well cultivated garden & Sophias boy gathering horse dung to manure it --- well in the house you find James Hart in health & his wife full of grievous ulcered & incurable sores. At the other end live Peter Solsbury, his wife together with their son Isaac, wife & 4 children --- happier than they were a few weeks ago for Isaac is just left out of limbo where he has been confined since Michs for robbing a maid servant wearing apparel at Bedford Fair --- Next is Mrs. Hurst & Hannah Wilby, they live as usual but enjoy indifferent health --- now to Mr. Balls, they are doing well in this world but Mrs. B. enjoys poor health --- their son is a sprightly lad & pert enough --- We'll now step on to Fishers Farm **(D)** --- here lives old Martha Dyson --- Tho. Maddoc & Billy Cox with his Charlotte & young family --- Polly Panters house is shut up, herself and family all gone to London where they live comfortably ----if we step across the Close to Fluton End **(E)** we shall find Winsalls family in the cottage by the Old Lane --- Philip Woodham & wife with their son Cotes & his little brats in their old home & John Sanford and his son Sam & Wife their next neighbour --- then you may come to old George & Nanny Rench & find them where you left them & Wm Ray Mr Gibbins shepherd their next neighbour a pious, steady & happy man with

51

3 or 4 rosy faced children & then there is John Sturges & his wife Bet still stewing & fretting & working away & afraid of everything & more than all of Bill Winsall who has lately fathered a dead child borne by their daughter Susan --- Wm Gore lives in the parsonage **(F)** with his housekeeper who he appears to like very well & they have his mother under their care, she being unable to do for herself in the Alms Houses. The cottages adjoining the Church Yard being demolished we may step into Mr. Gibbins **(G)** next, who with Mrs G. a little Bob & 2 girls are very well and very happy and if we walk down the farm yard we shall soon arrive at Jemmy Fosters --- Jemmy has grown grey --- his Molly meets sorrow before it comes --- her daughter Beckey Davis has lately lost a leg in the infirmary --- poor old Cowdal & his wife remain next door & by their very regular habits appear to prolong their days. Jack Cowdal is a creditable gentlemans servant & has been home & paid the Paris for his tricks at Baby Making --- Tho. Childs & his wife with their son Lewis & also Hannah who is married to Jas. Cowdal struggle hard along a thorny path thro life --- Now I'll go to Church **(H)** for it is Good Friday & we have no service at the Chapel till evening --- There is s conscientious clergyman with his worthy wife superintending a pleasing Sunday School with which they take great pains --- I observe some further improvements & more regularity in the Church --- but some sad hop-step & jump singing.

Now we will call at the new cottages built in old Clark Brown's garden --- here lives first W. Mark, 2nd J. Stokes, 3rd the old superannuated Clark with his blind Sarah together with their daughter Hannah their husband and children almost all sickly & could not sometimes attend to each other but for Hannahs oldest daughter. Hannah has a dreadful asthma & Tommy has not the right use of his limbs --- Next lives Mole the tailor --- Let us go to Mr Meads & we shall find them in the enjoyment of poor health --- their work apparently nearly done and afflicted in mind on account of the difficulty of getting up their bills & of their son in law Wm Abbotts being in difficulties for the want of work & account of his numerous family --- We will pass Bill Skinners on the bank and call upon Henry Hart who with Eliza are well and live snugly --- John Layton & his son Dick live in their cottage behind Henry Harts but the men & old nanny are from home & Dicks wife is ill in bed of the ague --- But we will go back to the almshouses, only we will first take a peep at Bill Ball & Tho Eyles cottages behind them **(I)** where the inmates live tolerably comfortable --- young Tom Ball is whipper in to a pack of Fox Hounds. --- with Eyles lives the widow of the late Baker Eyles of Risely formerly Mrs Hills of Keysoe quite reduced & infirm. Now to the Alms-houses **(J)** : 1st in old Sarah Gores house William Rench & wife & William Gores daughter have a temporary home, the old people appear nearly worn out --- poor old Will unable to work --- 2nd lives Sarah Lilley grown almost double --- 3rd is Nanny Church where late Ann Ball used to live --- poor old Nanny is a good Christian with all her weakness & a happy woman amidst all her poverty --- 4th lives that useful woman Molly Parrot the midwife & her son Bob who is a sly dog--- 5th lives Poll Tebbutt as you may tell by the windows which are mended with paper--- the house floor is strewed with dirt & straws & upon the hearth lie the remains of some scrolling bushes stolen from a neighbouring fence --- poor Polly she is as she were --- I could but laugh when I went in one stormy morning last Autumn, Polly had been out amidst the rain by 5 in the morning picking up wood which had blown from the trees --- she had made a good fire and was drying herself & actually pulled up her outer garments to show me how much her shift was dagged, this to me appeared new as well as curious, but I felt too shamed to examine such a thing & particularly in such a place --- last lives Rebecca Lord a tight clean & prudent woman but in the enjoyment of poor health and distressed in on account of her only son being now in prison* for helping Isaac Solsbury** thieve at Bedford Fair --- Next we find Tom Brown afflicted with ague & asthma yet sometimes tolerably cheerful yet his work is done --- he is thoughtful yet unhappy --- his only comforter is his houskeeper Ann Pain & with them live their daughter George Lords wife & 2 children. Under the same roof we find the Parish Clerk Bill Solsbury --- he is steady for his office'sake --- we would call on Makham the wheelwright where old George Odell used to live but they are busy preparing to open a beer shop on Monday --- Jerry Abbott still lives in yonder old cottage in Greens Close but as he is with the Sunday School children & his wife sickly and proud we shall only perplex her if we call. Yet the poor woman needs a comforter for her brother was at the last assizes sentenced to transportation for breaking into our Parsons stables & other robberies.

We must not go on to Low's for he is out of temper & then we know he is very violent, he lately gave me some hearty blackguardism & has since served Gibbins out in the same way --- he is angry with Gibbins for encouraging Makham to open a beer shop & also because he has got possession of Pecks house --- Low having offered Mole a bribe to get possession that he might play Harrison with it & cheat old Peck --- Lows son Ted also intended opening a beer shop next week --- we must then call & drink --- perhaps Low will then be in a better humour. It is too far to the mill to see Dickey Foster in the Mill House & if we go we may not fish nor can we see old John Abbot there for he has been many weeks in the Infirmary & tho' he is now at home he does not appear as tho he would ever be able to work again --- young John is miler & has to the present time supported his father & mother during their affliction --- may God reward him! --- Now we will just take a peep at Milton House **(K)** before the old offices are demolished & they soon will be for Lord Tavistock and friends have taken it and are directly going to make the necessary alterations for the accommodations of a studd of hunters and a pack of fox hounds. --- Our worthy Parson has no taste for such sports so is going away directly --- Alas! I am sorry tho' I have never sold him a loaf of bread

Marshy Lane

Babs Lane

Fig 33 – Enclosure Act Map of Milton Ernest dated 1803. This gives a good indication of the village at the time of John Turner. The two roads which no longer exist today have been highlighted. Places mentioned in the letter, which can be found on the map, have been marked with a letter to give an idea of the route that John Turner took in his narrative. They are: (A) Old Bakery; (B) Swan; (C) West Manor Farm; (D) Fishers Farm; (E) Flewton End; (F) Vicarage; (G) East Manor Farm; (H) Church; (I) Cottages behind almshouses; (J) Almshouses; (K) Milton Ernest Hall; (L) Home Farm; (M) Cook's Alley; (N) Workhouse; (O) River Lane; (P) London End.

--- he does more of our morals than a pack of fox hounds will tho they will encourage trade & are to make us all alive they say --- Ah! & I fear the grooms will make our girls too live if they do not take care --- Our Parson has improved the gardens & house too & wished to live & die here --- I wonder he did not secure the house because no doubt he is in circumstances to buy the estate but he has taken a home elsewhere & the workmen are coming --- If the Marquis of Abercorn who married the Duke of Bedfords daughter buys the estate I shall not wonder; Good bye peace and quietness at Milton House --- No wonder at new Tom & Jerry shops --- Mole means to have one too as soon as Gibbins has built him an additional room which is already begun and I suppose we shall be all Toms, Jeriries & Fox-hunters and fools before long. But we must go on --- we will pass by our fathers **(L)** --- Jo Brown looks gloomy & well he may --- Whitbread is busy and perplexed so we may go on, Cook the baker **(M)** does not want to see visitors but we'll peep down the yard --- there lives Jo Church, Jim Parrott and Widow Polly Farrer & her daughter Hannah with her ready to go to bed having last year gone into the mans bed at Mr. Pains by mistake (they say). We must pass by Daddy Croxton & Harry Hart & only peep in at Mary Skinner to see all the girls lace making. --- George Hart & Bill Sanford are busy, Russell is in the garden, Sophia in the shop --- John Dayton ill in bed --- Patty Odell & her Jem tired and poorly --- we don't want to go to the workhouse **(N)** , tho old Knight is not the worst master --- Harry Solsbury, John Davis & a little boy are the only inmates there, next door live T.Allen, Pointer, J.Childs & Mary Truett --- We must pay little London a visit next time. Sukey Witney & old Peck will at any time be glad to see us.

In my last I have taken you round our village, only we had not time to go to Little London, but as old Tommy Peck will perhaps be angry if we do not call we will now go to see both him & his neighbours. As we go down River Lane **(O)** we observe by the brook side a curious unfinished cottage intended by Thomas Allen for his future home & below it a more curious arrangement of hovels and pigsties & gardens which well nigh block up the road. On the right is George Lords cottage **(P)** & George himself just out of prison. Next is Dan Solsbury as rough as ever with 4 children, then we find Bill Robinson & his wife almost as thick as can be being ready to go to bed after being up 8 years --- their sons Jack & Christopher are models of old Tom Tebberitt --- the next perhaps will be a model of old Polly. Next door lives soldier J.Odell with his Peggy & only one daughter at home who is married to Mr Meads, journeyman. Next we step into Paul Sommerling with whom & Dad White live Blind Dick (only poor Dick is now in the infirmary) Solomon Witney & Betty Hartwell is queen over this company. Opposite still lives poor Bob Bettles with his old cottage about his ears. Then we come to Sukey Witney in the shed at the end of the Millers House --- very poor --- very old --- very short tempered, and very clean and as careful as ever. Next we find Molly Abbott at home but her husband in the infirmary & his case nearly hopeless. His son John is miller & has during the winter supported his father & mother by his labour --- a worthy example this --- may God help John for the deed --- but he will not lose his reward.

Now we call upon John Barcock --- his wife can only walk with crutches, having a white swelling in the knee, they are resigned, pious & happy. Elizabeth Barcock is dead --- Mary is married --- Ann is somewhere in service. Now we call upon Tommy Peck --- here he is, together with Sukey Sutton? Just as they were 5 years ago, only Sukey rather more lame & deaf yet looks well --- as to old Tommy there appears no alteration --- he is pester'd to death --- the hens lay away --- some will sit in their wrong nests --- the cursed poulterers give nothing for eggs nor fowls & the dev'lish farmers charge so dear for barley --- the plaguey boys want for ever looking after or they will destroy every thing so that he has no time for any thing --- the last years crop has not wholly been planted in the garden & that which was planted has not yet been gathered. The furniture which was brought from the Public House 8 or 9 years ago is not yet put up --- one table still stands before another --- there is a handful of fire on the hearth & a heap of rubbish under a table ready to be applied very carefully to keep the half expiring flame from dying --- the fruit trees are rotting to stumps --- the faggotts are rotting in the ground yet it would be a sin to have a fire that would warm them even in the coldest weather --- by the hedge stand 5, 6 or 7 haycocks the produce of the orchard during so many years, some of which are as rotten as the faggotts & more worthless. --- Now we'll pass the cottage where Bradsher used to live & where Joseph Foot & Cornelius Parrott now reside, & enter Walkers Close which the hunters have been looking at with the intents to purchase whereon to build kennels for their hounds --- yet they are nearly as partial to Rabletts & more so to our fathers Horse Croft, yet I hope such rubbish will be kept out of the village entirely --- I had believed they would help trade & find some employment but I can now more clearly see that they will do more harm than good in the village.......

* George Lord was sent to Bedford Gaol in 1833 for stealing a basket.
** Isaac Solsbury spent five months hard labour in 1833 at Bedford Gaol for robbing a cart.

Information taken from Bedfordshire and Luton Archives and Records Service (Reference CRO Z629/1 to Z629/60).

Robert Arkwright and the Oakley Hunt Kennels 1834 to 1972

By the eighteenth century the old sport of stag-hunting had given way to the hunting of foxes. In 1798 William Lee Antonie, Samuel Whitbread and the Duke of Bedford initiated the Oakley Hunt. As the name suggests the hunt was based in Oakley Park but by 1829 it had moved to Harrold Hall where it was to stay for five years.

Fig 34 - Robert Arkwright.

In 1834, the new master of the hunt, Mr Dansey, moved the kennels to Milton Ernest. Two and a half acres of land (formerly known as 'Rabletts Close' and now the site of 'Arkwright Road') was acquired for £341, and stables and kennels were built at a cost of £859. In 1873 the original property was enlarged by the purchase of a further two and a half acres. The site was completed in 1899 with the addition of a new puppy house.

Robert Wigram Arkwright, having returned from army service in Africa, began his long term as Master of the Oakley Hunt in 1850 when he bought the pack for £400 and continued this role until 1885, during the last nine years of which he shared the duty with Turner Macan.

Robert Arkwright, who was born in 1822 and based at Knuston Hall, near Wellingborough, Northamptonshire, was a skilful breeder and brought the Oakley pack up to an exceptional standard. So much so that between 1879 and 1896 the Hunt exhibited only at three shows without winning a first prize. Arkwright and his huntsman of thirty years, Tom Whitemore, both share the credit for being those that bred the brown into the coats of hounds. Up until then hunting hounds had only been black and white.

Fig 35 – Meet of The Oakley Hunt in 1850. Left to right: Tom Wells, George Beers, Robert Arkwright (standing to the left of the white horse), Barnett, Hollingworth Magniac, Duke of Bedford (seated on the white horse), Harry Thornton, SC Whitbread, WB Higgins, Captain Newland, Lord CJ F Russell, H Littledale, Major Magenis.

Fig 36 – A painting of Robert Arkwright.

In 1888, Robert Arkwright died in the hunting field and was buried at Bletsoe. But the family name was to continue to be associated with the Oakley Hunt as in 1904, Captain Esme Arkwright, grandson of Robert, became master of the hounds, a post he held until his death in 1934, a thirty year period only broken by the First World War when he was away on active service.

The cost of moving the Kennels to Milton Ernest in 1834 had been borne by four gentlemen in equal proportions – Marquis of Tavistock, Lord Ludlow, JB Praed and the wonderfully named, Hollingworth Magniac. By 1894 the 11th Duke of Bedford had acquired all of the shares and in 1903 he presented the property to the trustees of the Oakley Hunt.

Fig 37 – Pre WWI meet of the Oakley Hunt, near Milton Mill.

Before World War II the Hunt used to meet at least four times a week. Records from 1898 show that the Hunt met on 'Mondays, Tuesdays, Thursdays and Fridays or Saturdays (optional), during the season'.

The Kennels usually housed about fifty couples (hounds are counted in twos) with each one having an 'O' for Oakley branded on the inside of the right ear with a red hot iron. In 1963, for example, there were seventeen couples of old dogs, twenty-five couples of working bitches, and thirteen couples of dogs that had never been out with the pack. Amazingly, Stanley Hardiman, the huntsman at this time, knew all 110 of them by name!

Fig 38 – A postcard with a post mark dated 1904 of the Kennels at Milton Ernest.

The kennels were sold in June 1972, thus ending a one hundred and thirty-eight year association with Milton Ernest, and the Oakley Hunt moved to Cock Lane, Melchbourne. A housing estate, later named Huntsmans Way and Arkwright Road, was built on the site between 1976 and 1978.

Information derived and extracts taken from 'A History of the County of Bedford - Schools & Sport' by Arthur Ransom, 1908; 'A Short History of the Oakley Hunt' by Ralph Greaves; 'The Oakley Hunt' by Eric Rayner, Bedfordshire Magazine, Autumn 1963; 'The Oakley Hunt' edited by Joyce Godber, Bedfordshire Historical Record Society, 1965.

Richard Greenleaf's 1847 Day Trip to Milton Ernest

In 1847 Richard Greenleaf and his travelling companion, Will Ramble, visited many of the North Bedfordshire villages. Their thoughts and experiences were published in a serial of articles in the Bedfordshire Times under the title 'A Day's Drive from Bedford into the Country'. Whether Greenleaf and Ramble were actual visitors to the area as suggested or a local journalist using pseudonyms is not known. Will Ramble certainly did just that in the articles! However, it is interesting to note the views of an outsider compared to the Milton Ernest that John Turner described, as an inhabitant, some thirteen years earlier.

The following extract is taken from two issues of the Bedfordshire Times in 1847. It is reproduced in its entirety with the exception of a couple of long passages where Richard Greenleaf does indeed ramble about the need for the rich to educate the poor and his theories of what caused the mildew to ruin that year's crop.

Without any incident occurring worthy of observation we reached the village of Milton Ernest, through which the turnpike road from Bedford to Kettering passes. On our left, in a small park embellished with some fine trees in groups and in rows, on the eastern bank of the river, stood **Milton Hall**, the residence of Philip Booth, Esq. It is a plain building, with an extended stone coloured front. Adjacent to the mansion is an extensive kitchen garden, of a quadrangular form, bounded on three sides by a stone wall, and which seemed to take up no inconsiderable portion of the area of the park. The estate has, within these few years, been purchased by the present proprietor.

The carriage road to the mansion ran through an avenue of very noble elms, whose stately trunks appeared like parallel rows of columns supporting a long massy roof of interlacing boughs, covered with deep green foliage, which cast a twilight even at summer's noon. A little farther on the **road** branches off to **Thurleigh** a place which we had marked down on our route-sheet to visit, on account of its retaining some vestige of an ancient mansion where dwelt de Hervey, an ancestor of the present Marquis of Bristol, the noble owner of Ickworth park and its remarkable building, but we found it lay too much out of our way. Milton Ernest is one of those rural villages, of the beauty of which we cannot speak in cordial terms of commendation. The streets are badly formed, and its houses are chiefly old thatched buildings, built irregularly, and without neatness and elegance of style. Its natural site, unfortunately for its picturesque fame, possesses few of those bold interesting features of nature, which would otherwise give a charming effect to the whole; and redeem, in some degree, the meagre character of the buildings which compose the rural village. 'It looks,' said my companion, 'as if the ill constructed dwellings – certainly, like the old fashioned garments of our venerable grandmothers, fast getting out of date – had been picked up some murky night by a Michael Scott, and some of his coadjutors, of necromantic fame, and celebrated in legendary lore for like deeds in different localities in all directions of the cardinal points, and hurriedly thrown down at that place, to form a country village, in the promiscuous manner in which we now find them.' I pulled my friend's coat, and requested him to curb his imaginative faculty. He smiled. Some of the buildings we noticed could boast a roof of blue slate, or red tile. One **old farmhouse**, contiguous to the road side, had its walls mantled with pyrancanthus and ivy, the latter climbing over the eaves, and spreading its thick mat of leaves over one of the gables, forming a rich ornamental border to the roof. The house was inhabited, we were told, by a bachelor of shrewd intelligence and great benevolence of heart. On several of the damp slanting roofs of the houses, we could see that the soft velvety moss found moisture and a congenial soil to vegetate and flourish, as it painted the roofs from ridge to eaves with a brilliant verdure, far surpassing the elm's vernal foliage, or the new springing grass of the dew sprinkled lawn. One or two frightfully dilapidated buildings, with rafters sticking out at all conceivable angles, like the ribs of some broken up vessel, and the pendent thatch hanging over at one end, like a tattered shirt, vainly endeavouring to conceal the dismal ruin, were permitted to disfigure the village in one of its most conspicuous localities.

We left the **church** on our right: it is a fine structure, with battlemented tower and side walls. The churchyard, in which were some flourishing limes, did not seem to be overcrowded with graves. If quaint and striking epitaphs in a country churchyard be any test by which we can judge of the order of intellect which distinguishes a locality, we should say that this place has not been favoured with a very high order of that quality of mind in a former day, as we saw very few epitaphs sufficiently attractive to ensure a record in our memories. But we have had frequent occasion to deplore the sadly neglected condition of tombstone literature. My friend was somewhat puzzled to discover the true meaning of ecclesiastical edifices wearing the features of a fortress. On looking at the embrasures in the walls he observed, 'Surely, these were never meant for the purpose of pointing out iron-capped guns against the enemies of the church. Perhaps, however,' he added, 'the embattled walls are only symbolical. They symbolise that the church's mission is a spiritual warfare, and that the church is indeed a citadel well fortified, with the ordinance of the glorious gospel of Christ.'

At a short distance from the church across the road, embosomed in a fine shrubbery, in which we could notice some rare exotic trees and shrubs tastefully and ornamentally disposed, stands the retired residence of the clergyman. It is a neat and elegant stone building, erected within these dozen years *(in fact the extension was built in 1836 but the rest of the house dates back to 1694)*, on the site of the old **parsonage** house, and exhibits a tasteful style of domestic architecture, the angular character of the whole predominating. Last winter, we were informed, the house was broken into by some daring burglars, who effected an entrance in an ingenious manner at the nursery window, while the family slept, and stole money to the amount of about two or three pounds. The de-predators got clear off, and have never since been discovered, although the experienced services of the chief constable of the constabulary and his well organised force were called into requisition. Near the entrance gate is a small triangular plantation of young trees, which will have a fine effect from the village as the trees approach to maturity, shading with their deep umbrage the greatest part of the front of the building.

At the extremity of the village are the **kennels**, in which the hounds of the Oakley hunt are kept, and a good range of stables belonging to the hunt. A neat red-brick cottage, contiguously situated, serves for the residence of the huntsman.

Being favoured with a large development of that organ which denotes inquisitiveness on the part of the possessor, we, like curious children, were desirous of seeing and learning all that we could. We drove down a lane called **London End**. Why it has been so designated we could not divine: for certainly with respect to population or a real extent, it can lay small claims to resemble the 'ends' of its great prototype. What's in a name? The prince of poets has said, 'a rose by any other name would smell as sweet'. And probably the London End of Milton Ernest may smell as sweet as some ends of the Metropolitan London. 'I often think', observed my friend, after some remarks on the significant name, 'that the condition of the dwellings of the lower orders in the purlieus of towns and cities, from the crowded situation, and bad construction, are ill calculated for the nursing of the amiable virtues, and the propagation of peace and concord amongst the huddled, ill-consorted families.' My sentiments, I found were in perfect unison with those of W. Ramble, for I believe that comfortable dwellings of neat construction, in a cheerful situation, with a tolerable good prospect, would be greatly conducive to effect beneficially the occupiers, both physically and morally. There are certain secret ties between the external world of nature and our inner being, which are of such a subtle nature, that we cannot perceive them through the medium of vision; and we have not Milton's angel to purge our eyes 'with euphrasy and rue' to enable us to penetrate the veil which covers the mysterious links of nature. Nor is our auditory organ strung with that exquisite fineness to catch the soft sweet tones of their music: but we know that they exist, and that they are indissoluble with our being while life lasts,

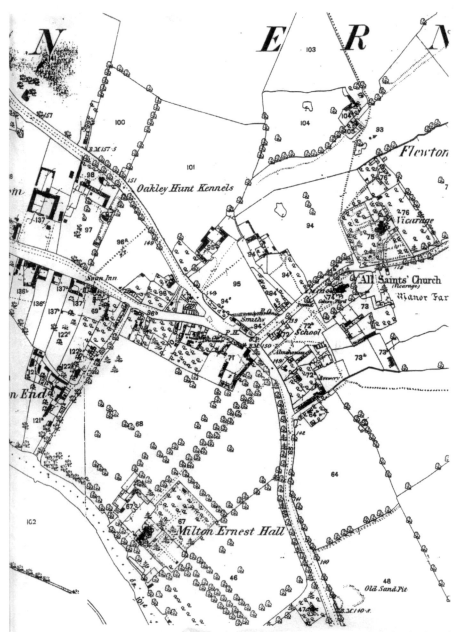

Fig 39 – Map of Milton Ernest dated 1884. This is how the village would have near enough looked at the time of Richard Greenleaf's day trip.

64

for we feel them attached to the emotional part of our nature. The bright sunshine – the lovely flowers – beautiful forms – melody of birds, and tinkling of rivulets, awake within us emotions of sweet delight; while the dark shades of broad-spreading trees – the thunder-gloom – the lofty mountain – or august ocean – affect us, in their turn, with a sense of deep solemnity, awe or sublimity. By the same law will the beauty and cheerfulness of human dwellings be conducive to promote cheerfulness of mind, and goodness of heart, for nature has got the key by which she can attune hearts to harmony and peace. We never pass a neat dwelling, whose walls are bright with cleanness, growing as it were out of a rich bed of odoriferous flowers, but we set down in our minds that peace dwells here. With these sentiments on our minds we left London End to visit the almshouses; but not without some misgivings that strife and discord sometimes disturbed the serenity of the former locality.

The **Almshouse** at Milton Ernest consists of six tolerably comfortable dwellings, and are kept in good repair by the worthy incumbent, who is the sole trustee during the time of his incumbency. On the front of the building is the following inscription – 'Amore et exemplo 1695, Dona Dei Deo.' The houses are for the habitation of six poor persons of the parish, and were originally founded and endowed, so far as we could gather information, by a Sir George Turnor (in fact it was Sir Edmund Turnor), with lands of the annual value of £40, but under the excellent management of the vicar the estate has within these few years increased considerably in value. During the winter months the inmates each receive the weekly allowance of 3s, and 2s 6d, during the summer months. There are other charities in place, one of which is a rather singular bequest, that is, twelve small loaves of bread are each Sunday distributed to as many persons, residents of the place, who attend the parish church. The recipients of this charity assert a hereditary claim to the bread gift, and we did not find that the claim was much disputed. To discharge the function of a charity trustee agreeably to one's best judgement, and satisfactorily to others, is not one of the least difficult tasks to accomplish, and it was with no small gratification we learned how well the affairs of the Milton Charity were administered by the clergyman. The rev. gentleman, who has within these few years been appointed to the rural deanery of Clapham, is also in the commission of the peace, and from his active habits we would auger he is a valuable acquisition to the Bench. He is represented as being a truly useful man, thoroughly devoted to his duties, of incorruptible integrity, of great liberality and generosity of heart, of fine scholastic attainments, and much endeared to the village people by his uniform kindness and watchful regard to their best interests, and by his readiness, whenever solicited, to assist them by his counsel and means in their straits and difficulties.

The gross income of the living of Milton, which is a vicarage in the archdeaconry of Bedford and diocese of Ely, is £242, and rated at £7 0s

8d. In 1803 the commutation of its tithes took place. The number of acres in the parish is reckoned at 2,070. According to the census of 1801 the population of the village did not exceed 300; in 1831 it had increased to 372, or 24 per cent in 30 years, being the mean rate of increase of 0.8 per cent annually – a considerably less ratio of increase than the average progressive increase of the population of the whole county during the same period of time, which was about 44 per cent, or an average of 1.466 per cent yearly. The annual value of the real property is £1468. Milton is without historical interest. There is a one day **school** in the place; it is conducted by a poor man, who certainly does himself great credit in adopting his highly honourable avocation in disseminating the seed's of instruction in the minds of the youth who attend his humble seminary. Why, observed my friend, and that very truly, is there no nobler effort made to mould by the force of education the young intellect of the place, to impart to the children more extensively the elements of wholesome knowledge, to extricate them from the entanglements of demoralising habits and practices, and to fortify their minds against the contaminating influences of profane and profligate associates, by a course of religious, virtuous, and industrial training, so as they may become the worthy and useful men and women of the next generation? We appoint our gaolers and chaplains, and police and constables, and fill our gaols with criminals, but what is done to purify the stream of corruption at its source? Is there any effective combined effort amongst the wealthy and the powerful of our villages throughout the land, to educate, so far as human instrumentality and power can do, the young heart of the lowly peasantry?

O that men were awakened from their sleep of social indifference to a lively sense of their immense responsibility………. There is a Sunday school in the village connected with the church, and one connected with a **Methodist chapel** in the place.

Although the season was a favourable one for the growth of corn, and a superabundance of it under the blessing of Almighty Providence covered the earth, yet this parish experienced a sad check in the production of its wheat crop. The baleful mildew attacked several fields of corn, which erewhile looked fresh and flourishing; and the poor barberry (berberis vulgaris) comes in for its share of blame for causing the injurious blight. This useful and ornamental shrub which adorns our hedgerows, has found, however, amongst eminent naturalists some powerful champions to defend it from dubitable imputation………. After all the impeached barberry may be unjustly traduced. It may be perfectly harmless; and the mildew may be traceable to some other combination with the atmosphere, or to some peculiar condition of the soil.

Information derived and extracts taken from 'Original Correspondence – A Day's Drive From Bedford Into The Country – Part 4 and Part 5' by Richard Greenleaf, The Bedford Times, 20th & 27th November 1847. Bedfordshire & Luton Archives & Records Service reference CRT 130 BED 168.

William Butterfield and Benjamin Starey in Milton Ernest, 1853 to 1872

In April 1838, Benjamin Starey married Anne Butterfield and they set up home in Highgate, London. This relationship had a major effect on the shaping of Milton Ernest as Anne was the sister of William Butterfield, the eminent Gothic architect.

Fig 40 – William Butterfield

Fig 41 – Benjamin Helps Starey

By 1853, Benjamin Starey, who was the director of a candle company, was convinced that recent gold discoveries would cause inflation and make land the safest form of investment. He bought an estate of 590 acres at Milton Ernest for £22,000 and went on to spend a further £14,000 on building work in the village, including a country house, all of which were designed by William Butterfield.

William Butterfield was born on 7th September 1814, the son of William Butterfield and Ann (nee Steven). Butterfield, senior, was a chemist and druggist and had a shop in the Strand, London.

William Butterfield completed his architectural studies, travelled abroad to study medieval buildings and then set up office at Lincoln's Inn Fields, London in 1840. He was a meticulous architect and decorative designer with an individual Gothic style. His first job was Highbury Chapel in Bristol (1842) and he ended his career with Saint Paul's Anglican Cathedral,

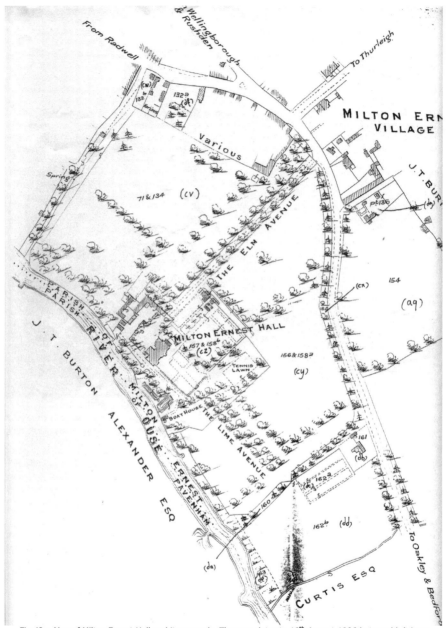

Fig 42 – Map of Milton Ernest Hall and its grounds. The map dates to 10th August 1906 but wouldn't have changed much from Butterfield's day.

68

Melbourne in 1886. In between he designed many ecclesiastical buildings at places such as Canterbury, London, Plymouth, Oxford, Manchester, Winchester, Cardiff and Adelaide, Australia.

Fig 43- Milton Ernest Hall.

Milton Ernest Hall, as a favour for his brother-in-law, Benjamin Starey, was the only country house designed by Butterfield. It was completed in 1858 and over the next few years he designed many buildings in Milton Ernest for Benjamin Starey. These included farm buildings, a boat house by the Hall, a mill and mill house, a number of cottages including homes for the coachman, gamekeeper and gardener of Milton Ernest Hall and he restored All Saints' Church, all at the expense of the Starey family.

Butterfield treated the Starey family as his own, always coming to Milton Ernest for Christmas and when William Butterfield, senior, died, such was the Butterfield association with Milton Ernest that he was buried on 1st Dec 1866 in the churchyard of All Saints' Church. However, after a number of setbacks on the Stock Exchange, Benjamin Starey was forced to sell Milton Ernest Hall in 1872 for less than a third of the money he had put into the estate. Two years later, his health seemingly broken by the shock of the failure, Benjamin died aged 67.

William Butterfield died, aged 86, in his home at 42 Bedford Square, Bloomsbury, London on 23rd February 1900 and was buried alongside his sister, Anne Starey, in Tottenham, London. His will demonstrated his attachment to the Stareys, as more than a dozen of the family were mentioned.

Information derived and extracts taken from 'William Butterfield' by Paul Thompson, 1971; 'MacMillan Encyclopaedia of Architects' edited by Adolf K. Placzek, 1982.

In Memory of Lucy Starey, 1866

Benjamin Helps Starey married Anne Butterfield in 1838 and together they had nine children, all of whom were born before they moved into Milton Ernest Hall in 1858. Their children were Anne (born 1839), Mary (1841), Elizabeth (known as 'Lily', 1843), Lucy (1844), William (1846), John (1848), Augustin (1849), Emily (1851) and Arthur (1854).

Lucy Starey, the fourth child, was born on 7th December 1844. Unfortunately Lucy was to die young, aged just twenty-two, after a long illness while living at Milton Ernest Hall.

Fig 44 – Lucy Starey photographed before her death in 1866.

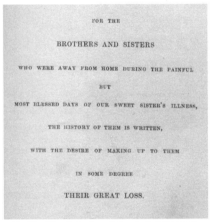

FOR THE

BROTHERS AND SISTERS

WHO WERE AWAY FROM HOME DURING THE PAINFUL

BUT

MOST BLESSED DAYS OF OUR SWEET SISTER'S ILLNESS,

THE HISTORY OF THEM IS WRITTEN,

WITH THE DESIRE OF MAKING UP TO THEM

IN SOME DEGREE

THEIR GREAT LOSS.

Fig 45 – The dedication at the start of the book.

What is unusual about this event is that the details of her final three months in 1866 were written and published in a book entitled 'In Memory of Lucy Starey'. Nobody is credited with the 57 page book but possible authors could be Lily or Emily Starey. Handwritten on the first page is 'Emily Starey, Feast of the Epiphany 1868'. The book, which has a white cover, embossed with the gold initials 'LS', was printed and produced for Lucy's four brothers and four sisters, many of whom were not living at Milton Ernest Hall at the time of her death.

The book chronicles how Lucy's illness, which she had endured for three years, steadily grew worse in the autumn months of 1866. Although the book doesn't name the illness, there are various references to symptoms. One was a difficulty in breathing - 'she said that she felt as if she had one of the kitchen weights upon her chest, and that she could not breath', 'she could not get her breath during all that time, and sat up in bed, mamma holding her in her arms, occasionally giving her chloric ether, which, however, seemed to have no power to relieve her'. Another was coughing - 'Lucy had coughed all night, and scarcely slept at all', 'Her cough was very trying, either by its violence, or by the oppression it caused her, which was even worse'. Lucy also had a problem with her hip - 'Besides her difficulty in breathing, the pain in her hip made her start up, it was so sharp, she had lain on the same spot for three years', 'Mr. Sharpin had sent a leather plaister for the hip, but this did not relieve her' and 'the pain in her hip, made tender by having lain so long on one side, also prevented her from sleeping, and continued to increase until the end'.

Although the book predominately covers Lucy's strong religious belief and bravery in dealing with her illness, it also gives an insight into life at Milton Ernest Hall. There are mentions of servants, "Uncle William" (William Butterfield, the eminent Victorian architect), the funeral of his father and Lucy's grandfather (William Butterfield senior) and Mr Sharpin (her doctor).

The following extracts have been taken from the book. They are reproduced in chronological order.

The book starts with a passage about Lucy's last boat journey. She would have taken a trip from the boathouse behind Milton Ernest Hall. Also mentioned are 'papa' (Benjamin Helps Starey), 'grandpapa' (William Butterfield), 'mamma' (Anne Starey, nee Butterfield) and 'aunt' (Ann Bletchley, sister of Benjamin Helps Starey).

Through the autumn months of 1866 our darling Lucy was evidently growing weaker; she was less capable of exertion; her breath grew shorter, and walking up stairs became very difficult to her.

On the 8th of October she first allowed herself to be carried up stairs, but she would not submit to it constantly. About that time she began to have those severe attacks of pain in her side, which lasted two or three days, and returned every week, leaving her always very much exhausted, so that she had not time to recover her strength in the intervals.

On the 20th of October my mother went to London, where she was unexpectedly detained on account of grandpapa's illness. The 23rd was a very lovely day. Lucy thought she should like to go out in the boat, so I rowed her and papa up the river, and we all enjoyed the soft autumnal beauty of the afternoon. We talked of the day of auntie's funeral, of which this was the tenth anniversary. Papa and I carried Lucy up the bank to the house again. That was the last time she went in the boat. It had been the one pleasure she really enjoyed all the summer, as it was no fatigue to her.

72

While mama was in London nursing grandpapa, papa used, on Sunday evenings, to bring out old letters and diaries of our aunt's, which were very interesting, and Lucy especially enjoyed them, as they told us so much we did not know before of her early life and trials, and the beauty and devotion of her character.

On Thursday, November 15th, she had a sharper attack than usual, and on Friday mamma came home to see her, and stayed until the following Monday, when she was again summoned by grandpapa. He fell asleep on the 26th.

In the book, a letter written by Lucy to Mrs Brown, dated December 3rd 1866, has been transcribed. The following is an excerpt of the letter which relates to the funeral of William Butterfield, who was the grandfather of Lucy and father of William Butterfield, the architect. The funeral was held at All Saints' Church, Milton Ernest on 1st December 1866.

It had been decided, to his great satisfaction, that he should be buried here, so there were many preparations to make. Mamma could not get home till Thursday. The coffin was brought down on Friday night, and placed in the prayer-room. It was of such a simple, grand design, - elm, with a raised wooden cross the whole length of the lid, and white iron ornaments at the sides. They say the inside was radiantly beautiful, more so each day, but it was not thought well to open it again. Uncle William came down the night before, the rest came to luncheon on Saturday, mamma's two older brothers, aunt Jane and her husband, and Mr Alder, grandpapa's most kind friend and doctor. The funeral was at three. I was not able to go, to my great disappointment. I watched them start, it looked so nice – six bearers with long cloaks, and six mourners. Mamma, aunt, and Lily drove up. We had a new bier of orthodox design, a framework of iron carrying the pall over the coffin, which was partially visible. The pall was from St. Matthias, violet, with a large white cross, and red trimmings.

The writer of the book suggests that Lucy's illness may have been hastened by her mother's absence nursing Lucy's grandfather, William Butterfield, in the weeks before he died. Throughout the book it is evident that Lucy and her mother had a very close bond.

She clung to mamma all through her illness, and could not bear to be out of her sight, though she was so unselfish, she would send her in the garden or to lie down, when she knew she should be restless all the time mamma was away.

On the 11th November, the twenty-fourth Sunday after Trinity, she wrote to mamma in the evening :-

"My OWN DEAR MOTHER, -

"It seems, indeed, that our separation is to be a long one. I hope I may not miss the lesson intended, but learn to love and value your dear presence more when it is restored to me. The hymn for to-day in the Lyra is 'Separation.' I wanted you much the last two days, when I had a great deal of pain, but I am much better to-day. I did not feel nervous at all, which was a comfort, and could always sleep so comfortably that I had reason to be thankful. I seem to get more and more sleepily disposed, which rather annoys me, it seems to waste so much time. And if I am quiet for a few minutes, I find myself beginning to dream, which is very dreadful at one's prayers and in church. I suppose it is partly opium and chlorodyne, but the effects last very long."

The Starey family were very religious and Lucy, who was very aware that she was dying, had no fear of death. Mr Pownall was the vicar of All Saints' Church, Milton Ernest.

At this time she whispered, "How is it, mother dear, that I of all your nine children should be chosen first to be gathered out of the temptations and trials of the world, and made safe in the heavenly fold?" Presently she said softly to mamma, "Do not let me go without the church's blessing; watch me, mother dear, and if at any time you think the end is near, be sure you send for Mr. Pownall."

The next two extracts relate to comments made by Lucy about flowers and the Good Shepherd. Both would be honoured by her family after her death – her grave was designed to have flowers grow on it and a stained glass window in All Saints' Church, dedicated to her, depicted the Good Shepherd.

On Saturday night, Mrs. Trapp sent her a basket of Christmas roses and late rosebuds; they had been gathered for her birthday. We laid them out one by one on the couch for her to see before putting them in water. She was charmed with them, they were so pure. She said, "I never used to care much for Christmas roses, though they have always seemed to belong to me. I think I learnt to appreciate them last year; they looked so nice in my Church bouquets." Mamma said, when she was born she was our Christmas rose. As she gazed on the flowers, she softly said, "I hope you will be able to get plenty of flowers by-and-bye. I should like to be covered in flowers".

During morning service mamma stayed with her. Reminding her of all the dear ones who had gone before, and would be ready to welcome her in paradise – her godparents, Miss Pontet, grandpapa and others, Lucy answered, "I don't think we ought to dwell too much on those friends who will be there, lest we lose sight of the Divine Presence that fills all. I have always tried to picture our Lord as the 'Good Shepherd,' and now my mind dwells upon the thought of going to be with the Good Shepherd for ever!"

The following two extracts give an insight into the terrible pain that Lucy suffered in her final days.

She said, "While it lasted I thought I must be dying, but I hope I may be calmer than that at the last; it would be dreadful to die in such agony. I had not the least idea what pain was before." It must indeed have been terrible to witness. She did not lie down all that night, but sat up in the bed with a great many pillows round her. She said it was such a comfort she found out a way she could rest, leaning her cheek on a hard cushion, with her knees up to her chin. In this position she slept for an hour after the attack, thoroughly exhausted. She also invented a greater comfort still, which was a rope made by fastening a towel to the end of the bed, which she held in her left hand, and she said it was wonderful how pulling at this relieved her spine and supported her. She was never without her friendly rope after this; and the way the stuff was stretched and dragged showed how much she leant upon it.

Her feet were beginning to swell and be very painful. When she was settled she said, "I am so *very* weary!" This was now her constant cry. The aching of her back from her cramped position, with all the other pains in her limbs, together with the total absence of sleep, were, indeed, sorely trying. She said to me, "I am more and more trouble, and I am weaker every hour. I cannot move at all now; I wonder how long I could go on like this." I asked her if she could at all remember or imagine what it felt like to be perfectly well, with no pain or weariness of body? She smiled as she answered, "No, I cannot. I have just been saying to mamma what a wonderful – most wonderful – part of my joy *rest* will be. I cannot remember what it is like to be at rest."

The final pages from the book are replicated below. These describe Lucy's death (12th December) and her funeral at All Saints' (19th December).

The day before, when she had recovered from her attack of tremor, she had said to mamma, "I had a longing at the worst for you to take me in your arms as a little child." And now she asked her to take her. But practically, it would not do; she could not bear to be touched anywhere, and Annie resumed her place, as she supported her best. So we remained, I kneeling on the other side, mamma at her feet. I read the prayers she wished for from the "Churchman's Guide," and some verses from the Psalms. Papa came and kissed her, full of grief, and she exclaimed, "Oh, papa, you must rejoice;" and added, to mamma, as he left the room, "Tell him he must rejoice." Her great wish had always been that she might depart with the Church's blessing, and she had before asked mamma, when she saw the end coming, to send for Mr. Pownall. At that moment he came to the house to inquire for Lucy, and especially to ask when she would be ready for his visit. There would not have been time to send for him. Mamma begged him to come up, and then asked her if she would receive the Holy Sacrament. She answered, "How can I, mother, in this agony? If I could be calm!" But Anne said, "Oh, let him come." Just before this, she had thrown herself back into Annie's arms, but instantly cried, "Oh, lift me up, I can't breathe," and she resumed her former posture. Then I feared she was going, for I heard her murmuring, "Mysterious, the dark valley," and I repeated, "When thou passest through the waters, I will be with thee," and some part of the twenty-third Psalm. Mr Pownall quickly prepared her last Communion. His own hands placed the little cross on the table which all night had supported her head, and now the struggle was over, and she was calm – exhausted, but perfectly conscious. Her voice joined in the Confession. Then, as Mr. Pownall seemed delaying after the Consecration, she said, "Make haste," and he administered the sacred elements to her first, instead of last. Afterwards, in the Lord's Prayer, I distinctly hear her whispered words, and in the Gloria her lips still moved. Hardly had Mr. Pownall's hand left her head and the service was ended, then she again threw herself back into Annie's arms, as though she would have said, "Lord, now lettest Thou Thy servant depart in peace." Mr. Pownall began the Commendatory prayer; her face, turned to the window with wide opened eyes, had a look that made one tremble, but it was momentary, the struggle between life and death. Three hard slow breaths succeeded the quick ones we had long been used to: there was a slight noise, and all was still. We waited but no breath came. Closing her eyes, Anne signed the cross upon her forehead, and I could only say from my heart, "Thank God". All the pain and sorrow were fast leaving the pale worn face, and sooner than one could have thought it possible, the look of peace began to settle there – the look which grew each day so much more bright and heavenly, that at last, one could hardly believe it was the same face of the last four-and-twenty hours of her earthly life. It was so wonderful to us to see her lying down, to try and realize that the long-desired rest had finally come.

"Then are they glad because they are at rest, and so He bringeth them unto the haven where they would be."

It was at half-past twelve on December 12th, the eve of her own Saint's Day, S. Lucy, virgin martyr, that she entered into rest. Day by day she was covered with fresh flowers, - a cross of Christmas roses always on her breast below her crossed hands, and two candles, always burning at her head, filled the room with glorious light. There was no gloom in any thought of her.

Those who had loved her among the villagers came to see her at rest, and their sympathy with us was very touching.

In the afternoon of Wednesday, December 19th, she was laid to rest beneath the church's eastern wall, by the side of our grandfather, who had been laid there only a fortnight before. There rest two simple child-like hearts.

Fig 46 - Lucy Starey's grave, with flowers growing as she requested, alongside her grandfather William Butterfield's grave. Photograph taken in 1868 and can be found in the book 'In Memory of Lucy Starey'. Lucy's headstone reads 'LVCY STAREY, DEPARTED THIS LIFE, DECEMBER 12TH 1866, AGED 22 YEARS.

The following Easter, the two graves were completed. Our grandfather's is entirely covered with stone, but Lucy's has only a stone at the head, and a small one at the foot, so that the green turf still remains over the mound, and we are still able to carry out her wish that she should be "covered with flowers."

At the same time, the window in the south aisle, behind the font, was filled with stained glass – "To the Glory of God, and in Memory of Lucy Starey." And in the three lights are three representations of "The Good Shepherd".

A copy of Lucy Starey's death certificate records the cause of death as being 'Phthisis'. Pronounced TIE-sis, phthisis is an archaic Greek name, meaning "a dwindling or wasting away", for tuberculosis. A person afflicted with tuberculosis in the old days was destined to dwindle and waste away.

Tuberculosis disease, often shortened to TB, most commonly affects the lungs (75% of cases or more), where it is called pulmonary TB. Symptoms include a productive prolonged bloody cough of more than three weeks duration and chest pain. Other symptoms include fever, chills, night sweats, appetite loss, weight loss, and fatigue. TB was also known as consumption because sufferers appeared as if they were "consumed" from within by the disease. TB is a long relentless wasting disease which can also affect the bones and joints and in Lucy's case it would seem it was her hip.

The cause of TB, Mycobacterium tuberculosis (MTB), is a slow-growing aerobic bacterium that is spread by droplets expelled by people with active TB disease of the lungs when they cough, sneeze, speak, or spit. In those people in whom TB bacilli overcome the immune system defences and begin to multiply, there is progression from TB infection to TB disease. This may occur soon after infection or many years later, so Lucy could have had been carrying the infection for a long time.

It was not until 1946 with the development of the antibiotic streptomycin that treatment rather than prevention became a possibility. Treatment of TB before then was of little benefit and unfortunately, Lucy Starey was one of the many who succumbed to this terrible disease.

Information derived and extracts taken from 'In Memory of Lucy Starey' published in 1868 by the Starey family, courtesy of the Trustees of Mrs G.C. Starey Deceased.

Milton Ernest Lower School Log Book
1912-1945

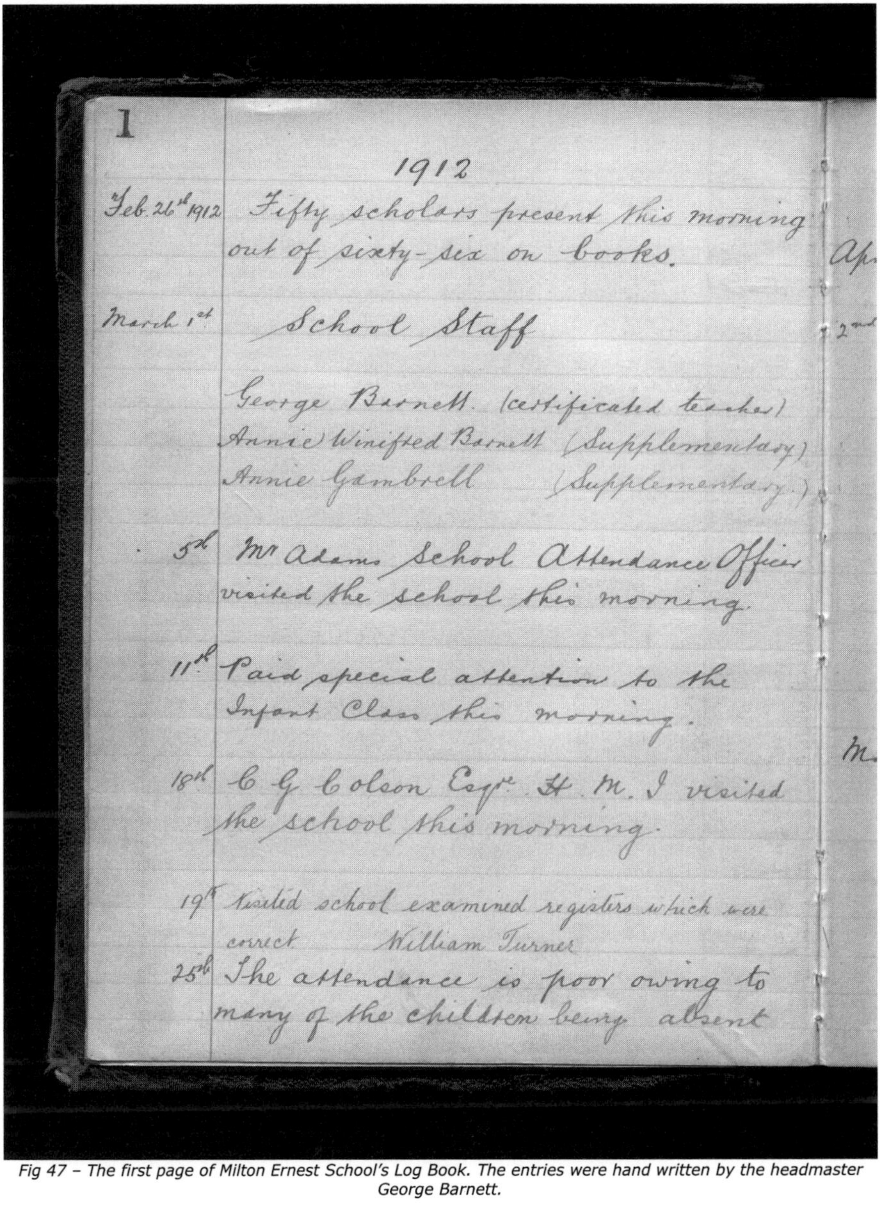

1

1912

Feb 26th 1912 — Fifty scholars present this morning out of sixty-six on books.

March 1st — **School Staff**

George Barnett (certificated teacher)
Annie Winifred Barnett (Supplementary)
Annie Gambrell (Supplementary)

5th — Mr Adams School Attendance Officer visited the school this morning.

11th — Paid special attention to the Infant Class this morning.

18th — C G Colson Esqr H.M.I visited the school this morning.

19th — Visited school examined registers which were correct   William Turner

25th — The attendance is poor owing to many of the children being absent

Fig 47 – The first page of Milton Ernest School's Log Book. The entries were hand written by the headmaster George Barnett.

Milton Ernest School was required by law to keep a log book. Key events, attendance figures, school visitors and illness records were all captured. Unfortunately the first log book which would have covered the period 1872, when the school opened, to 1911 has not survived. The second log book does still exist and covers the period 1912-1975. Replicating the log book in its entirety would require a book of its own, so only the more interesting entries have been included from the start of the book to the end of World War II.

The following extract is every entry from the school year 1912-1913. This gives a good indication of how Milton Ernest Lower School was managed almost one hundred years ago.

Sep 15th 1912 - Re-opened school this morning after five weeks Harvest Holiday.

Sep 19th 1912 - School closed for the day to allow the Master to attend the Revising Barristers Court at Sharnbrook.

Sep 24th 1912 - Mr Adams School Attendance Officer visited the school this morning.

Oct 2nd 1912 - Checked registers. Found them correct. William Turner.

Oct 8th 1912 - Paid special attention to the Infant Class.

Oct 15th 1912 - Mr Adams School Attendance Officer visited the school this morning.

Oct 16th 1912 - Paid special attention to the Infant Class this morning.

Oct 22nd 1912 - Paid special attention to the Infant Class.

Oct 28th 1912 – Posted up a notice of the Diocesan Inspection.

Nov 4th 1912 - Registers closed at 8.40 this morning to allow the scholars to go to the opening Meet at the Mill at 10.45.

Nov 12th 1912 - School examined in Religious Knowledge by the Rev A D Perrott, Diocesan Inspector.

Nov 14th 1912 - Mr Adams School Attendance Officer visited the school this morning.

Nov 16th 1912 - Registers close at 1.45 in the afternoon from today.

Nov 20th 1912 - School closed in the afternoon to allow the master to attend the Audit at Bedford.

Nov 21st 1912 - Paid special attention to the Infant Class this morning.

Dec 4th 1912 - Paid special attention to the Infant Class this morning.

Dec 6th 1912 - A jumble sale was held in the schoolroom. School closed for the day in consequence.

Dec 10th 1912 - Mr Adams School Attendance Officer visited the school this morning.

Dec 12th & 13th 1912 - Gave the older scholars an examination.

Dec 19th 1912 - Examined the Infant Class.

Dec 24th 1912 - Broke up school this afternoon for Christmas Holiday.

Dec 25th 1912 to Jan 6th 1913 - Xmas Holiday.

Jan 6th 1913 - Re-opened school this morning after the Xmas Holiday.

Jan 10th 1913 - The attendance has been very good during the week.

Jan 16th 1913 - Registers Close at 2.10 in the afternoon again.

Jan 17th 1913 - Mr Adams School Attendance Officer visited the school this morning.

Jan 22nd 1913 - Several of the infants away with bad colds.

Jan 27th 1913 - Checked registers including garden register found them correctly kept. William Turner.

Feb 3rd 1913 - Attendance poor owing to sickness especially amongst the infants.

Feb 5th 1913 - Ash Wednesday. Registers closed at 9.5 in the morning to allow the scholars to go to Church at 11.15.

Feb 7th 1913 - Mr Adams School Attendance Officer visited the school this morning.

Feb 13th 1913 - Dr Parbury reported two cases of Whooping Cough in the village.

Feb 17th 1913 - J L Fishwick Esq Sub Inspector visited the school this morning.

Feb 25th 1913 - Received a supply of garden seeds from Messrs Laxton Bros.

Mar 7th 1913 - Mr Adams School Attendance Officer visited the school this morning.

1913 – School Staff: George Barnett (Certificated teacher), Annie Winifred Barnett (Supplementary), Annie Gambrell (Supplementary).

Mar 14th 1913 - Attendance still low owing ringworm and whooping cough.

Mar 19th 1913 - Paid special attention to Arithmetic in Standard III.

Mar 20th 1913 - Broke up after afternoon school for the Easter Holiday.

Mar 21st to 25th 1913 - Easter Holiday.

Mar 26th 1913 - Re-opened school this morning after three days Easter Holiday.

Apr 2nd 1913 - Registers closed this afternoon at 1.50. Mr Slack paid a visit of inspection to the school gardens this afternoon.

Apr 4th 1913 - Finished the term examination.

Apr 9th 1913 - Mr Adams School Attendance Officer visited the school this morning.

Apr 18th 1913 - The attendance is still low owing to ringworm and whooping cough.

Apr 21st 1913 - Sowed special manures on the school garden plots.

Apr 29th 1913 - Mr Adams visited the school this morning and checked the stock book.

May 5th 1913 – Visited school this afternoon and checked registers. Found them correctly marked. Alfred Bonham.

May 8th 1913 – Dr R J Herdman Asst School Medical Officer paid a visit of Inspection this afternoon.

May 9th 1913 – Broke up after afternoon school for Whitsun Holiday.

May 19th 1913 – Re-opened school this morning after Whitsun Holiday.

May 23rd 1913 – Empire Day kept and County Council Time Table followed in the morning. The Rev E L Holmes distributed the prizes at 12 o'clock.

May 27th 1913 - Mr Adams School Attendance Officer visited the school this morning.

Jun 4th 1913 – Mr Slack paid a visit of inspection to the school gardens this morning.

Jun 9th 1913 – Paid special attention to the Infant Class this afternoon.

Jun 12th 1913 – School closed in the afternoon to allow the master and some of the scholars to attend the Scouts' Rally at Bedford.

Jun 20th 1913 - Mr Adams School Attendance Officer visited the school this morning.

Jun 25th 1913 – Several children absent with bad colds.

Jun 26th 1913 – School closed in the afternoon to allow the teachers to attend a Sunday School Teachers' Gathering at Turvey.

Jul 7th 1913 – G C Colson Esq H M I visited the school this morning.

Jul 10th 1913 – School closed in the afternoon to allow the choir boys to attend a choir festival at Turvey.

Jul 11th 1913 - Mr Adams School Attendance Officer visited the school this morning.

Jul 14th 1913 – Feast Monday. School closed for the day.

Jul 18th 1913 – An excursion to Yarmouth. Several children away from school in consequence.

Jul 22nd 1913 – I visited the school this morning – I examined registers which were correctly marked. E L Holmes.

Jul 29th 1913 – Paid special attention to the Infant Class this morning.

Jul 31st 1913 – Milton Ernest Horticultural Show, school closed for the day.

Aug 4th 1913 – Bank Holiday. School Closed for the day.

Aug 6th 1913 – Mr Slack visited school gardens.

Aug 8th 1913 – Broke up after afternoon school for Harvest Holidays.

Fig 48 – Children at Milton Ernest Lower School. Photograph taken by the headmaster, George Barnett.

1912/1913 was a typical school year. The following extracts are exceptions to normal school years.

Mar 6th 1914 – A case of diphtheria in the Church family.

Apr 15th 1914 – Copy of Inspector's Report 2.3.1914. "This school continues to maintain its reputation for careful and conscientious work on the part of the teachers and steady progress on the part of the scholars. Much of the work is very praise worthy and order and tone are excellent".

Oct 5th 1914 – A case of Scarlet Fever in the Russell family. Four scholars kept away in consequence.

Oct 16th 1914 – The Sanitary Inspector called this morning and reported that three of the Bonhams had been removed to the hospital suffering from Scarlet Fever.

Oct 27th 1914 – Dr Parbury, M. O. H. visited the school this afternoon and ordered it to be closed for a fortnight on account of Scarlet Fever.

Scarlet Fever (scarlatina) is an acute infectious disease. Symptoms include a sore throat, high fever and a rash of very fine spots. There could also be complications of inflammation of the kidneys and middle ear infection.

Nov 26th 1914 – Attendance still very low owing to Scarlet Fever.

Jan 7th to Feb 14th 1915 – School closed on account of an epidemic of Influenza and Measles.

May 18th 1915 – Mr J Barnett gave a lecture to the scholars in School this afternoon on alcohol and the Human body.

Oct 22nd 1915 – An aeroplane came down at Milton Ernest during the dinner hour and as only 11 scholars came to the school in the afternoon the managers decided to close the school.

It must have been really exciting to have seen an aeroplane in those early days of flight (the first Wright Brothers flight had been in 1903), hence the reluctance of the children to return to school.

Mar 28th 1916 – Owing to he inclement weather only 18 scholars came to school this morning, the registers were not marked in consequence.

May 1st 1916 – Several of the girls absent this morning having gone "Maying".

This was a regular occurrence every year. Presumably it was a May Day celebration and included dancing around the May Pole.

Jun 12th 1916 – Registers closed at 9.30 this morning to allow the master to be at the wedding of an old scholar of his at 11.30.

Milton Ernest Wedding Register: 12th June 1916, Algernon Woodyatt, aged 35, married Victoria Church, aged 20.

Dec 21st 1916 – School attendance low this afternoon owing to the heavy rain, only 21 scholars present.

Jan 11th 1917 – There was a heavy fall of snow last night. Only 27 scholars present this morning in consequence.

Apr 2nd 1917 – There was a heavy fall of snow between 8 and 9 o'clock this morning. The attendance is low in consequence.

Jul 2nd 1917 – The master absent with an attack of Gout.

Jul 30th 1917 – A case of German measles has broken out in the Parrott family causing the absence of three scholars.

Oct 2nd 1917 - School closed in the afternoon to allow the scholars to gather blackberries.

Oct 3rd 1917 – School closed in the afternoon to allow the scholars to gather blackberries.

Oct 5th 1917 – Dr Walsh visited the school this afternoon and ordered Mabel Woods to be excluded for a week on account of her verminous head.

Oct 10th 1917 – School closed for the day to allow the scholars to pick blackberries for jam for the Army and Navy.

Jan 24th 1918 – William Church left the playground this morning without leave to follow the hounds. His attendance was cancelled.

Fig 49 – Milton Ernest Lower School. Note the bell tower.

Nov 11th 1918 – Re-opened school this morning with 18 scholars present. School closed in the afternoon to celebrate the armistice with Germany.

Nov 22nd 1918 – Only 12 scholars present this afternoon owing to Influenza.

Between September 1918 and June 1919 there was a worldwide influenza pandemic. More people died from this infectious disease than in World War I. It has been estimated that between 20 and 40 million people died, making this the most devastating pandemic in recorded world history.

Nov 25th 1918 – School closed for a week by order of the School Medical Officer.

Dec 2nd 1918 – Owing to the prevalence of influenza the school closed for another week.

Dec 9th 1918 – Re-opened school this morning with 33 scholars present out of 51 on books.

Jan 28th 1919 – There was a heavy fall of snow last night and only 16 scholars turned up, registers not marked in consequence.

Feb 18th 1919 – Only 19 scholars present this morning owing to a heavy snow storm.

Jul 22nd 1919 – A wet morning. Attendance low in consequence.

Oct 1st 1919 – The Assistant Mistress absent being at Lincoln and unable to get home owing to lack of trains through the Railway strike.

Oct 7th 1919 – The Assistant Mistress able to get back to school today.

The national railway strike ran from 27th September to 5th October 1919.

Dec 2nd 1919 – A very wet morning. Attendance low in consequence.

Mar 12th 1920 – One blackboard renovated this morning.

Mar 15th 1920 – Snowing hard this morning. Attendance low in consequence.

Mar 1st 1921 – Mr F S Cooper, L. D. S. and Nurse Maltby visited the school this afternoon and extracted some of the children's teeth.

Feb 28th 1922 – School closed for the day in honour of Princess Mary's wedding.

Princess Mary, only daughter of George V and Queen Mary, married Viscount Lascelles in London.

Oct 5th 1922 – Mr G Barnett's duties as Head Master of the Milton Ernest School terminate today.

Oct 17th 1922 – School dentist examined the mouths of the children. Treatment required in 30 cases.

Nov 1st 1922 – I entered upon my duties as Headmistress of this school. Amy Heritage.

Nov 15th 1922 – School closed on account of room being used for Election purposes.

Conservatives won the election under Andrew Bonar Law with a majority of 75. The first time that they have been in power since 1906.

Feb 2nd 1923 – Four children are away from school with "ringworms".

Ringworm is a contagious skin disease, characterized by circular patches, pinkish in colour, due to a parasitic fungus. The superficial layer of skin peels off either in flakes or powdery form.

Feb 27th 1923 – Report by H. M. I. Mr A E Kenny Herbert. The last report on the school was submitted in 1914. A new Head Teacher has recently been appointed and the condition of the school is as follows. Reading begins well in the Infant's Room, and is a good subject through the school. Writing varies from poor to very poor except in the case of three or four children who write fairly well. Arithmetic is rather below fair as regards mechanical work. Problems are not well set out, and seem to have been neglected. Singing has been taught entirely by ear: the tone is not bad, but theory, reading and production have not been taught. Drawing is very poor indeed: it has been simply copies from cards. The records are meagre and worthless. Very little recitation has been done. Composition (apparently a fair copy per week in the past) is very poor. History and Geography have not been taught intelligently: there are no draft books for Needlework, and it is not easy to find what any child has ever made. The last year's examinations did not include tests on any subject except Composition, Reading and Arithmetic, and show very inferior work. At the last visit of inspection Physical Exercises were found to be practically of no value. The new Head Teacher is aware of all this: she has been granted temporary help in order to enable her to get to the root of all the weaknesses; and seems able and willing to make a fresh start on good lines.

Apr 26th 1923 – A days holiday given on account of the wedding of the Duke of York.

The Duke of York and Lady Elizabeth Bowes-Lyon married at Westminster Abbey.

May 31st 1923 – The school dentist came this morning and extracted teeth from five children.

Jun 13th 1923 – School closed for the day as the Head Teacher wished to attend a wedding.

Sep 12th 1923 – The school was closed for the afternoon session for the wedding of the Vicar's elder daughter.

Milton Ernest Wedding Register shows Frederic Hunt, aged 40, marrying Elizabeth Holmes, aged 23, on 12th September 1923.

Oct 1st 1923 – Five cases of whooping cough and three suspected cases were reported to the School Medical Officer this morning.

Oct 3rd 1923 – Owing to an outbreak of whooping cough only thirty eight children were present out of a possible fifty seven.

Oct 8th 1923 – The school to be closed for three weeks owing to an outbreak of whooping cough. To be re-opened on 29th Oct, if the cases have diminished in numbers.

Oct 29th 1923 – School re-opened this morning after being closed for three weeks for whooping cough. Only 26 were present.

Whooping cough (pertussis) is an infectious disease characterised by acute respiratory catarrh with sudden attacks of coughing. These terminate with a long noisy drawing in of breath giving the typical whoop.

Oct 30th 1923 – School closed at 12pm until Monday 5th Nov owing to low attendance.

Nov 5th 1923 – Only 19 children were present this morning owing to whooping cough and also to its being the opening meet of the hunting season.

Apr 30th 1924 – I resign the charge of this school today. Amy G Heritage.

May 1st 1924 – I take charge of the school today as Head Mistress. Lilian M Tysoe.

Jul 9th 1924 – The Inspector of R. S. P. C. called this afternoon and found the five Luff children with very dirty heads. They will be excluded from school for the rest of the week.

Oct 31st 1924 – I resign the charge of this school today. L. M. Tysoe.

There wasn't a permanent head teacher until 1927. Various teachers were temporarily in charge, including Lilian Tysoe, Charles Broad, Ethel Linger, Bertram Perryman, E Ballard, Mary Hebbes and Emily Wingrove.

Nov 3rd 1924 – 15 children absent owing to Meet of Oakley Hunt at Milton Mill.

Fig 50 – Opening Meet of the Oakley Hunt at the Mill, Milton Ernest, on the first Monday in November, circa 1908. Note the heaps of granite lying beside the A6 for re-surfacing the road.

Reginald Parratt recalls this annual event in his memoirs: "The highlight of the year was the opening Meet of the Oakley Hunt. This always took place on the first Monday in November, the venue being Milton Mill. On the Monday morning we would go to school at 8.30 am instead of 9 am with no lunch break, so that we could be excused by 11.30am. Our headmaster was very keen on witnessing this occasion. On being released from school, a host of boys and girls would run down the road to the Mill, a distance of about a mile, so that they could be there in time to see the stirrup cup being handed round by – at that time – the jolly miller. It was a great sight to see some of the nobility of the Victorian era. There would be about three dozen or more gentlemen wearing scarlet coats and top hats. This indicated that each one had subscribed £100 or more to the Hunt. The ladies of that day always rode side-saddle, looking to me very unsafe. The pack would move off about mid-day to the nearest wood or spinney which usually held a fox, and away would go the field with us following. Before anyone could say 'Jack Robinson' we were miles away from home; forgetting that we had promised our headmaster faithfully that we would return for school at two o'clock in the afternoon; instead we often did not return home until four, five or six o'clock tired, hungry and bedraggled. The next morning at school we had to face the music, for being absent without leave and this could entail the bigger boys receiving six strokes of the cane, and the smaller ones two strokes. I often wonder if it was worth it!"

Nov 28th 1924 – The children are disorderly and inattentive. They are very loquacious and fond of making irrelevant remarks: their chief interest is shown in a task deputed to somebody else. Writing is poor. Reading is monotonous and Recitation even worse. Singing is harsh and there is a local absence of life and spirit.

Feb 26th 1925 – Form E sent to the School Medical Officer and Medical Officer of Health reporting that 17 children are suffering from Influenza colds.

Jun 8th 1925 – 32 present. Mumps. Form E posted to M. O. and S. M. O. re outbreak of mumps.

Jun 16th 1925 – Albert Mitchell left school at break without permission. His attendance this a.m. was cancelled.

Jun 30th 1925 – School closed for the day Sunday School trip to Clacton on Sea.

Jul 1st 1925 – 23 children were present this morning and 27 this afternoon. It would appear that a number of children is still suffering from the effects of a visit to the sea side.

Aug 6th 1926 – The attendance during the week since Monday which was a holiday for Bank Holiday, has been very poor. Albert Denton & Brenda Norman were suffering with bad throats and the doctors were afraid of diphtheria. Herbert & Ethel Taylor were taken to hospital suffering from diphtheria & Ethel died on Aug 4th.

Milton Ernest Burial Register: Ethel Taylor, aged 11, buried on 7th August 1926.

Diphtheria is an infectious disease caused by bacteria which most often infects the fauces and tonsils, causing a greyish white membrane to form. A powerful toxin is produced which poisons the blood and can attack the heart muscle.

Jan 21st 1927 – A snowy morning: 30 present only this morning and 31 in the afternoon. A number of absentees enjoyed a snow fight in the street!

Apr 1st 1927 – I Gertrude Hazlett began duty this morning as Head Mistress of this school. There were seven admissions to the Infant Department. Number on register 62.

Apr 26th 1927 – School re-opened this morning after Easter vacation – Attendance 47. There are two cases of Scarlet fever amongst the children who are absent.

May 16th 1927 – Another pupil – Audrey Bell has developed Scarlet fever and has gone to hospital. Both medical officers notified.

Jul 26th 1927 – Copy of H. M. I's Report. Inspected on 2nd May 1927. Report by H. M. I. Mr Kenny Herbert.

This school has been most unfortunate in the last few years. Since the last report a series of teachers have been in temporary or, nominally permanent charge. No one has been there long enough to effect any lasting change; and the present newly appointed Head Mistress has a very exacting task before her. The Infant's teacher is promising; but the Head Mistress has she says, left the elementary matters to the junior teacher in her previous appointments. They must work together and see that methods correspond in this school, if any improvement is to come. There is some shortage of up to date books of all sorts and of storage: and the teacher's desk is not very convenient; but it is hoped that papers will be properly sorted and arranged and the school given a suitable curriculum before much more time has elapsed.

Aug 2nd 1927 – Attendance in senior room reduced from 36 on reg to 26. Whole family of Luff absent with impetigo – Also 3 other pupils in this room absent for same reason.

Impetigo is an acute contagious inflammation of the skin marked by pus filled pimples and scabs.

Sep 12th 1927 – Three pupils struck off register. Two children have left the village; one has left because he was 14 years old.

Jan 9th 1928 – Electric light has been installed in the school during the holidays.

Feb 21st 1928 – Dr Herdman, S. M. Officer visited school this afternoon at 2.50 – in company with another medical officer for the purpose of making an exhaustive examination of the heads of the pupils – fifteen were found to be verminous and one child to have very extensive ringworm – two children are already excluded for same. The matter now rests in the hands of the S. M. O. who will notify all parents as to course of treatment. Luff and Woods families are excluded.

Feb 29th 1928 – 4 children absent with ringworm. 4 excluded with unclean heads.

Mar 6th 1928 – Three excluded children attended this morning. The nurse examined their heads and those of three other children (two brothers of the Luffs – and Fred Woods – Emily Woods' brother). Out of these six children examined five were found to be still in a condition to cause them to be excluded. The boy Woods, who has been absent until today for over a month, and who is a M. D. case, ran home at the recreation hour. The grandmother of these Woods children has just come down (11.15 am) and cursed and abused because her grand-daughter has again been excluded for a verminous head.

Mar 13th 1928 – Today Nurse Shorthouse called to examine the Luff and Woods children at their homes and came to me and reported that they are still not fit to return.

Mar 30th 1928 – From 1st April School will be reorganised on the "Eleven Plus" principle according to instructions for the schools in the county.

Apr 16th 1928 – 49 present. 61 on the register. Several pupils absent with ringworm and whooping cough.

Jun 7th 1928 – Officer for Prevention of Cruelty to Children called and inspected those children who at one time were excluded for unclean bodies and heads. He reports a great change for the better.

Jun 21st 1928 – School Medical Officer visited today at 10.30 o'clock and inspected all pupils suffering from ringworm. He gave fresh instructions about all children wearing caps who are allowed to attend with ringworm in their heads. One case was excluded.

Sep 28th 1928 – Two children - Frances and Joseph Keech absent suffering from Scarlet Fever – M. O. notified.

Oct 3rd 1928 – Miss Hazlett absent – suffering from scarlet fever.

Oct 4th 1928 – School closed for disinfection.

Nov 1st 1928 – School re-opened at 9am this (Thursday) morning. 19 children attended. 6 of these from infected houses were sent home as they produced no medical certificate.

Dec 10th 1928 – G. Hazlett (Head Mistress) and Mrs Hunt resumed duty this morning.

Mar 13th 1929 – Captain Starey has most generously decided to lend the School a most valuable set of wireless. He hopes to have it installed in a very short time and we shall then be able to take the lectures.

Jul 9th 1929 – Only 34 children present this morning because of an excursion to Wickstead Park, Kettering.

Nov 4th 1929 – 32 children present this morning out of 59 (percentage 54.2). This because the opening Meet of the Oakley Hounds takes place in the village at eleven o'clock. As this is a much looked forward to event I have asked the managers' permission to take those pupils who are present to see the meet at quarter to eleven o'clock and all return when the hounds have moved off – not later than 11.30 am. The managers through Mr Clark (the vicar being absent) have given their sanction.

Fig 51 – Oakley Hunt Meet, Boxing Day at Milton Ernest.

Mar 28th 1930 – At 11.40 am I was called upon to attend immediately Sharnbrook Police Court to give evidence in a case being hear there. Ivor Willars, one of the pupils had to attend for the same purpose. I left the school in Miss Hollis' care. The vicar visited some ten minutes after I had left. I was not free to leave Sharnbrook till 5.50pm.

Nov 11th 1930 – Report by H. M. I. Mr Allam. Inspected on 7th October 1930.

There are 61 children on the books with an average attendance for the year of 56. These are divided unevenly into two classes and the Head Mistress has a class of 42 in five different groups for arithmetic. The infants division has a new teacher, the fifth change since the head mistress came three and a half years ago. The present condition of this section is not very satisfactory but the teacher who has had only one month with them has begun on good lines and improvement seems probable. probable. The work of upper class might be better. The children are intelligent but they are listless and careless. They are on the whole well behaved but they cannot concentrate on what they are doing. This lack of mental discipline is reflected in the careless spelling of simple words, in a lack of punctuation and in too many ill formed sentences. The arithmetic lacks proper statement with consequent errors in the conclusions reached. A silent reading test particularly showed this lack of concentration. In oral response the older children showed intelligence and a keenness to answer in subjects in which they are interested. Indiscriminate answering by the better informed spoilt the efforts of the remainder. Singing is good and some of the colour book very creditable. It is a school with possibilities. More training in systematic work and self discipline would do much to effect improvement.

Oct 20th 1931 – This morning I was informed that Peter Hooker, a pupil who has been absent about a week has been removed to Isolation Hospital with Scarlet Fever.

Feb 23rd 1932 – Sent George Smart home at 3.35 this afternoon for insubordinate behaviour and impertinence.

Dec 7th 1932 – Report by H. M. I. Mr Kenny Herbert. Inspected 24th Nov 1932.

Considerable improvement has been effected in this school during the last 12 months. Reading is very good, even the Infants being able to answer questions on subject matter. Recitation, especially of the older children, shows a good deal of natural dramatic power: Singing is tuneful: and in all these branches of speech work much better aspiration and purer vowel sounds are evident. Handwriting has much improved also, and some of the older children spell very well. In arithmetic progress has been made, but it is still a weaker subject.

Dec 9th 1932 – Practice of fire drill today at 11.50. Time taken two minutes. Not very successfully done in senior room. More practice needed.

Jan 19th 1933 – The influenza epidemic is on the increase. The attendances this morning are 11 out of 37 in the Senior Division and 3 out of 17 in the Junior Division.

Jun 12th 1933 – 53 on register. 16 absent – 9 cases of measles – and the remainder colds.

Jan 22nd 1934 – Two days before the Christmas vacation four new pupils attended school. They are a family of the name of Slater – 3 girls and one boy – they are very dirty and completely ignorant – the youngest (7) cannot read – all the other three are only able to work with the second standard tho' their ages are 9, 10 and 11.

Oct 18th 1934 – This afternoon upon assembly only 18 children, out of 39 on reg, were present. The absentees were away to see an aeroplane on the Radwell Road. I shall ascertain as far as possible how many had their parents permission to be absent from school and deal with them accordingly.

Oct 19th 1934 – Received notes from all parents of children absent yesterday afternoon with one exception (Broughtons).

Nov 23rd 1934 – Received official notice of a days holiday to be given on Thurs next Nov 29th on the occasion of the Royal Wedding.

Prince George, Duke of Kent, married Princess Marina of Greece.

Fig 52 – Milton Ernest School photograph, circa 1935.
Back row (left to right): Bob Haycock; Bimbo Woods; Bert Defrain; Ted Slatter; Syd Garner; Unknown; Cliff Willett; Tom Bradshaw; Jack Haycock (Died in WWII); George Willars; Unknown; Unknown.
Third row (left to right): Shelia Stanton; Marjorie Denton; Unknown; Peggy Slatter; Rose Slatter; Winnie Purser; Frances Osbourne; Sylvia Willars; Kit Marsh; Rhoda Garner; Joyce Gammons; Unknown; Ken Barrett; Stan Darnell.
Second row (left to right): Gladys Slatter; Unknown; Doreen Broughton; Winnie Murray; Dot Quinney; Elizabeth Smith (daughter of head mistress, Ivy Smith); Mary Wrench; Pam Hooker; Daphne Slatter; Nigel Stanton; Olive Darnell; Connie Stanton; Jean Murray; Johnny Wrench.
Front Row (left to right): Frank Woods; Gerald Willars; Jim Smith (son of head mistress, Ivy Smith); Charlie Knight; Gordon Brown; Fred Murray; Don Willars; Ray Bradshaw; Dick Denton; David Willett; Tom Barrett; Unknown.

Dec 7th 1934 – 5 boys (J. Quinney) (Fred & Clifford Willett) (George & Gerald Willars) absent as they have to appear on summons at Sharnbrook Police Court, under a prosecution by the L. M. S Railway Company.

Dec 14th 1934 – A pane of the class room window was broken by George Willars (IV) kicking a ball at playtime this morning.

Mar 14th 1935 – The Oakley Hounds met at the Kennels this morning at 11.30am. This afternoon 7 or 8 children were absent ostensibly following hounds. I have given out that these children must bring notes from their parents to say they were away with their consent, otherwise they would be punished as truants (notes were brought by all absentees).

Apr 1st 1935 – I Ivy Alice Elizabeth Smith commence duties as Headmistress in this school today.

May 6th 1935 – School closed today on account of the Silver Jubilee of His Majesty King George V.

Nov 4th 1935 – School closed today on account of the opening Meet of the Hounds.

Nov 6th 1935 – School closed today in honour of the wedding of HRH The Duke of Gloucester and Lady Alice Scott.

Nov 14th 1935 – School closed today as the building was being used as Polling Station for the General Election.

Stanley Baldwin (Conservative) elected as Prime Minister.

Fig 53 – School children on the Green, circa 1935. Left to right: Gordon Brown, Fred Murray, Connie Stanton, Unknown, Charlie Knight, Unknown (obscured), Nigel Stanton, Winnie Murray, Doreen Broughton, June Marsh, Dick Denton and Tom Barratt.

Jan 28th 1936 – School time table suspended this morning and time devoted to lessons on our late King George V, the Royal Family, the new King Edward VIII etc. School closed this afternoon owing to this being the day of King George V's funeral.

Jan 13th 1937 – Numbers very low today. Only 20 children present owing to an epidemic of influenza.

Jul 26th 1938 – Nurse called at 11.15 today and examined children's heads. 15 were found to have nits and 6 vermin. These have been excluded until clean.

Nov 11th 1938 – Mr Pinnock called at 9.40 this morning and stayed until noon. We discussed problems of untidiness of children and school – windows have been broken for months – window cords are of no use – cupboards are falling to pieces – fence in playground is dangerous – pegs broken in porch – ceiling falling down in porch – offices in bad condition. All these things have repeatedly been brought before managers with no result.

Dec 13th 1938 – Copy of H. M. I's report.

There are at present 46 children on the books of this two teacher school. The Headmistress who was appointed April 1935 has maintained and developed the good features which existed at the time of the last report (November 1932). She has also brought about improvements in other branches of the work, notably in arithmetic, in handwriting and in physical training. The infants are taught by a kindly and painstaking teacher. The older children are making favourable progress in Reading, Writing and Numbers. Singing is well taught and suitable provision is made for other subjects, particularly Handwork and art.

Dec 21st 1938 – Heavy fall of snow attendance very low in consequence.

Dec 22nd 1938 – Snow fall heavier attendance still low.

Feb 27th 1939 – The new iron fence in the girl's playground is now completed. Running water is installed.

Mar 14th 1939 – Boys playground finished.

Mar 16th 1939 - Cloak room ceiling collapsed today.

Jun 29th 1939 – This morning we receive the news that a scholar in the infant room, Peter Slatter aged 6, was knocked down by a lorry on his way home from school and received injuries from which he died within 4 hours.

Jul 3rd 1939 – School closed at 3.30 today to enable the choir boys to attend the funeral of Peter Slatter. 4 school boys acted as bearers.

The following entries give a fascinating insight into life at Milton Ernest School during World War II.

Aug 31st 1939 – Today I received notice from the Director of Education to report at school and to get into communication with the school staff at once as a state of emergency has arisen. Further instructions were to postpone the re-opening of school for instruction until Sept 15th. Meanwhile fresh schemes of work to be considered as school will be worked on "double-shift" system. All instructions received have been carried out.

Sep 1st 1939 – Today, with the billeting officer and his clerk, I received 99 children (evacuated from London) together with 12 teachers and several helpers. Children assembled in the schoolroom and were conveyed to various billets by Guides and Scouts from this school.

On August 31st 1939 the exodus of children from Britain's cities and towns began with 1.5 million of them being evacuated to safe areas within the country over the next seven days. Parents wishing to evacuate their children were told to send them to school with no more than spare clothing, toothbrush, comb, handkerchief and a bag of food for the day. Parents didn't know where their children were going to be sent. For many of the children it was to be their first sight of cows and other farm animals.

Sep 6th 1939 – The Director of Education called today and discussed problems of school during war time. Mr Culmer the headmaster of the school evacuated was also present. We received instructions on registration, double shift scheme, stock etc.

Sep 11th 1939 – Re-opened school at 9am today. Admitted 2 children, 3 left. No. on roll – 44. Morning session only today 9 – 12. School used by Walthamstow children in the afternoon while the scholars of this school were taken for a nature walk. Singing, poetry, games were taken in the fields.

Sep 12th 1939 – Miss Wagland a member of the visiting staff assisted in my school today and will continue to do so until further instructions are received. Children were taken for a walk from 2-4 pm today. Baskets of blackberries were gathered. Many species of berries were noted – dangers of poisonous ones pointed out.

Sep 14th 1939 – S. A. O. called at 3pm today when the Walthamstow school were in possession. The senior scholars went swimming this afternoon. Juniors took a nature walk; only about 20 scholars however attend these "off-shifts".

Sep 15th 1939 – Emergency stock received today for use by the evacuees.

Oct 9th 1939 – Admitted one new child today. He is Welsh and cannot read English.

Oct 11th 1939 – HMI Mr Burkitt visited this school this morning at 11am – 12 noon took particulars of staffing and working arrangements of this school and the guest school (Markhouse Road Walthamstow).

The only school on Markhouse Road today is Kelmscott School, 245 Markhouse Road, Walthamstow, London, E17 8DN.

Oct 17th 1939 – Too wet for an off-shift today. Mr Pinnock called this morning and discussed working arrangements with the two head teachers. It was agreed to try a single shift scheme the infants of Markhouse Rd to use Capt Starey's room thus leaving 89 children to be accommodated in this school.

Oct 23rd 1939 – Started single shift today at 9am. 18 London children are in the smaller room. 44 children of this school at one end of the Senior room and 26 London children at the other.

Nov 17th 1939 – Acknowledged receipt of furniture for use of visiting Infant's school.

Dec 13th 1939 – Air raid warning practice was carried out at 3.15pm today.

Jan 18th 1940 – Air raid warning practice was held at 3.15 today. Children have been instructed to bring gas masks to school but only a few scholars do this.

Jan 29th 1940 – A heavy fall of snow. Attendance is very low – only 14 children present this morning and 10 this afternoon.

Jan 30th 1940 – Only 7 children present at 9.00 this morning. Temperature 40 degrees.

Jan 31st 1940 – Weather is still very severe. Only 3 children present today.

Feb 19th 1940 – Only 14 children present owing to colds and coughs.

Feb 20th 1940 – Attendance very low. Only 7 children present – many have coughs.

Mar 19th 1940 – An air raid practice (dispersal of children) was held at 11.45 this morning.

May 27th 1940 – An air raid warning practice was successfully carried out at quarter to 12 this morning.

May 28th 1940 – A curtain has been fitted in the main room today.

Jun 24th 1940 – School closed today (instructions having been received during the weekend) in order for provision to be made for protection in case of air raids. Mr Baines and Mr Pinnock called at 11.30 this morning to discuss this matter. The staff were told to remain on duty to receive material to be posted on windows (these to be treated later). No further practices of dispersal to be held. In case of air raids children are to remain in school.

Jul 1st 1940 – Received further instructions to close the school for 2 weeks. This to be the summer holidays.

Jul 15th 1940 – Received further instructions. The school to remain closed until the windows have been made splinter proof and the school made as safe as possible. The staff of each school meanwhile is taking 2 weeks holiday in turn. Head teacher remaining on duty.

Jul 18th 1940 – Material arrived today. Staff cut it to shape while workmen pasted it on windows. Bricklayers have laid a foundation for a wall to be built outside the infant classroom. School is still closed.

Jul 29th 1940 – Re-opened school this morning. Admitted a new child from Riseley. It has been necessary to make a completely new Time Table as the "Refuge Room" is only possible for one oral lesson. Each class will take turns in using this.

Aug 21st 1940 – Air raid practice was held today.

Sep 3rd 1940 – Air raid warning 11.10 – 11.30.

Sep 12th 1940 – Air raid warning 11.05 – 11.30.

Sep 16th 1940 – Air raid warning 2.45 – 3.05.

Sep 19th 1940 – Air raid warning 3.30 – 4.10.

Sep 25th 1940 – Air raid warning 10.30 – 10.40.

Sep 30th 1940 – Air raid warning 10.25 – 10.35.

Oct 4th 1940 – Air raid warning 9.35 – 11.00. A further warning from 11.15 to 11.50. Children were all in the Refuge Room but it was impossible to do normal lessons. However singing, poetry, mental arit, stories etc were all carried on. A warning was received at 1pm today. No wardens were in the street however to warn the children; some children therefore arrived at school at 1.10pm. As this was the dinner hour I dispersed the children, they could all get home within 5 mins. The visiting teacher however opened the school and assembled the London children. The news of this soon got around the village and several village children arrived and entered the premises before the "all clear" was received. Consequently I came into school to take charge as I felt dispersal was unwise. The children spent the whole afternoon in the Refuge Room – same procedure being followed as in morning. Some children bringing knitting. The "all clear" was not received until 5pm. Some parents called for their children but Miss Racher and I remained with the children until 5.00. The London teachers took some of their children home. One child however returned as his foster parents were not at home.

Oct 9th 1940 – Air raid warning 3 – 3.30 (approx).

Oct 14th 1940 – I admitted 4 unofficial evacuees this morning. Air raid warning 10.40 to 11am. Another from 11.35 – 12.50. A warning was received in the dinner hour. The "all clear" was heard at 2pm. A warning was heard at 2.45. Scholars all in the refuge room.

Oct 17th 1940 – Air raid warning at 9.40 till 10.10.

Oct 21st 1940 – Air raid warning at 11.30 this morning. Several parents called for their children between 12 and 12.30. The remainder were in the Refuge Room. The London teachers personally conducted some of their scholars to their houses. Miss Racher and I remained in the Refuge Room until the all clear which was received at 12.58. School was re-opened at 2pm this afternoon. An air raid warning was received at 2.20. The "All Clear" was received at 3.10.

Oct 28th 1940 – An air raid warning from 11.15 – 11.40.

Oct 31st 1940 – An air raid warning was heard at 1pm today. The all clear at 3.15.

Nov 6th 1940 – A warning received at 9.45 – all clear at 9.55. An air raid warning from 2.30 to 3.35.

Nov 11th 1940 – Air raid warning from 3- 4 pm.

Nov 13th 1940 – Air raid warning at 3.40 – 4.10 today.

Nov 15th 1940 – Several more cases of measles. 25 children absent today.

Nov 21st 1940 – Air raid warning 2.30 – 2.40 today.

Dec 3rd 1940 – Air raid warning 11.30 – 11.50. Warning 2.30 – 2.40 this afternoon.

Dec 5th 1940 – A warning was rec'd this afternoon 1.50 – 2.20.

Dec 6th 1940 – Air raid warning received 11.15 – 11.30 this morning.

Dec 12th 1940 – Warning rec'd 2.15 today. Miss Racher acted as "watcher" and school was carried on as normal except for about 5 mins when a plane was heard. Children were in the Refuge Room until the plane had passed over.

Jan 6th 1941 – Air raid warning 10 o'clock.

Jan 7th 1941 – Air raid warnings 9.15am to 9.40, 12.10pm to 12.20pm, 2.10pm to 2.45pm. All in Refuge Room.

Jan 10th 1941 – Air raid warning 11.10 am. All in Refuge Room.

Jan 21st 1941 – Air raid warning 10.29 am Miss Haley acted as "Watcher". All clear at 10.45 am. Air raid warning at 11.40. Miss Goodman "Watcher". All clear at 12.20 pm. Warning 1.35 pm. All clear 2.10 pm.

Jan 23rd 1941 – Air raid warning 10.20 – 11 am. Miss Haley – watcher.

Jan 28th 1941 – Air raid warning 11 – 11.30 this morning. Miss Haley "watcher". A warning from 3 – 3.10 this pm. Miss Goodwin "watcher".

Jan 31st 1941 – Air raid warning at 1.10 pm. 3 infants attended school at normal time ignorant of warning. Several evacuees arrived. All children were retained and informal work was done. Registers were not marked. All clear was received at 3.40.

Feb 3rd 1941 – A warning at 11.45 "all clear" at 12.05.

Feb 5th 1941 – "Alert" at 2.35 – "All Clear" at 2.50. Miss Racher watcher.

Feb 6th 1941 – A very bad morning – snow several inches deep. Further cases of mumps reported. 17 children present. No. on roll 44.

Feb 14th 1941 – Attendance very low. Eleven present.

Feb 18th 1941 – Air raid warning at 3.00 today. Miss Goodwin, Miss Haley, Miss Racher acted as "Watcher" in turn. "All clear" at 3.30 pm.

Mar 5th 1941 – Air raid warning at 11.30 – 11.45. Miss Racher "watcher".

Mar 10th 1941 – School milk started today.

Jul 29th 1941 – I have today received notice that the 3 schools will merge after the Summer holidays and that all children will be divided into 3 classes – Seniors, Juniors, Infants – taught by myself, Miss Goodwin and Miss Racher.

Sep 8th 1941 – We re-open school today. School is divided in 3 groups. Seniors under Mrs Smith H. T, Juniors under Miss Goodwin, Infants under Miss Racher.

Jan 22nd 1942 - HMI Mrs Loch visited this school at 1.30 this afternoon and took particulars of numbers, classes etc. She suggested that bricking up of window in Refuge Room was not necessary.

Jul 13th 1942 – Several children absent with permission to help farmers with hay.

Jul 23rd 1942 – Air raid warning 8.55 – 9.15 am. Children on premises were admitted. Miss Goodwin acted as watcher.

Oct 6th 1942 – PC Wheeler visited school this morning at 11.30 and talked to the children of the danger of objects lying about which might prove to be bombs or grenades.

Oct 15th 1942 – Mr Pinnock called at close of school today and suggested that as the numbers are now 60 (both schools) the services of Miss Goodwin might be dispensed with.

Nov 6th 1942 – Miss Goodwin's duties terminated today.

Nov 26th 1942 – The LMS Railway Company have today collected 19 Walthamstow desks for return to Walthamstow.

Dec 17th 1942 – LMS Railway Company have today collected a teachers table and 2 cupboards to return to Walthamstow.

Oct 12th 1943 – The remaining equipment belonging to the Walthamstow authority was collected this morning.

Jan 3rd 1944 – Re-opened the school at 9.30 this morning. On arriving at 9 am I found the fires had not been lit and that no caretaker had been appointed. The temperature was 40 degrees.

Jan 4th 1944 – Still no caretaker. I personally, have today, before school, swept, dusted, cleaned the grate and lit the fires ready for morning school. I found that the lavatories were in a filthy condition someone having used them during the evening. They cannot be locked.

Jan 5th 1944 – Mr Tatman commenced work today as caretaker, although it has not yet been found possible to dispose of the contents of the lavatory pails.

Jan 24th 1944 – The school has been open 3 weeks now the pails have not been emptied once.

Jan 29th 1944 – The lavatory pails were emptied and refuse taken away by Tuisley of Clapham at 11 am today (Saturday).

Apr 3rd 1944 – On opening school today I found many desks had been deliberately cut and scratched. The caretaker also reports that the school was left very dirty and untidy after a function held on Friday. The playground being particularly so.

Apr 5th 1944 – I terminate my duties here today. I A E Smith.

Jun 20th 1944 – I received news this morning that Clifford Poulter was killed yesterday evening by a farm machine.

Milton Ernest Burial Register records Clifford Poulter, aged 6, killed under a tractor, buried 23rd June 1944.

Sep 18th 1944 – I, Monica Boielle, commence duties as acting Head Teacher of this school. I received word that I had been appointed Head Mistress of the school, took up duties at an earlier date, because of the illness of Mrs Burke, former *(acting)* Head Mistress.

Jan 8th 1945 – No. on roll now 38 (+ 3 evacuees).

Jan 15th 1945 – Fire drill and ARP practice held. Good results.

Mar 21st 1945 – The Director of Education, Mr Lucking, the Assistant Director, Mr Pinnock, and Canon Cockbill visited the school this morning, to examine the buildings. It was suggested that a new school be built.

Apr 9th 1945 – One evacuee Grace Underwood had returned to London. No. on roll 18 boys 21 girls Total 39 children (+ 2 evacuees).

May 8th & May 9th 1945 – School closed for VE and VE+1 day.

May 16th 1945 – Baffle wall for blast removed.

May 28th 1945: School re-opened today. The two official evacuees Joan and Reginald Littlechild have returned to London.

Sep 20th 1945 – Three panes of glass broke in south window of large room – due to demolition of ammunition in this area. House badly damaged.

Fig 54 – Mrs Boielle, Head Mistess of Milton Ernest Lower School, 1944-1965, and some of her scholars. The back of the photograph is annotated "In School Milton Ernest, Madam and some of the mob, 1951".

Information derived and extracts taken from 'Milton Ernest Log Book, 1912-1975' as written by the Head Teachers of Milton Ernest Lower School during that period; 'Sixty Years A Thatcher', W. R. (Reg) Parrott.

Milton Ernest Hall During World War II

In 1939 at the start of Second World War the Starey family moved out of Milton Ernest Hall to live in nearby Home Farm. During the early part of the war the Hall was thought to have been used as a Special Operations Executive (SOE) base. Milton Ernest Hall was ideally placed to assist Thurleigh and Tempsford Airfields from where the heroes of the SOE flew out to their missions in occupied Europe.

In February 1943, the United States Army Air Force chose the Hall to be the headquarters for their 8th Advanced Air Service Command. It was given the official name of Station 506.

Fig 55 – Milton Ernest Hall under American control during World War II. Note the American flag.

In preparation for the arrival of the Americans, Milton Ernest Hall was surrounded with barbed wire; 'no admittance' signs were put up; and there were two guard posts. Once the Americans were in situ, six military policemen (MP) guarded the main entrance to the hall. Two stood opposite the main gates on the far side of what is now the A6 while another two faced the main road. Two further MPs were stationed on the approach to the Hall. At another entrance, near to the barracks, there were two sentries and inside the Hall wall there was a MP hut. Even the river was guarded by up to three MPs with a machine-gun pit and children were prevented from swimming up to the Hall in that direction. The reason for this high level of security has led to much conjecture of what the Americans were doing at Milton Ernest Hall that warranted such high security. Other seemingly more important American sites during World War II had a much lower level of security. By comparison Milton Ernest Hall was Fort Knox.

Officially the work undertaken at Milton Ernest Hall was to oversee and co-ordinate activities at advanced supply and repair depots. The 8th Advanced Air Service Command was important to bombing operations as it helped provide the parts which kept bombers airborne. However, even if the headquarters at Milton Ernest Hall had been put out of action, the Command would still have had the necessary communications and back up bases to keep up the flow of parts to the bases.

Fig 56 – A nissen hut in the grounds of Milton Ernest Hall.

Milton Ernest locals soon became curious about the activities at the Hall. The Americans had constructed several brick and corrugated metal huts in the grounds of Milton Ernest Hall and radio transmitters were spotted in one of these, but Service Command had no need for radios. Land lines, with scramblers, and teletape machines were used to pass on operational information. Radio transmitters were more likely to be used to contact personnel where the usual forms of communication were either unavailable or impractical, such as occupied Europe. To add to the intrigue a local Police Constable, passing the hut with the radio transmitters, overheard operators speaking in German.

Milton Ernest Hall had an Operations room which was located in the large former dining room. Wooden shutters covered the bay windows which overlooked the lawns at the rear. These would have prevented visual access to the maps and charts. Although Service Command could have needed an Operations room it is interesting to note that Brigadier General Edmund W. Hill, who had overall command of several specialised units, made frequent visits.

Fig 57 – Construction of the bailey bridge, alongside the boathouse, during WWII.

Fig 58 – The bailey bridge to the rear of Milton Ernest Hall, circa 1945

Pierced steel planking was laid in the field on the other side of river to the Hall. This enabled single-engine aircraft to land and take-off. General Hill was a good pilot and he was able to quickly fly between Milton Ernest Hall and his headquarters at Cheddington, near Leighton Buzzard,

Bedfordshire. A bailey bridge was put across the river to allow easy access to the hall.

General Hill continued to use Milton Ernest Hall until late 1944 when he was named Commanding General, AAF Units, Installations and Activities in Russia. His presence at Milton Ernest Hall, along with the high security, begs the question, was Milton Ernest a divisional OSS (American Office of Strategic Services) headquarters or a link in the chain of the entire Allied clandestine war effort? Either would explain the tight security in and around the Hall; the need for a radio transmitter; and why a company of British MPs were stationed at the Grange, a large town house on the main road, a few hundred yards to the south of the Hall. Such evidence supports the theory that Milton Ernest Hall was central to a wider group of 'stations' concerned with secret allied radio and propaganda, transmitting political warfare and undertaking undercover operations by both British and American units.

Fig 59 – An envelope sent from Station 506 (Milton Ernest Hall) to Christopher Haycock at Ousebank Farm, Milton Ernest. The post mark is dated 8th December 1944, exactly a week before Glenn Miller's final flight.

At the end of the war an American unit took a month to thoroughly cleanse the hall and grounds of any signs of military occupation. Sadly, it is highly unlikely that the true importance of the Second World War activities at Milton Ernest Hall will ever be revealed. Such information will probably always remain classified.

Information derived and extracts taken from 'The Bedford Triangle. US Undercover Operations from England in World War 2' by Martin W. Bowman, 1988; 'Miller's tale just one of many Hall secrets' by Liz O'Reilly, Bedfordshire on Sunday, 27th February 2005.

John Michael Bryan, a World War II Hero

On the war memorial in the graveyard of All Saints' Church are inscribed the names of thirteen Milton Ernest men who died during the two world wars. All of them heroes, as were the many other men from the village who were fortunate enough to survive the conflict. John Michael Bryan's story has been included in this book because there was more material available; however, his story should be seen as a representation of the bravery displayed by all of the men from the village when they fought for their country.

John Michael Bryan was born in 1922 at South Norwood and was educated at Tunbridge School and Cambridge. His parents, John Ingram and Lucy Silver Bryan, moved the family to Milton Ernest in 1935. This was because John Ingram Bryan succeeded Ernest Holmes as the Vicar of All Saints'. John Michael Bryan would have been thirteen years of age when he came to live in Milton Ernest Vicarage. George Willars remembers John Michael playing in the grounds of the Vicarage before the start of the war. John would often confront George and his friends with the words "Halt, who goes there!" when they walked alongside the grounds of the Vicarage.

In 1940, aged eighteen, John Michael Bryan, known as Mike Bryan, enlisted in the Royal Air Force Volunteer Reserve. He trained in Canada and was commissioned as a pilot officer on 22nd June 1941. War details, if they still exist, are only released with the permission of the person or next of kin; therefore, it is hard to put together a complete war record. In John Michael Bryan's case all we know is that by 1943 he was part of Squadron 137. Before that is a bit of a mystery. Squadron 137 wasn't formed until 20th September 1941, so Bryan must have started his active military service in another squadron.

Squadron 137 started at Charmy Down in Somerset. Six officers were posted from 263 Squadron to form the core of the new squadron, one of whom could well have been John Michael Bryan. 137 Squadron moved to RAF Coltishall, Norfolk, in November 1941 and then was based at Matlaske, Norfolk, a month later. In September 1942 Squadron 137 became associated with RAF Manston, Kent, and took on the role of ground attacks.

The squadron used the Westland Whirlwind I, then the Hawker Hurricane IV, before being equipped with the Hawker Typhoon 1b in January 1944.

A report in the Bedfordshire Times dated 19th March 1943 headed 'VICAR'S SON PAYS FLYING VISIT' stated that Flight-Lieutenant J M Bryan, younger son of the Vicar of Milton Ernest paid a 'flying' visit to his parents.

After lunch he took off again from a nearby aerodrome for his operational station. George Willars remembers John Michael Bryan flying his Whirlwind just over the top of the Vicarage on a number of occasions.

The Bedfordshire Times also reported that Bryan belonged "to a squadron which has an outstanding record for "intruder" activities over enemy occupied territory". John Michael Bryan was credited with attacking twenty-one locomotives and his squadron had shot up twenty-seven goods trains. It would seem that John Michael's sudden visit to Milton Ernest had been to pass on some good news to his parents, as four days later it was announced, in the London Gazette, that John Michael Bryan had been awarded the Distinguished Flying Cross.

© R N Pearson 1999

Fig 60 – Westland Whirlwind Mark I with the markings of 137 Squadron.

The DFC had been established on 3rd June 1918 for officers and warrant officers of the Air Forces for "an act of valour, courage, or devotion to duty performed whilst flying in active operations against the enemy". The DFC was open to those pilots who had scored eight or more aerial victories.

The entry in the London Gazette, dated 23rd March 1943, confirmed that John Michael Bryan was in 137 Squadron. It stated that "This officer has taken part in a large number of sorties and patrols. On one occasion he assisted in the destruction of a Dornier 217. In attacks on enemy transport in Northern France and Belgium, Flying Officer Bryan has damaged 15 locomotives. His skill and keenness have been worthy of high praise". The Bedfordshire Times also reported the accolade and their newspaper report, interestingly, noted that John had three elder brothers all fighting in the War. He had two brothers, Squadron Leader A. L. Bryan and Major Paul Bryan, in the African Campaign and another brother, A. Ingram Bryan, who was in the Canadian Army. Major Paul Bryan was later awarded the Military Cross and Distinguished Service Order in the North African and Italian campaigns respectively.

When John Michael Bryan was invested with his DFC at Buckingham Palace he was accompanied by his mother and another brother, Mr Arthur E Bryan, Canadian Trade Commissioner in Liverpool. The number of Canadian references suggest that the Bryan family originated from that country.

In June 1943 Squadron 137 moved to RAF Rochford at Southend-on-Sea. Here the pilots practised in the Hurricane IV and used 40mm cannon and 3 inch rockets which were so new that they were still officially a secret.

The London Gazette reported on 30th July 1943, that Bryan had added a bar to his DFC. It reported that "Flight Lieutenant Bryan is a skilful and tenacious pilot. Since being awarded the Distinguished Flying Cross, he has damaged 2 minesweepers, 3 barges and an E boat. In addition he has executed 13 destructive attacks on locomotives; he has also participated in several successful attacks on enemy airfields. Flight Lieutenant Bryan has displayed high qualities of leadership, setting an inspiring example". The Bedfordshire Times, dated 6th August 1943, added that "in a sweep, leading his squadron over enemy territory, he personally destroyed seven locomotives, which makes thirty-four now to his credit". Locomotive attacks would have been spectacular as the 40mm cannon could blast the boiler clean off a train.

To put his honours into perspective, 4,018 DFC's were awarded during WWII, plus 214 first and 5 second bars. John Michael Bryan was, therefore, one of just 214 officers to be awarded a bar to his DFC.

In August 1943, 137 Squadron returned to RAF Manston. During this month Bryan left 137 and became Commanding Officer of 198 Squadron who were also based at Manston. Bryan was Squadron Leader of 198 Squadron, which was one of the first Typhoon squadrons tasked with ground attack duties to the continent, from August 1943 to November 1943.

On 23rd September 1943, 198 Squadron were in action along the Mastgat (Netherlands) where they found a large tug towing barges. They left it smoking but quite a bit of flak came up and Bryan's Typhoon was hit and badly damaged.

Four days later, on 27th September, Bryan once again led 198 Squadron to the Dutch coast. At Oosterschelde they found tugs and barges escorted by three 800 ton naval auxiliaries. These vessels put up a good protective screen which brought down two Typhoons. Bryan was again hit, this time in the starboard ammunition pan by a 20mm shell which exploded the remaining ammo, blowing a hole two feet across in the main plane. This caused such a loss of lift that Bryan had to use both arms and one leg to keep the stick hard over in order to fly back to base. Here again his troubles were not over for his right wing dropped suddenly as he came in to land, causing the Typhoon to twist over to the right in mid air. The right wing banged down hard and the whole aircraft swung so much that he changed direction to run through forty degrees to the right and covered quite a distance before rolling to a halt.

On 7th October 1943, John Michael Bryan and Vaughan Fittall shared a Focke-Wulfe 190 near Blankenberge, Belgium. The 190 came down in a field south-west of Tielt. Fittall recalls that he and Bryan enticed two of these German planes by pretending to be slower Hurricanes. Crossing the sea they throttled back with a bit of flap down and chased them back inland. Flight Lieutenant Fittall, who survived the war and moved back to his native New Zealand, said "Mike Bryan I can only describe as a good bloke and if you know anything about New Zealanders, you will know that it's high praise".

The Bedfordshire Times of 15th October 1943 reported that John Michael Bryan "has been engaged in some exciting encounters over enemy territory. Last week, in a running fight of fifty miles over tree-tops, he brought down a Focke-Wulfe 190". This report is probably referring to the action encountered with Fittall.

The same paper then printed on 5th November 1943 that "some dramatic pictures of an attack by Typhoons on enemy supply shipping off the Dutch coast, which were published in the week-end newspapers, were taken by Squadron-Leader John Michael Bryan (DFC and Bar), youngest son of the Rev. Dr. J. Ingram Bryan and Mrs. Bryan of Milton Ernest, by means of a small cine-camera fitted in his plane which led the attack".

On 30th November 1943, 198 Squadron supported a B-17 deep penetration raid into Germany. On this sortie the squadron caught a number of FW190s as they came into land at an airfield near Deelen. Four were claimed, of which one was destroyed by Bryan and one was damaged.

At the end of November 1943, John Michael Bryan was posted away for a rest. However, on 13th January 1944, he briefly visited 198 Squadron and took the chance to take part in a Ranger operation led by Squadron Leader Johnny Baldwin. Six Typhoons took part, taking advantage of bad weather to sweep airfields in the Montdidier, Juvincourt and Laon areas of France. At Poix, Bryan shot down a Caudron Goeland transport plane and a Messerschmitt 109.

Bryan returned as Commanding Officer of 198 Squadron in April and May 1944. He was then promoted in May 1944 and became Wing Leader of 136 Airfield and led 164 Squadron.

On 18th May 1944 Bryan, flying with 164 Squadron, encountered a number of Messerschmitt 109s. He fired at one from below, of which the results aren't recorded, and another he fired at exploded. Bryan's aircraft was hit during the engagement and one of his rockets had been dislodged, hanging down all the way back to base.

Fig 61 – Hawker Typhoon Mark 1b with the markings of 164 Squadron.

D-Day, 6th June 1944, saw Bryan lead 164 Squadron on a late morning operation strafing trucks and lorries. Late in the afternoon he led 164 to the Bayeux area, finding targets, such as trains and bridges, for their rockets. A battle ensued between the Typhoons and FW190s in which one from each side was lost. Two days later Bryan was back in action in the same area. This time they found a number of Messerschmitt 109s in the air. The ME109s attacked the Typhoons and Bryan claimed two in the ensuing scrap.

On Saturday 10th June 1944, John Michael Bryan's luck ran out and he was shot down by flak two miles south-east of Falaise in Normandy. He was buried in the Bretteville-Sur-Laize Canadian Cemetery, in Calvados, France.

John Michael Bryan died at the age of just twenty-two. The few records that exist of his war record paint the picture of a very brave man and an exceptional leader. Like so many of his generation he was a true hero. The people of Milton Ernest and the rest of the country should be very thankful for him and for his like.

Obituary

FALLEN OFFICERS

"THE TIMES" LIST OF CASUALTIES

We have received news of the death of the following officers in addition to those whose names have been published in the official list:—

THE ARMY

ALDERSON, Captain R. C., Coldstream Gds.
BAINES, Major R. G. T., Hampshire Regt.
DOUGLAS, Major A. S. K., Cameron Highdrs.
HEAD, Lieutenant A. L., Notts Yeomanry.
KER, Captain P. M., R.A.
MARTIN, Lieut. E., 6th Airborne Division.
OSLER, Major K. S., R.C.A.
RIVERS, Lieutenant E. A., Essex Regiment.

ROYAL AIR FORCE

WING COMMANDER JOHN MICHAEL BRYAN, D.F.C., killed while leading his wing over Normandy, was 22 years of age, and the youngest son of the Rev. Dr. and Mrs. J. Ingram Bryan, of Milton Ernest Vicarage, Bedford. Born at South Norwood in 1922, he enlisted in the R.A.F.V.R. in 1940, was trained in Canada, and commissioned in 1941. He was awarded the D.F.C. in March, 1943, as a flying officer, for skill and keenness worthy of high praise in a large number of sorties and patrols in No. 137 Squadron. On one occasion he assisted in the destruction of a Dornier 217, and in attacks on enemy transport in France and Belgium he had damaged 15 locomotives. Four months later he gained a Bar to the D.F.C. as a flight lieutenant with the same squadron. In the interval he had damaged two minesweepers, three barges, and an E-boat, had made 13 destructive attacks on locomotives and had attacked airfields.

Fig 62 – Obituary of John Michael Bryan, taken from the Saturday 24th June 1944 edition of The Times.

Information derived and extracts taken from '137 Squadron – RAF' by Charles Shepherd at 'www.137squadron.com'; 'History of No. 137 Squadron' at 'www.raf.mod.uk'; The Bedfordshire Times; The London Gazette; The contributors to Key Publishing Ltd Aviation Forum at 'http://forum.keypublishing.co.uk'.

Glenn Miller in Milton Ernest, 1944

Alton Glenn Miller was born in Clarinda, Iowa, USA, on 1st March 1904. He dropped out of university to become a full time professional musician and joined his first big band in 1925. Eleven years later he formed his own band but it soon fizzled out. In 1938 he formed the Glenn Miller Orchestra and almost immediately hit the big time. Seventy top ten hits were achieved in the US including "Pennsylvania 6-5000", "String Of Pearls", "Moonlight Serenade", "In The Mood" and "Tuxedo Junction". Such was Miller's success that he was reckoned to be earning $20,000 per week! However, such was his love for his country that Miller joined the US Army Air Forces and on September 27th 1942 disbanded his successful Orchestra.

Fig 63 – Glenn Miller (right) with Chaplain Joe Luck, outside Milton Ernest Hall, 1944.

Captain, later Major, Miller's wish to perform to America's fighting forces overseas was finally granted and on June 18th 1944 he flew into England. Ten days later, the sixty members of his band arrived on the liner *Queen Elizabeth*. They had intended to be billeted in London, but the constant attacks of the V1 flying bombs meant that this wasn't an option. David Niven, the film star, suggested Bedford as a safer location and so, on

Sunday July 2nd, Glenn Miller and his band settled into their new base in Ashburnham Road in the town.

Fig 64 – Glenn Miller's Band being dropped off, what is thought to be, outside the entrance to Milton Ernest Hall, 1944.

The US Army personnel at Milton Ernest Hall were responsible for the day to day administration of the band. Brigadier General Donald Goodrich, the commanding officer at Milton Ernest Hall, allowed them to have their meals in one of the nissen huts in the grounds of the Victorian mansion, as there was nowhere suitable in Bedford. This meant that army trucks took Glenn Miller and his band to and fro between Bedford and Milton Ernest. Miller and his executive officer, Lieutenant Don Haynes, were billeted at the American Red Cross Officers' Club, while the band were based in two large detached houses in Ashburnham Road. In return for Goodrich's hospitality, Glenn Miller arranged for his American Band of the Supreme Allied Command, to play a concert in the grounds of Milton Ernest Hall. This took place at 4pm on Sunday 16th July 1944 and was a huge success with 1,600 officers, enlisted personnel and civilian guests from the village present.

Glenn Miller and some members of the band often stayed overnight in rooms at Milton Ernest Hall. After meals they used to frequent 'Club Castle', the Officers' Club located in the grounds near the enlisted men's barracks. Miller and his band also drank in the Milton Ernest public houses,

The Swan and The Queen's Head. They visited the Swan the most as they were very friendly with the landlord, Tom Larkins, and sometimes brought him bottles of scotch, a rare treat in wartime Britain.

Fig 65 – Glenn Miller and his American Band of the Supreme Allied Command in the grounds of Milton Ernest Hall, Sunday 16th July 1944.

Having toured England for six months, Glenn Miller and the Allied Expeditionary Force (AEF) Orchestra were booked to play to front-line troops in France. On December 14th 1944, Glenn Miller rang from the Mount Royal Hotel, London, to advise Don Haynes at Milton Ernest Hall that bad weather meant that all flights out of Bovingdon, Hertfordshire, had been cancelled and he wouldn't be able to precede the orchestra to France the following day as planned. Colonel Baessell overheard the conversation and informed Miller that he was flying to Paris the next day. Haynes drove to London in a staff car to pick up Miller and later that evening, back at Milton Ernest Hall, Miller played poker with Haynes, Baessell, Major William Koch and Warrant Officer Neal Earlywine until the early hours.

The next morning, Bedford was fogged in. Miller and Haynes left their quarters at Goldington Road and drove to Milton Ernest Hall, which was shrouded in fog and swirling mist, to meet up with Baessell. Here they had lunch before receiving confirmation that the flight would go ahead. Lieutenant Don Haynes drove Miller and Baessell to the RAF station at Twinwood Farm. Their aircraft appeared through the overcast cloud, circled the airfield and then landed. Haynes drove to the end of the runway to the waiting plane. As Miller and Baessell boarded the plane, Miller looked up at the horrible weather and said "Haynsie. Even the birds are grounded today!" At 13:55 on Friday 15th December 1944, Glenn

Miller and Lieutenant Colonel Norman F Baessell took off from RAF Twinwood Farm in a Canadian built single-engine Noordwyn Norseman piloted by Flight Officer Johnny 'Nipper' Morgan. They were headed for Villacoubley, France, but were never seen again and no trace was ever apparently found of the plane.

Fig 66 – Glenn Miller (centre) in the grounds of Milton Ernest Hall. Note the nissen hut in the background.

There have been many theories about the fate of Glenn Miller. The more extreme include that he died in the arms of a Paris prostitute and that he didn't die in 1944 but languished in a mental institute before dying some years later. Rumours within Milton Ernest also suggest that there never was a plane flight but Major Glenn Miller died from syphilis and was secretly buried in an unmarked grave in All Saints' Church.

For the past sixty years, despite the speculation, experts felt that Glenn Miller's death was nothing more than a tragic accident with his plane probably ditching into the English Channel. However an article in the 29th November 2005 edition of the Daily Mail suggests that at last the mystery of Miller's disappearance has been solved.

The article quotes Mark Montoya who was a U.S. military policeman based at Milton Ernest Hall in 1944. Montoya alleges that Colonel Baessell used to make twice weekly trips to an U.S. airbase in Northern France. Here he would bring back an illicit cargo of French contraband which was then shipped to the United States. Montoya states that he saw Chanel No5 perfume and other luxury goods inside the crates. Such items, including champagne, would have fetched massively inflated prices on the black market and so the trips were very lucrative for Baessell.

Fig 67 – Don Haynes, Glenn Miller (centre), and another officer are served dinner by Sergeant Ming of the catering staff at Milton Ernest Hall.

On that fateful 15th December day, Montoya insists that Miller's plane landed safely at Merville, in Normandy, and not Paris which has always thought to have been its destination. Montoya didn't think that Miller was directly involved with the black market trade, he had simply 'gone along for the ride' with the aim of having lunch with Baessell in France. However, the weather deteriorated and they had to cancel their plans for a meal.

Miller helped Baessell load the contraband and then the plane took off from Merville headed north towards the French coastline. Nearing the Channel, the temperature plunged and it is thought that the aircraft's wings started to freeze. Johnny Morgan, the pilot, struggled valiantly to keep the Norseman in the sky. He issued several Mayday messages which were received by American servicemen at Merville. However, the combination of the icy weather and the heavy cargo meant Morgan's efforts were in vain. The plane crashed onto a beach somewhere between Calais and Dunkirk killing the three men on board instantly.

Montoya states that the wreckage was buried on the beach and the bodies of Miller, Baessell and Morgan were secretly flown to America. The reason for the cover-up, according to Montoya, was because news of Baessell's 'racketeering' would have been highly embarrassing to the U.S. Army and Glenn Miller's involvement on this one trip would have tarnished his reputation.

Interestingly, in 1949, Glenn Miller's widow, Helen, purchased a six grave burial site in Mountain View Cemetery in Altadena, California. This was despite there only being five members in her close family. When researchers asked Helen Miller whether they could scan the empty grave to see if Miller's body was in fact buried there, she refused them permission.

The question that remains is why has it taken sixty years for this story to emerge? Mark Montoya, who celebrated his eighty-first birthday in 2005, would seem to have reached an age where he simply wants to put the record straight. He stated that "...it does bother me when I see all the different theories and they have not come up with the truth." Has Montoya ended the speculation once and for all? Only time will tell.

Information derived and extracts taken from 'Dictionary of American Biography 1941-1945' edited by Edward T. James; 'Glenn Miller in Britain Then and Now' by Chris Way, 1996; Glenn Miller article by Ben Raza, Bedfordshire Times & Citizen, 17th December 2004; 'Miller's tale just one of many Hall secrets' by Liz O'Reilly, Bedfordshire on Sunday, 27th February 2005; 'Is this the answer to one of the greatest mysteries of the war?' by Andrew Kelly and Paul Bracchi, 29th November 2005.

Moving Milton Ernest Water Tower, 1952

In 1952, a wind tunnel was planned at the new National Aeronautical Establishment, Bedford, but a concrete water tower, which had been erected by Bedford Rural District Council in 1936, stood on the designated site. The tower was going to be demolished and a completely new tower erected nearby at a cost of £30,000. However, J. L. Kier and Company (London) Ltd, won the contract when they advised that they could move the 1,800 ton, 79-feet-tall, 53-feet-wide, tower bodily to its new position and at half the cost!

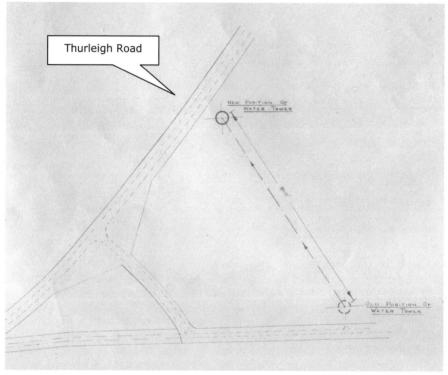

Fig 68 – 1952 plan of the proposed Water Tower move.

Before work was undertaken to move Milton Ernest water tower, which has a capacity of 150,000 gallons, a new tower had to be built at Turvey to ensure that water supply was maintained across the North Bedfordshire villages. This was brought into operation on 3rd September 1952.

Starting in May 1952 a team of twelve workmen built two narrow concrete roadways, each 8 feet wide, from the base of the tower to its new position close to Thurleigh Road. The water tower was emptied and then separated from its foundations by small blasting charges of gelignite and a hexagonal concrete cradle built at its base. Then a series of concrete blocks was placed onto the twin roadways and on top were put steel channels like railway lines. Ball bearings, each 2.5 inches in diameter, were inserted in the channels and the tower was lowered onto them.

Fig 69 – Milton Ernest Water Tower on the move, 1952.

On 19th September 1952 Milton Ernest water tower started to be moved slowly along the ground. Underneath the tower at any given moment were 800 ball bearings, 400 on each rail. Another 400 were placed in front of the tower and as it moved the concrete blocks, channels and ball bearings, over which it had travelled, were moved around to the front to be used again. The tower was towed 810 feet by a crawler tractor using a block and tackle system exerting a pull of about seventy tons. Originally a steam traction engine was used but it suffered a mechanical breakdown.

The structure was moved at the rate of about 50 feet a day and reached its new position on 17th October 1952. The Milton Ernest water tower move was a successful engineering movement performed for the first time in Britain. Throughout the process the tower remained vertical to within 1/8th of an inch. People were impressed at the smooth, almost effortless, movement of the tower. This engineering achievement generated much local and even some national interest.

Fig 70 – Base of the Water Tower.

Fig 71 – Ball bearings on the tracks.

Fig 72 – Men working on the concrete blocks.

Fig 73 – Cables attached to the tractor.

Fig 74 – Milton Ernest Water Tower being moved by the tractor.

SKILFUL ENGINEERING FEAT TRANSFERS TOWER

Milton Ernest Landmark
Moved Bodily

Bedford Rural Councillors and officials stood on a bleak Bedfordshire hilltop on Wednesday afternoon and witnessed an engineering achievement performed in this country for the first time.

Slowly before their eyes, Milton Ernest water tower, a landmark for many miles around, was moving along the ground It was no optical illusion but part of a revolutionary method of transferring the massive concrete tower in one piece to another spot 800 feet away.

Weighing nearly 2,000 tons, the tower interfered with plans for the National Aeronautical Research Establishment. It was going to be demolished and a completely new tower erected near by.

But in stepped a firm of civil engineering contractors Messrs. J. L. Keir and Company (London) Ltd., who said they could move the tower bodily to its new position and at half the cost.

Working since last May a team of 12 workmen built two narrow concrete roadways from the base of the tower to its new position at the boundary of the Aeronautical Establishment against the Milton Ernest—Thurleigh road.

HOW IT IS BEING DONE

Mr. J. F. Dickinson, 40-year old civil engineer in charge of the project tells the rest of the story

He told this newspaper that the 82-feet-tall tower was separated from its foundations by small blasting charges and a hexagonal concrete cradle built at its base.

Then a series of concrete blocks, made on the site, were placed on to the twin roadways, and on top were put steel channels like railway lines Ball bearings, each 2¼ inches in diameter, were inserted in the channels, and the tower was lowered on to them

Underneath the tower at any given moment were 800 ball bearings, 400 on each "rail way line." Another 400 were placed in front of the tower, and as it moved the concrete blocks, channels and ball bearings over which it had travelled were moved around to the front to be used again.

Mr Dickinson estimated that the cost of demolishing the tower and erecting a new one would be about £30,000, but the total cost of this operation was half that amount—£15,000. The tower was towed by a crawler tractor using a block and tackle system exerting a pull of about 70 tons.

mal rate of progress was 50 feet a day. On Wednesday it had been moved 170 feet, leaving another 630 feet to traverse. Mr. Dickinson estimated that this would take another fortnight before being in position over its new foundation.

The Councillors were all impressed by the smooth, almost effortless, movement of the tower and took a keen interest in the project. Among them were the Council Chairman Ald. P. Raymond Smith, and the Clerk (Mr. C. B. Townsend) with the Surveyor (Mr. D. T. Matthews).

For many of the Councillors it was their second visit to the tower. The first occasion was the opening ceremony in 1936. The tower supplied water to

The tower photographed before the operations were begun.

"To my knowledge," said Mr. Dickinson, "this is certainly the first time in this country that a permanent concrete structure has been moved by this method. The Mulberry Harbours made during the war were moved by the same system, but they were constructed with such a method of movement in mind."

The structure was first moved on Friday, and the nor-

most North Bedfordshire villages, and there would have been serious inconvenience during the removal operations but for a new water distribution scheme in the area.

"LIKE OILED SILK"

Mr. Townsend said after the visit, "All of us thought it a marvellous engineering achievement. It was one of those things that people would not believe unless they actually saw it with their own eyes. The thing that most amazed us was its smooth movement—just like oiled silk."

Fig 75 – Bedfordshire Times article on the Milton Ernest water tower move, Friday 26th September 1952.

Information derived and extracts taken from 'Skilful Engineering Feat Transfers Tower – Milton Ernest Landmark Moved Bodily', Bedfordshire Times, Friday 26th September 1952; 'Milton Ernest Water Tower' document by P. G. Clark, December 1955, kindly provided by Mollie Foster of Clapham Historical Society.

Milton Glebe, 1989

In 1989 Bedfordia PLC proposed the construction of a new hamlet within the Parish of Milton Ernest between the villages of Milton Ernest and Radwell. This new settlement would be set within a 300 acre 'bow' of the River Great Ouse and would be called Milton Glebe.

A planning document and a glossy pamphlet highlighted the total development package which was:

- a new railway station and car park.
- a new hamlet of 150 executive homes.
- a new golf course and clubhouse.
- a landscaped riverside walk.
- a low cost village housing development of 45 dwellings in Milton Ernest.
- improvements to the sewage works.
- improvements to the road network.
- possibility of a shop/Post Office.

The electrified railway line would be extended from Bedford Station. Milton Glebe Railway Station would be used by people living in the North Bedfordshire villages to travel to Bedford Railway Station before catching another train to commute to London. This would mean that they would not have to contend with the traffic congestion in Bedford. There would be no northern service from Milton Glebe. It was also proposed that the golf course would be built around the executive homes.

On 25th July 1989 a Special Parish Council Meeting was held at Milton Ernest Village Hall to discuss the proposal. Bedfordia and their partners, including British Rail, presented their proposal and answered questions from the audience, which consisted of 180 members of the general public plus representatives from three parish councils. After two hours of a "lively and interesting" meeting it was agreed that there should be a vote on the proposal. This was done by a show of hands and resulted in 13 abstentions and no votes in favour. Everyone else voted against the proposal. Clifton Ibbett of Bedfordia accepted that the forceful show of hands against the proposal meant that the villagers did not want such a development.

The rejection was based on the consensus that although there was the need for a railway station north of Milton Ernest but it should not be at the expense of a large scale housing development. This it was felt would change the villager's quality of life and alter the character of the village.

Information derived and extracts taken from 'Proposed Residential Development at Milton Glebe, Bedfordshire by Bedfordia PLC', Phillips Planning Services, Ref YAP/JMS/87264/PPS1277/95, 31st May 1989; Milton Ernest Parish Council Minutes, 25th July 1989.

Fig 76 – Cover of the Milton Glebe pamphlet.

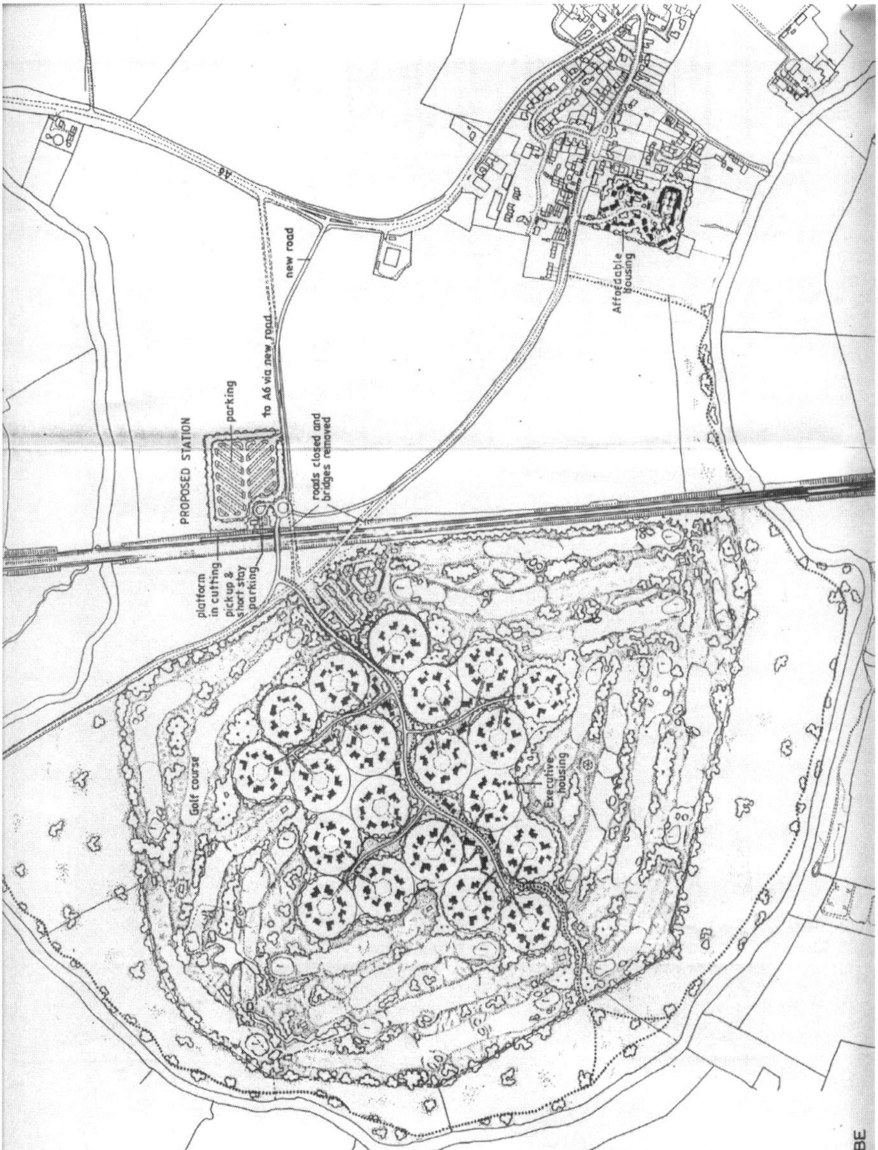

Fig 77 – The proposed Milton Glebe development.

PROPOSED STATION

parking

to A6 via new road

new road

roads closed and
bridges removed

platform
in cutting

pickup &
short stay
parking

golf course

Executive
housing

Affordable
housing

MILTON GLEBE

129

Fig 78 – An artist's impression of Milton Glebe Railway Station.

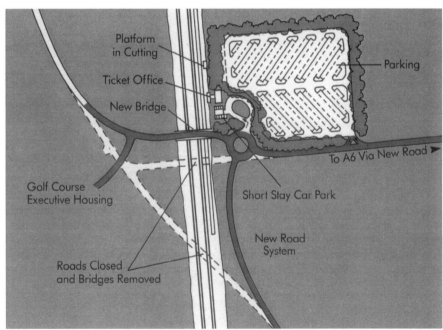

Platform
in Cutting

Ticket Office

New Bridge

Parking

To A6 Via New Road ➤

Golf Course
Executive Housing

Short Stay Car Park

New Road
System

Roads Closed
and Bridges Removed

Fig 79 – Map of the proposed Milton Glebe.

The Importance of Milton Ernest

Section Three:
The Heritage Trail

The Importance of Milton Ernest Heritage Trail

The 'Importance of Milton Ernest' Heritage Trail is 3.2 miles (5.2 kilometres) long. The route has been designed to cater for all ages and abilities. For the major part the walk covers the tarmac footpaths of the village making it accessible throughout the year. However, there are additional parts of the walk which use grassed areas which could be difficult for wheelchair users or become muddy at certain times of the year. Bearing this in mind alternative routes have been included on the map to ensure that everyone can complete the walk, no matter the weather conditions, without missing any of the historic buildings.

Please note that walkers must respect the privacy of the householders and not enter gardens or properties marked and mentioned in the text.

The walk has been designed to start and finish at the Queen's Head. However, you can obviously start anywhere on the route as by following the map you will eventually end up at the point where you began! The numbers within the text of the walk denote the reference to the building on the Heritage Trail map which can be found at the very end of the book.

An abridged version of the heritage trail has been included at the rear of the book for ease of use when actually walking. This conveys all of the key facts of each building that you will visit.

If you require something to eat or drink during or after your walk then why not enjoy the delights of the Queen's Head or the Coffee Shop at the Garden Centre!

Fig 80 – David Green's 1999 painting of Radwell Road, Milton Ernest. Left to right are Butterfield's Cottage, The Old Bakery, Hooker's House and Swan House. All four properties are visited during the Heritage Trail.

Heritage Trail (Part I) – The Queen's Head

Start the walk at the Queen's Head Hotel **1** which dates back to the late seventeenth century.

Fig 81 – The Queen's Head, 25ᵗʰ November 2004. Note the outlines of the two previous entrances.

In the early eighteenth century a pair of cottages were converted into a single unit as a public house. The original front doors to these cottages have been blocked and their outlines can still be seen today. This public house has been called 'The Queen's Head' from at least the start of the eighteenth century. A mortgage exists, dated 23ʳᵈ October 1733, showing the owner as being Thomas Rolt of Milton Ernest Hall and the occupier as John Robinson.

Fig 82 – The Queen's Head, circa 1930. Note the different location of the pub sign.

There was a brief period when the name of this establishment was changed to 'Booth's Arms' after Philip Booth, who lived at Milton Ernest Hall and was the major landowner at the time. Records show that Susanna Brown was the innkeeper between 1839 and 1862 and these name the pub as 'The Queen's Head' up until 1847 and then again from 1861. For some of the period between, certainly 1851 to 1854, the pub name was recorded as 'Booth's Arms'.

Fig 83 – The Queen's Head, circa 1910.

Sale particulars for Milton Ernest Hall, dated 26th June 1871, show the Queen's Head as being part of the Hall Estate. The exact wording being "A LICENSED PUBLIC HOUSE, known as the QUEEN'S HEAD, with YARD AND GARDEN, let to Mr. W. H. Gibbins, on lease expiring in September 1879, at the very low rental of £14 per annum. The lessee being under stringent conditions to ensure quiet occupation."

Ownership of the Queen's Head has changed over the years. The earliest records of a brewery owning the pub date back to 1876 when Allfrey and Lovell of Newport Pagnell were shown as being the proprietors. In 1919 Charles Wells bought Newport Pagnell Brewery for £30,000 in order to expand their estate. The Queen's Head was at this time owned by Newport Pagnell Brewery and so became a Charles Wells pub. It stayed this way until the 1990s when the Queen's Head was sold to a company called Old English Inns. Recently, Greene King of Bury St Edmunds took over Old English Inns and therefore the ownership of the business.

Fig 84 – Newport Pagnell Brewery Dray outside the Queen's Head. Note the sign which reads Newport Ales & Porter. The name on the sign, which is almost obscured by a barrel, is William Heritage. He was the landlord of the pub from circa 1914 to circa 1928. The photograph is circa 1915.

Fig 85 – The Queen's Head circa 1925. Note there are doors to the pub and to the next door cottage. Both are now blocked and the current pub entrance is between the two. The sign above the pub door reads 'Accommodation for Transport. Teas Provided'. The sign to the left of the door advertises 'Shell'. The other two signs read 'The Queen's Head'.

In Victorian times, the Queen's Head innkeepers had more to do than 'just' run a pub. Robert Makeham, who was landlord circa 1869-1885, was also a carpenter and wheelwright! The pub was also a good place to buy horses as occasionally fifty to one hundred horses would be brought into Milton Ernest by traders en route to a distant village or town. A halt would be called outside the Queen's Head and the local farmers would make a deal for the odd horse or two from the heavy cart horses, hunters, cobs, ponies, brood mares and their foals.

Fig 86 – Mr. Bradley, landlord of The Queen's Head, 1951. Note the black paint at the base of the walls.

In 1987 plans were submitted to convert the pub into a hotel with thirteen bedrooms. A large threshing barn, situated between the Queen's Head and Home Farm, was made part of the hotel and converted into bedrooms. This barn had a date stone of 1666, which is the date of the Great Fire of London.

One interesting fact is that the ceiling of the public bar is so low that the only way that darts could be played was by the construction of a trap door in the floor. Players had to open the trap door and stand in the hole which ensured that the dartboard was at the correct height! The trap door can still be seen just inside the car park entrance to the bar.

Fig 87 – The Queen's Head and Bedford Road.

Fig 88 – The Queen's Head and Bedford Road

Fig 89 – The Queen's Head, 1975. Note the whitewash on the walls.

Fig 90 – Another photograph of the whitewashed Queen's Head, 1975.

Heritage Trail (Part II) – Parkside and Radwell Road

From the Queen's Head car park turn left into Radwell Road.

The car park and the land before Parkside used to house a row of old cottages including the home of James Parrott the local shepherd and a bake house which was owned by William Cook between 1841 and 1871. A butcher's shop run by Mr Mole was also in the vicinity. The area was known as 'Cook's Alley' **2** .Today there is no sign that these buildings ever existed.

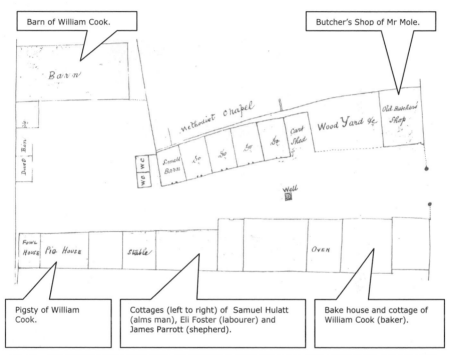

Barn of William Cook.

Butcher's Shop of Mr Mole.

Pigsty of William Cook.

Cottages (left to right) of Samuel Hulatt (alms man), Eli Foster (labourer) and James Parrott (shepherd).

Bake house and cottage of William Cook (baker).

Fig 91 – Map of Cook's Alley dated 1860. An earlier map of the same area, dated 1857, but in not such good condition, has the names of the owners or inhabitants. These have been added around this map.

Now turn left into Parkside, walk to the end of the road and you'll end up behind the Queen's Head. In front of you is Home Farm, which has been converted into two homes.

Home Farm **3** (10 & 11 Parkside) is thought to date back to 1660. It was renovated in the 1730s and a date stone on the street gable end commemorates this fact. William Butterfield then largely rebuilt the farmhouse in 1859.

Fig 92 – Home Farm before the extensive renovation.

Fig 93 – Home Farm, 25th November 2004.

Previous occupants include John Turner, the author of the letters describing Milton Ernest in 1834, and his father who was the farmer, and Edward Peck in 1871. In both cases the farm was named after the farmer by the locals and was known as Turner's Farm and then Peck's Farm.

Edward Peck farmed 228 acres and employed twelve men, nine boys, a governess and a servant.

Later, in the early part of the twentieth century, the Starey family moved into the property after selling Milton Ernest Hall. Captain Stephen Starey hired the Bedfordshire architect Sir Albert Richardson (1880-1964) and he transformed Home Farm into a dignified country residence. Richardson, who was based in Ampthill, extended the gable wing north eastwards and added an elevated first floor balcony entrance , with a staircase on the south-west front.

Fig 94 – The old stables and barns of Home Farm, now residential properties, 25th November 2004.

Stephen Starey was Bedfordshire County Scout Commissioner and he put Home Farm at scouting's convenience. The grounds of Home Farm were used as a temporary camping site until the scouting organisation found a permanent camp site.

John Starey recalls the farmhouse during the Second World War, when twelve children lived there including eight evacuees. At the time the farm had 370 poultry, 200 sheep and 20 cows. Home Farm used to have an outbuilding called 'The Hovel', which was a misleading name as it was an immaculately kept building which Stephen Starey let out for village functions. The Hovel was also used as a cinema enabling villagers to watch movies on a screen.

In 1985 the Stareys moved out of Home Farm and Parkside was created. As part of this development some outbuildings belonging to Home Farm were converted into five private dwellings **4** (3, 4 5, 6 & 7 Parkside). Three of them have names: 'East Barn', 'West Barn' and 'The Old Stables', which sheds light on their purpose before they became homes.

You now need to retrace your steps in Parkside, past number 2, which is built on the site of tennis courts, and head towards Radwell Road. Just before you leave Parkside, stop! This is the site of the Wesleyan Chapel.

Location of the Chapel

Fig 95 – Aerial photograph depicting the location of the Chapel on Radwell Road. In the foreground of the photograph note the football pitch on the village green and the original position of the school swimming pool.

The Wesleyan Chapel **5**, was built in 1839, a charming little neo-classical building with simple pilasters and a delicate fanlight over the entrance door. Inside were seven pews facing a pulpit at the far end of the Chapel.

It must have been quite a boost for the village Methodists to have a place to worship, as previously they had to obtain official registrations to worship at their own homes in Milton Ernest. These meeting places included the houses or buildings of William Barnett (1798), Samuel White (1800), James Odell (1806), Ruth Hart (1807), Richard Gower (1819) and James Lamb (1838).

The Chapel opened in 1839 and the first baptism, Selina Gibbins, quickly followed on 17th June of that year.

By 1851 the Sunday evening service attracted 120 people and there were 65 members of the Sunday School. Over a century later on 28th June 1970, Roger Wormold was the last person to be baptised at the Chapel.

Fig 96 – The Chapel, 1939.

Fig 97 – View of the pulpit which was at the rear of the Chapel.

Fig 98 – The Chapel pews. This photograph was taken from the pulpit facing the Radwell Road door.

Fig 99 – The Chapel on 26th July 1973. No longer used and in a state of decay.

George Willars recalls that the children of the village used to look forward to the 'Lantern Lectures' at the Chapel. This was a slide show which many children would gather to watch inside the Chapel. George also remembers that the village was split into Chapel people and Church people. Being one of the latter, he was dismayed that he wasn't allowed to watch let alone take part in the annual Chapel Sports Day which was only open to Milton Ernest people who attended the Chapel. All Saints' Church had the same attitude, as Church goers were the only people allowed at their events.

The Chapel Sports Day was held in a field opposite what is now called 'The Old Post Office' on Rushden Road.

By the late nineteen sixties the congregation had dwindled considerably and soon afterwards the building was no longer used for worship. In 1972 an application was made to demolish the building and erect a single dwelling. The worship registration was cancelled on 28th June 1973 and, after standing empty for over five years, the Chapel was duly demolished in 1976.

The Chapel, which was renovated in 1885, stood in Milton Ernest for 137 years and would have been an important building within the village, but today there is no visible sign that it ever existed.

One little known fact of this long history is that Glenn Miller's American Band of the AEF performed at a chapel service on the Sunday morning of 6th August 1944.

Leaving Parkside turn left onto Radwell Road. The first building you encounter is a restaurant known as 'The Strawberry Tree'.

Fig 100 – The Strawberry Tree, 25th November 2004

The Strawberry Tree 6 (3 Radwell Road) is a seventeenth century thatched cottage. It was originally three separate cottages, a sweet shop at the front, a laundry in the middle and a small cottage at the back. By the first half of the twentieth century the Marsh family owned what was by then one cottage. This was a marine store, which today would be called a scrap dealer's yard, and the garden used to be covered in various items of scrap. George Willars can remember that there were pig sties in a large yard with plenty of rats!

Fig 101 – Radwell Road circa 1910. Post mark on the post card is 1921. The cottage which became the Strawberry Tree is on the right.

Fig 102 – Close up of swing and seat which used to be the village play area.

Fig 103 – Close up of Forge Cottage and Bedford Road. An advert for 'Lyons Tea' was by the roadside.

During the Second World War, the Starey family bought the cottage and added the stone extension. Freda Starey and her sister lived at the property. At this time the house was known as 'The Old Cottage'.

In 1982 the cottage was converted into a tea shop called 'The Strawberry Tree' and by 1993 it was developed into a restaurant. The Strawberry Tree (arbutus) is an evergreen tree which produces edible strawberry like fruits in late summer. There are three such trees in the garden of the cottage, hence the name given to both the tea shop and restaurant by the Bona family, who established the business in 1982 and have been there ever since, winning many awards along the way.

Fig 104 – Ernest Milton.

If you look closely at the car park entrance wall immediately to the left of the cottage you can see a stone carving of a face. This was carved and built into the wall by Alfred Hall, a stone mason from Kempston. It is alleged that Alfred was unhappy with the owner of the cottage and incorporated the caricature as an act of defiance. The stone carving has since become known to the villagers as Ernest Milton!

Opposite the Strawberry Tree is a small piece of grassland, once known as 'Barton's Folly', with a bench. Here stood a large three storey red brick building which fronted onto Radwell Road and had no backyard. It was known to the villagers as the the Barracks **7** and housed a number of different families. The building filled the entire grassed area and would have dominated the landscape as people entered Radwell Road from Bedford, which is evident from some of the photographs in this book.

In the Village of Milton Ernest.

Fig 105 – Radwell Road looking towards the Old Bakery. The Barracks are on the right of the photograph.

Fig 106 – The Barracks. The six doors give an indication of the number of families who lived in this building.

150

Locally the building was also known as 'Gawp Row' because the inhabitants used to peer out of the windows at anyone who passed! George Willars recalls that the women who lived in the Barracks weren't that friendly. He and his friends were often told to "get back to your end of the road"!

The Barracks was demolished in November 1962.

Continuing down Radwell Road you'll soon come to a large red brick building known as 'Bob's Shop'.

Fig 107 – The Barracks.

'Bob's Shop' 8 (9 Radwell Road) is named after the proprietor Mr Robert Haycock and is sadly the last remaining shop in Milton Ernest. This grocery shop was originally run by his father Christopher Haycock. Interestingly, Bob believes that, prior to becoming a grocery shop, the premises were used as a Gentleman's Club.

Next on the trail is another red brick house immediately before the turning into River Lane.

Fig 108 – Bob's Shop, 25ᵗʰ November 2004

Fig 109 – Butterfield's Cottage, 25ᵗʰ November 2004

Butterfield's Cottage, (13 Radwell Road) **9** was designed and built by William Butterfield in 1859 at a cost of £259. William Butterfield (1814-1900) designed many ecclesiastical buildings in Britain as well as two cathedrals in Australia. He was a decorative designer with an individual Gothic style. Being a relative through marriage of the local Starey family meant that the village benefited from his skills. In Milton Ernest he built the Hall and Mill, restored All Saints' Church and built other cottages and farm buildings.

Fig 110 – Rose Cottages, circa 1910. The cottage on the left, now demolished, was the village workhouse.

On the other side of Radwell Road facing the entrance to River Lane are a row of three cottages (18, 20 & 22 Radwell Road). There used to be two other cottages in the row, where number 24 Radwell Road now stands, but these were demolished in the late nineteen sixties. This row of homes was known as Rose Cottages **10** and at least one of the demolished cottages was the village Workhouse.

Under the Old Poor Law the primary responsibility for poor relief rested with the parish. In 1723 Knatchbull's General Workhouse Act empowered single parishes to erect workhouses. The Act introduced a 'workhouse test' whereby a pauper would only be granted poor relief through being admitted to a workhouse. Generally the poor were restricted to the building every day of the week except Sundays.

Parish workhouses were generally small establishments, and often in rented buildings rather than specially built premises. The running of workhouses was often handed over to a contractor who would, for an agreed price, feed and house the poor. He would also provide the inmates with work, in the case of Milton Ernest, lace making, and benefit from any income generated.

The earliest records of the Milton Ernest workhouse show payments being made in 1783 for thatching and repairs. On 22nd April 1794 there were nine paupers living in the workhouse. These were John Stocks (aged 90), Elizabeth Geaney (75), Elizabeth Bonham (50), Sarah Prat (40), Thomas Walduck (15), David Walduck (9), Elizabeth Cox (9), Elizabeth Hand (9) and Sarah Hall (7).

Workhouse

Fig 111 – Rose Cottages, circa 1940, viewed from River Lane. Walking down the lane, left to right, are Les Goodman, Gerald Willars and Gordon Brown.

In another record, a letter dated 1812, the unknown author writes ".... The poor house at Milton in its present state is not by any means fit for a human being to live in – it might however with some alterations be made to accommodate the people at present there tolerably well. The first floor consists of four apartments having only damp dirty floors..... small windows, not properly ventilated.... There are two rooms on the upper storey, one of which is unoccupied and is the most filthy place I was ever in".

It is not known when the workhouse closed down but it was still around in 1834 as it is mentioned in a letter by John Turner: "we don't want to go to the workhouse, tho old Knight is not the worst master --- Harry Solsbury, John Davis & a little boy are the only inmates there, next door live T. Allen, Pointer, J. Childs & Mary Truett".

Heritage Trail (Part III) – River Lane and London End

Now continue the walk by turning down River Lane. Where the electricity sub station now stands, on the left hand side of River Lane, used to be a saw pit surrounded by felled trees. At the end of the nineteenth century, Mr Makeham hired two men from Luton who sawed timber all winter.

Fig 112 – A public water tap in River Lane, 1939. Although this tap no longer exists, other taps still survive in the village.

Fig 113 – The spring in River Lane, 1939.

Further down the left hand side of the lane you'll come to a ditch which houses a stream and a natural spring. This mineral spring was first recorded in 1806 and was thought to have medicinal properties. It flows directly from the oolite into the bricked-up cavity, which has a stone slab above. Water from the spring was used by people in the village to wash their clothes right up until the twentieth century.

There is also a view that a mill was once situated in River Lane. In the 1841, 1851 and 1861 censuses, John Abbott lived in the area and his occupation was listed as 'Miller', giving some credence to the idea.

Continue until you reach the river at the end of the lane.

The River Great Ouse **11**, which flows for 250 kilometres (155 miles) from just south of Silverstone in Northamptonshire to just north of Kings Lynn in Norfolk where it enters the sea at The Wash, was probably the main factor in a settlement starting at Milton Ernest. Although it is only six miles from Turvey to Bedford, the River Great Ouse meanders for twenty six miles through many North Bedfordshire villages, including Milton Ernest, before it reaches the county town.

Evidence has been found that this part of the river, at the end of River Lane, was a Roman ford. During pipe laying work large slabs and roman coins were unearthed. Also, when the pumping station was constructed in 1964, a local resident, Mrs Boielle, remembers the workmen finding part of a roman road which headed for the river. The causeway was discovered under fifteen foot of clay with one of the stones measuring 10" x 8" x 6.5". Roman coins were also dug up by some scouts in this area. It is fascinating to think that a Roman Legion might have marched along what is now River Lane!

Fig 114 – Punts for hire at the bottom of River Lane, 1939.

River Lane could also have been part of a lost road which ran from Harrold to Biggleswade. Maps show the road as still being in existence in 1743 but there are no records after this date. The route ran from Harrold to Pavenham via the old village of Chellington, across the river at Milton Ernest, over the top of Clapham and Ravensden, down to a river crossing at Great Barford and so onto Biggleswade via Moggerhanger. The point where this road crossed the river at Milton Ernest could well have been the River Lane ford.

It is probably not surprising to learn that many a life has been lost in the river at Milton Ernest, especially when you consider that it used to run ten to twelve feet deep in places. Although only ten percent of burial records in the parish register record the reason for death, there are fifteen entries entered as 'drowned'. Extrapolate this up to take into account the ninety

156

percent without a reason and statistically there could have been as many as one hundred and fifty people who lost their lives in this stretch of water in the last four hundred and fifty years. Although this is probably an exaggeration, it does highlight that the River Great Ouse should be treated with respect.

Fig 115 – Punting on the Ouse at the bottom of River Lane. The river was a lot wider in those days

The worst tragedy at the river and probably in the history of the village occurred in 1576 when George Newcom, Richard Emerye, Nicholas Kinge and Arian Aprupe all drowned in this stretch of the Ouse. The entry in the parish register reads: 'Upon the second day of July 76 were buried these four men that were drowned in the water by misadventure'. What exactly caused them to drown hasn't survived time, but the sense of loss must have been immense in such a small village.

The Bedfordshire Mercury records another sad story. On Sunday 3rd February 1895, a boy named Frank Solesbury was sliding on the frozen river with his friends when he broke through the ice. George Mitchell, aged 16, went to his assistance but the ice gave way. Some men succeeded in getting Frank Solesbury out of the water but George Mitchell drowned.

On a happier note John Starey recalls the days when you could hire a punt on this part of the river. One of the punts was called 'Primrose' and could be hired for a shilling. Reg Parrott in his book 'Sixty Years A Thatcher' recalls fishing, rowing and that by July the water was warm enough to make swimming enjoyable.

Fig 116 – George Barnett (white hat), headmaster of Milton Ernest School, fishing at Milton Ernest, circa 1910. His wife, Elizabeth, is in front of the parasol.

Charlie Peck, of London End, was an early commuter. He used to row along the River Great Ouse to his work at Hurdlefoot, near Pavenham, every day. Not bad for someone who couldn't swim! Hurdlefoot used to be an entertainment area. People came from Bedford and the surrounding area to eat at the restaurant, play on the amusements and swim in the river on which there were springboards erected to add to the fun.

Turn away from the river and walk back up River Lane. The first building on your left is Ousebank Farm for which there are surprisingly few surviving records. It was owned by the Haycock family, of whom Robert Haycock of Bob's Shop is a relative. A receipt dated 3rd February 1950 states that the Haycocks were builders, decorators, joiners and undertakers. They also repaired and varnished boats and punts. George Willars remembers many a happy childhood day spent playing in the

Haycock's orchard which ran down to the river. Many of the village children would play here in the nineteen thirties.

In this area used to stand two thatched cottages which were burnt down on 25th July 1906. At 12.50 smoke was seen emitting from the roof of the cottage owned by Humphrey Haycock and occupied by Mrs Wilshire and her four children. A telegraph was sent to Bedford Fire Brigade who arrived at 13.55. They were just in time, as sparks were setting fire to other thatched cottages in the immediate area. It took two hours to put the fire out, by which time Haycock's cottage and an unoccupied property adjoined at the back were completely gutted.

The River Ouse at Milton Ernest.

Fig 117 – The River Ouse at Milton Ernest.

A short way and you'll walk past the entrance to London End. There seems to be no surviving record of why a small close in a small village should be named after the capital city. Maybe the name was derived from someone called London, but it was certainly linked to the capital in 1851 as census records refer to London End West End and London End City.

Continue walking up River Lane, past the row of red brick cottages (6, 8, 10 & 12 River lane), and you'll come to a stone building known as 'Stone Barn'.

Stone Barn (2 River Lane) was an old tumble down cottage which was ready to fall down before it was renovated. It used to be attached to the bakery.

Fig 118 – River Lane, 1961.

Now walk to the end of River Lane and turn left into Radwell Road.

Heritage Trail (Part IV) – Radwell Road Revisited

You have just walked past the side of the Old Bakery and are now at the front of the building.

The Old Bakery **12** (15 Radwell Road) was until recently known as 'Nookery Corner', but the name change is more befitting this old bake house which is one of the oldest in the country. Parts of the building date back to the 15th Century but mostly it is 17th Century. The ovens would have originally been heated by faggots before being rebuilt and heated by coke.

Fig 119 – The Bakery in 1939. Note that it was a row of buildings at that time.

The baker was a key figure in Milton Ernest, as many of the cottage homes in the village didn't have good ovens. On Sunday mornings a steady stream of people would carry their meat in a tin to the bake house with the yorkshire pudding mix in a can. The villagers went to All Saints Church or the Wesleyan Chapel and after the service collected their cooked meal, walking home with it wrapped in a cloth. Many people also took pastries and cakes throughout the week to be cooked in this bake house. Obviously the baker made a good trade from the lack of good ovens in the village!

The grounds used to have a pigsty, a cart shed and an orchard. In 1871 the bakery held seven and a half acres of land and employed a labourer and a servant.

There are no records of who owned or worked at the Milton Ernest bake house until the censuses and trade directories of Victorian times. John Pool is the earliest known baker at these premises circa 1825 and he was succeeded by John Turner, circa 1830-1840. After that Milton Ernest Bakery was owned by the Newell family for almost a century. In 1847 Edward Newell was the first of the family to work as a baker at these premises. He was succeeded by his wife Jane in 1869; then his son George Clayton Newell in 1877; and finally his daughter Fanny Jane Newell was baker from 1909 to 1931.

Fig 120 – Milton Ernest Bakery. The children in the photograph are evacuees, dating the picture as circa 1940.

George Clayton Newell had customers from the surrounding villages, and his only means of transport was a horse drawn open box cart. At 4pm he would leave his yard loaded with bread and visit a nearby village, with each village having a special day for delivery. He took with him a local lad to help with the running about, as some houses were in fields approached by muddy cart tracks, but winter, rain or shine, the bread was delivered. George would arrive back in the bake house yard by 10:30pm and still have a couple of hours work to do before he could take a well earned rest.

Fig 121 – The Old Bakery, circa 1940. Left to right are Doreen Goodman, Les Goodman, Gerald Willars and Gordon Brown.

Fig 122 – The Old Bakery, circa 1981. Note the gap due to the demolition of part of the bakery. This gap has since been closed through the extension work to the Old Bakery and once again looks like the scene above.

Fig 123 – A bread delivery from the Milton Ernest bakery, circa 1910. Note the name FJ Newell on the side of the cart. This represents Fanny Jane Newell.

Miss Fanny Jane Newell, affectionately known as Jenny, was the last of the Newell bakers. She delivered bread around Milton Ernest on foot, pushing a barrow made of wickerwork. When she died in 1937 the business was taken over by George Bull.

Fig 124 – Jenny Newell delivering bread in Milton Ernest.

An article written by Beatrice Gillam in 1939 describes the bakery in some detail. It states that the bakery was the central part of three little whitewashed thatched cottages. It only had two small windows and a door. The baker at the time was Mr Bull. Inside, the bakery was twelve feet long by ten feet wide with whitewashed walls and a stone floor. There were wooden benches all around the walls except at the end where the oven was situated. In fact there were two ovens, one above the other, which went back seven feet into the wall and were four feet wide. Built in 1910, the ovens were lined with bricks and each could hold between 120 and 130 loaves.

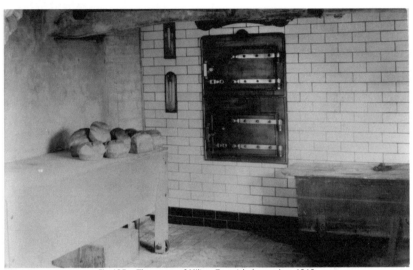
Fig 125 – The ovens of Milton Ernest bakery, circa 1910.

Every Saturday twelve two penny loaves would be produced in the bake house and placed in a special box in the church. These were then distributed on Sunday to the poor people in the village. But the practice stopped when the bake house closed in 1956.

Near to the bake house used to be the shop of Robert Hart, a high-class shoemaker, who undertook work for all of the local gentry.

Continue along Radwell Road to the large double fronted pale brick house. The address of the property suggests that this was once three homes. Numbers 19 and 23 Radwell Road **13** used to be the home of Stephen Hooker who ran an agricultural threshing business from at least 1891 to 1940. His machinery was kept in a barn on Thurleigh Road, near the Church. Stephen Hooker was a jack of all trades, with the 1891 census listing his profession as 'Agricultural engineer, machinist, cycle and motor manufacturer & threshing machine proprietor!' He retired in 1941 and auctioned his three complete sets of threshing tackle at Peacocks in Bedford.

Fig 126 – Hooker's House, 25th November 2004

Fig 127– Stephen Hooker's Threshing Gang. It is not known whether Hooker is pictured.

166

Fig 128 – Swan House, 25th November 2004

Next is Swan House (25 Radwell Road) **14**, a red brick building with a white colour washed front that dates back to the eighteenth century. Swan House used to be called 'North View' but has since been named after the village pub which used to be situated next door. Two large detached houses (27 & 27a Radwell Road) now stand on the front of the plot of land which used to house the pub.

Fig 129 – Radwell Road (circa 1900). The original Swan building can be seen on the right of the picture.

Deeds relating to the The Swan **15** date back to 1785, although it probably was built before this date. A printed sale catalogue, dated 15 June 1859, describes the Swan Public House as being principally made of stone and as having an 105 foot frontage with a large yard, garden and paddock. The house consisted of a tap room, sitting room and a large club room. There was also a kitchen, dairy, three bedrooms, cellar, laundry, butcher's shop, wood barn with loft, chaff barn, stabling and loose boxes for seven horses, piggery, hen house and a large barn.

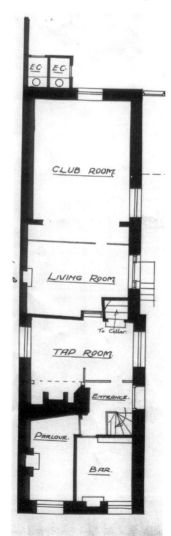

Fig 130 – Plans depicting the layout of the original Swan before it was demolished in 1934.

By 1876 the Swan was owned by the JW Nash Brewery of Bedford who became Newland & Nash in the latter stages of the nineteenth century.

The Swan's longest serving publicans were the Russell family who ran the inn from the middle of the nineteenth century to 1908. John Russell is recorded as the inn keeper in 1851. On his death in 1870 his wife, Mary Ann Russell, took over the role until she passed away in 1896. Their son, Charles, then ran the pub until 1908 when he too died and after almost sixty years the Swan was no longer kept by a Russell.

Fig 131 – The original Swan Inn. According to the plans the ground floor windows are for the parlour and the bar. The entrance to the pub was in the alley between the pub and the other building with shuttered windows which was a Swan outbuilding.

During this period The Swan occupied 25 acres of farm land for which the Russell's employed three men and two boys. A female servant was also employed and lived in the house. Mary Ann Russell, a widow at 45, ran the pub, cared for her seven children, managed the farmland and was also the village's butcher!

The second week of July used to be the time of the annual village feast. Stalls, swing boats and flying horses were erected near the Swan. A dancing booth was constructed in the Swan yard and a fiddler was engaged for the whole week. This was a big event in Milton Ernest, with villagers inviting their friends and relatives over for the feast.

Fig 132 – The Swan circa 1945. Note the gate which leads to open fields on the right of the picture.

By 1934 Wells & Winch's Ales were the owners and on 8th March in that year had their plans approved to demolish the old stone building which they replaced with a new brick version. The pub retained its name.

In the summer of 1944 The Swan became a regular drinking haunt of Glenn Miller and members of his band. They became good friends with the then landlord, Tom Larkins, who had become landlord in January 1942.

Towards the end of the twentieth century The Swan became famous locally for its annual pig roast. Villagers would roast the pig overnight ready for the next day celebrations which took place in the pub garden. The event grew each year and raised money for local charities. However, this all ended in 1998, when Greene King, the owners, announced plans to close the pub.

A campaign was started by the villagers to save the pub, but Greene King called last orders for the final time on Sunday 21st February 1999, two weeks ahead of schedule, which killed off the fight to keep the pub open. The next day The Swan was boarded up and it was never to reopen.

Fig 133 – The Swan.

Fig 134 – Julia Grimwood Payton and Mary Daniels Grimwood outside The Swan, May 1991. Mary is the daughter of James Daniels, Vicar of Milton Ernest 1959-1964. This is a rare surviving close up photograph of The Swan.

171

Between The Swan and Village Farm used to be the house of Thomas Griggs who was the village carpenter and undertaker from approximately 1839 until his death in 1877.

From the site of The Swan continue walking along Radwell Road until you reach a converted stone barn. Opposite at 42 Radwell Road, a schoolboy, named Adrian Dunn, found a lead papal bull of Clement V (1305-1314) buried in his garden.

'The Barns' **16** used to be part of Village Farm and is now a private residence. As you stand facing the building the left hand part, which is at a right angle to Radwell Road, was originally stables. The two buildings stood empty for some time before being converted into a house in 1994. To the right of 'The Barns' stands an old farmhouse which used to be 'Village Farm'.

Fig 135 – The Barns and Village Farm, 25th November 2004

Village Farm House **17** is a thatched property which has the gable end to the street. The words 'RTM 1670' have been carved into the stone on the central stack. The initials RTM represent the stonemasons who built the house. In this case it was Robert and Thomas Morris. Thomas was based in Pavenham while Robert lived in Milton Ernest. Both were born in Pavenham. Robert was baptised there on 2nd August 1640 and Thomas on 26th March 1643. These brothers also built 'Stone Cottage' in 1669, which you'll see, at Flewton End, later on during this heritage trail.

This could well have been the last house that Robert Morris built as he died the following year, aged just 30, and was buried on 11th May 1671 at All Saint's Church. Sadly he was buried on the same day as his son, John, and just four months after his wife Margery. Unfortunately, the burial records give no reason for the deaths of three family members in such a short space of time, but it is fairly safe to assume that they all succumbed to the same contagious illness.

Fig 136 – Village Farm. The Farmhouse and barns at the bottom of the photograph still exist but the rest of the site has made way for the 'Riverside View' housing development.

For a seventeenth century property there are surprisingly few records remaining to shed much light on its history. The earliest information from 1841 shows it to be in the hands of John Banks, a thirty five year old farmer, who employed one servant. Village Farm never had any extensions added which would suggest that it was always a working farmhouse.

During the Second World War an air raid shelter stood next to Village Farm. There was also a wooden building within the farm compound which was used to house first Italian and then German prisoners of war. Six or seven would be housed here while they helped on the farm. It was around this time that Claude Ibbett bought the property and eventually built up the local 'Bedfordia' company which farms most of the land in the area today.

Across the way from Village Farm is another old farmhouse which is situated at a right angle to Radwell Road. This building was originally called 'West Manor Farm'. Bedfordia combined the West Manor and Village Farm buildings into one farm unit as they owned both farms. When West Manor Farm was sold as part of the housing development, everything was transferred to Village Farm. This gave Village Farm the distinction of being the last working farm within the Milton Ernest village envelope. Having once housed dairy herds and Clydesdale horses, Village Farm ended its days as a pig breeding unit. Most of the time there were over a thousand animals on site including three hundred sows and ten boars. The last animal was moved out in 1994 ready for the start of the Riverside View development.

Fig 137 – Village Farm with Radwell Road in the background. Rearing pens in the foreground, sow house is left rear and boar house is right rear.

Fig 138 – Village Farm which has been replaced by 'Riverside View'.

Fig 139 – Furrowing House at Village Farm.

Fig 140 – Rearing Pen at Village Farm.

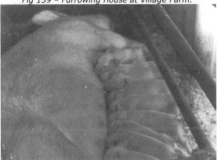
Fig 141 – Sow and piglets in the Furrowing House.

Fig 142 – A feeding piglet in the Furrowing House.

Fig 143 – The Stall House at Village Farm.

Fig 144 – Village Farm, 1971.

West Manor Farm **18** (52, 54 & 56 Radwell Road) is thought to date back to the early seventeenth century. Once, as the name suggests, a manor farmhouse, the building was converted into two homes in the twentieth century. When permission to demolish the farm house, to make way for new housing as part of the Huntsmans Way site, was refused, an extension was built on the back and two homes became three.

Named West Manor Farm to distinguish itself from the other manor farmhouse, you will visit East Manor Farm later during the walk, this could be the site of Babs Manor. However, as there is a Babs Lane and a Babs Close to the south of East Manor Farm, it is more than likely that that manor was located there. The only contradictory evidence being that Thomas Fisher sold West Manor Farm in 1804 to a Serjeant Vaughan and it was sold as the Manor of Babs.

In Victorian times the farm consisted of 329 acres and Benjamin Crisp, who was farmer for at least twenty years circa 1861-1881, permanently employed ten men, three boys, a governess and two servants. In the summer months six additional men came from Ireland to help with the harvest. They lived in a barn on the farm. The same men were to return year after year.

The farm must have been at its peak at the time of Benjamin Crisp. Previously James Lamb had farmed the land but only employed five labourers and, after Crisp, Hugh Andrew was the occupier (circa 1894-1924) and he was shown as having no permanent labourers!

Fig 145 – West Manor Farm, 25th November 2004

West Manor Farm is today split into three residences. The middle dwelling (54 Radwell Road) was the original entrance to the manor farmhouse and has some beautiful carved ceiling beams depicting leaves. These are thought to date back to Jacobean times (1603 to 1625). The final home (52 Radwell Road), furthest from the road, is the part of the farmhouse which used to house the servants.

Fig 146 – Aerial view of West Manor Farm.

Locals recall stories of the ghost of a 'Green Lady' who appeared at a window of West Manor Farm in the 1940s and 1950s. The window in question has since been bricked up, so it is unlikely that you will see her during your walk!

Fig 147 – West Manor Farm.

Continue along Radwell Road and you will reach the entrance to Riverside View.

Heritage Trail (Part V) – Riverside View & Milton Ernest Garden Centre

Riverside View was built on the site of Village Farm. Figure 136 shows the location of the farm buildings which were demolished to make way for the development.

Fig 148 – Advert placed by Holmes Estate Agents for the Riverside View development, Bedford Herald, 12th September 1996.

The 41 houses built by Bewick Homes Limited were sold between July 1996 and January 1998. Initial prices ranged from £139,950 for a detached house with four bedrooms, to between £158,500 and £215,000 for five bedroom homes. Two and three bedroom houses were advertised at prices between £59,950 and £82,500.

Walk down Riverside View and you will come to an open area of land which is a wild flower meadow **19** and picnic area. Walk across the grassland and you will once again come to the River Great Ouse.

Fig 149 – Wild flower meadow with access to the River Great Ouse, 25ᵗʰ November 2004.

Now turn back, retrace your steps along Riverside View, turn left onto Radwell Road and left again into the entrance to Milton Ernest Garden Centre.

Fig 150 – Milton Ernest Garden Centre, 25ᵗʰ November 2004

Milton Ernest Garden Centre **20** was originally based in the gardens of Milton Ernest Hall and first opened for business, under Maureen Catlin, on Good Friday, 20ᵗʰ April, 1973. After twenty years it moved to its present site which Bedfordia developed and own. The grand opening at this new Radwell Road site took place on 26ᵗʰ August 1993. Today Maureen Catlin still owns what has become a very popular Garden Centre business.

A Post Office was also sited here in November 1993, its fifth different location in the village. There was quite a lot of interest in the opening of this post office as it was the first post office ever to be based within a garden centre.

Before leaving Milton Ernest Garden Centre, why not stop for some refreshment at the Coffee Shop or browse the site which contains a pet shop, art centre, books, crafts and, of course, many plants!

From Milton Ernest Garden Centre cross over to the other side of Radwell Road. Here you can either go left and enter the gate to the playing field or right into Huntsmans Way via the path with the sign 'Radwell Road, Even No's. 58 to 64 & Huntsmans Way'.

Fig 151 – Milton Ernest Post Office inside the Garden Centre, 15th January 2006.

The 1.9 acre playing field **21** is rented from Bedfordia for the sum of 5 pence per annum and is maintained by Milton Ernest Playing Field Association. For a village the size of Milton Ernest it is very well equipped. It is also in a nice position with north and westerly views from the village. From the top of the field you can see the river, railway line, Pavenham Park Golf Club course, the village of Radwell and many acres of farmland.

On 1st May 1975 Bedfordshire County Council applied for planning permission to build a new lower school on what is now the playing field site. The paperwork states that "negotiations for the site have been developing over many years", "the land is cheap and available" and "the site will act as a buffer against westward development". Planning permission was granted on 20th August 1975, with the stipulation that vehicular access would be via the proposed adjoining new housing estate road.

However, the new school was never built and Milton Ernest Parish Council successfully obtained permission on 13th August 1979 for the site to be used as a playing field. This was despite 19 residents having written letters opposing the entrance being via Huntsmans Way, though their petition was withdrawn at a public village meeting in July 1979. Initial consent was for a three year period and the playing field opened in 1980 with a football pitch.

Fig 152 – Milton Ernest Playing Field, 25th November 2004

On 9th August 1982 consent for the land to be used as a playing field without the need to re-apply for permission every three years meant that Milton Ernest Playing Field Association felt able to invest in play equipment. In early 1983 the swings and slide were installed. There have been regular additions ever since, including the basketball pitch which was provided in April 1997. All of the equipment has been purchased through the hard work of the Playing Field Association, which was formed in October 1978, via grants and village fund raising activities.

Once you've walked around the playing field, and no doubt had a sly play on the swings for old times sake, leave via the once controversial Huntsmans Way gate.

Heritage Trail (Part VI) – Huntsmans Way & Arkwright Road

You will now walk through the Huntsmans Way and Arkwright Road housing estate. The aerial shot and maps on the next few pages clearly show how things have changed over the last two hundred years. Huntsmans Way is predominately on the land of West Manor Farm whilst Arkwright Road was built on the kennels site.

Fig 153 – A view of the Swan and Radwell Road from the Kennels. Note how open the area was in those days.

The kennels **22** were built on a 2.5 acre piece of land known as Rabletts Close in 1834. Almost forty years later in 1873 the site was extended when an additional 2.5 acres were purchased. The kennels were enlarged again in 1899 with the addition of a new puppy house.

The Oakley Hunt bought Rabletts for £341 and spent a further £859 building the kennels and stables. The 1873 land purchase cost a further £325.

The 1841 census records three homes on the site. These were occupied at the time by George Beers, the 40 year old huntsman; George Wells, an 18 year old groom; and Thomas Barringer, the boiler aged 25. It is unclear as to the actual role of a boiler at the Kennels. The huntsman and the groom both had a female servant living with them. The stables would have been home to 30 horses and the kennels usually contained 50 couples of hounds. The 1851 census mentions Joseph Orchin, a whipper-in, who was the hunting hound organiser.

Fig 154 – Land when Huntsmans Way & Arkwright Road were just a twinkle in the developers eye! A = West Manor Farm, B = the Oakley Hunt buildings and C = the kennels and stables of Oakley Hunt.

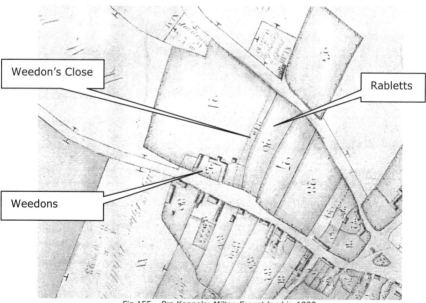

Weedon's Close

Rabletts

Weedons

Fig 155 – Pre Kennels: Milton Ernest land in 1803.

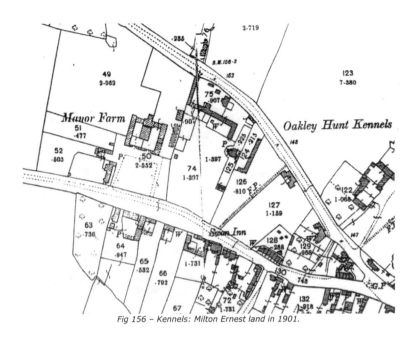

Fig 156 – Kennels: Milton Ernest land in 1901.

Fig 157 – Post Kennels (Huntsmans Way & Arkwright Road): Milton Ernest land in 2000.

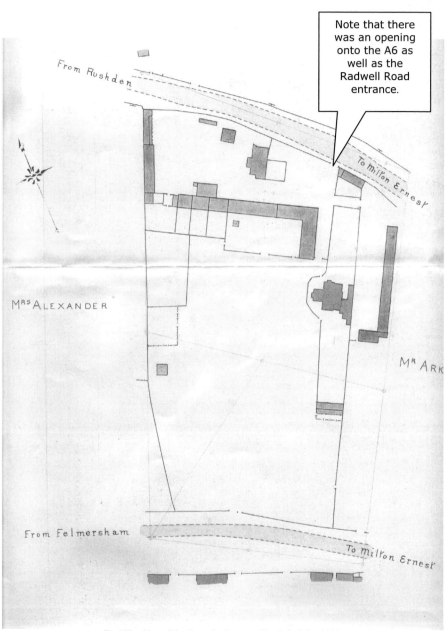

Note that there was an opening onto the A6 as well as the Radwell Road entrance.

Fig 158 – Plan of the Kennels. Surveyed by G. L. Pain, 1898.

Fig 159 – A postcard, with a post mark of 1920, of the Kennels at Milton Ernest.

Fig 160 – A close up section of Fig 159. The Oakley Hounds and Kennels, circa 1920.

187

Robert Arkwright, whom Arkwright Road is named after, was a successful Master of Oakley Hunt. He shares the credit with Tom Whitemore, who was based at the kennels, for introducing brown patches into the coats of hunting hounds. Previously all hunting hounds had just black and white coats.

Fig 161 – The stable block at Milton Ernest Kennels.

At midnight on April 4th 1933 Bedford Fire Brigade received a call and arrived at Milton Ernest in the "remarkable" time of fifteen minutes. Upon arrival they found that the staff's sleeping quarters, hay lofts, machine room, saddle rooms and store rooms were burning furiously. Flames rapidly burned through the beams and flooring, sending the contents of the upper floors crashing to the ground. A passing motorist had shouted the alarm in the yard which awoke the chief whip and kennel and stable lads. They escaped from their rooms which were filled with dense smoke but were unable to save any of their possessions. Seven horses and one hundred hounds had to be moved to safety. Bedford Fire Brigade were assisted by the Rushden Brigade in putting out the blaze.

Fig 162 – An aerial view of the Kennels site.

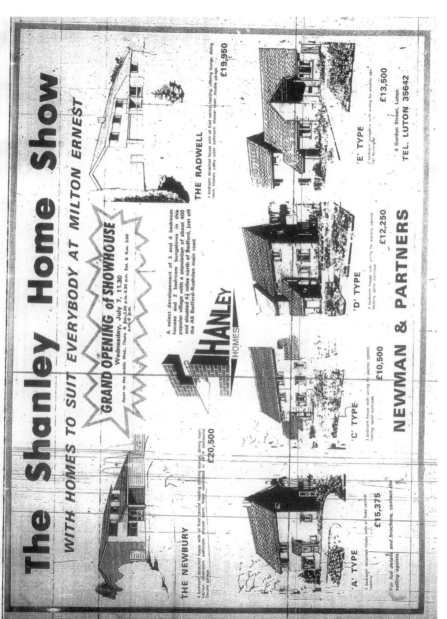

Fig 163 – New houses for sale on the old Oakley Hunt kennels site. Advert taken from the Bedfordshire Times, 2nd July 1976.

189

The hounds used to be exercised along Radwell Road and beyond every day. George Willars remembers this and being thrown a crown by the huntsmen for opening gates into fields when there was an Oakley Hunt meeting in the area. Roger Harris recalls that sometimes villagers would look after the puppies at their homes for six months before returning them to the kennels.

The kennels were a major part of the village for almost 140 years before being sold in 1972. The Oakley Hunt moved to Melchbourne the next year.

Between July 1976 and July 1978 eighty-one homes were sold on the old Kennels and West Manor Farm site. These were constructed by Shanley Homes on Huntsmans Way (45 homes), Arkwright Road (25 homes) and part of Radwell Road (11 homes). Prices ranged from £9,950 for a three bedroom terrace to £26,500 for a four bedroom detached house.

Fig 164 – Puppy show at Milton Ernest Kennels, 1949. Left to right: Lord Luke of Pavenham, C. Abbott (Oakley Huntsman), Captain T. W. Fitzwilliam, P. Barker (Whipper-in) and Will Pope (Huntsman to the Grafton).

Continue the walk along Arkwright Road until you come to the public footpath sign on the left hand side. The area of land in front of you used to be rented out by the Oakley Hunt as a pig farm. Alex Scarlett used to run this farm and some land just off Thurleigh Road until his death in 1951. He used to feed the pigs with swill during the Second World War collected from USAF bases and the isolation hospitals at Thurleigh Road and Clapham. The farm continued for a few years after his death before eventually being consumed by the Arkwright Road development.

Walk through the alley marked by the footpath sign and you will be faced by Rushden Road which is part of the A6.

Heritage Trail (Part VII) – Rushden Road

Turn right and walk along Rushden Road, which has previously been called 'Bletsoe Road' and 'Kettering Road'. The next three houses that you walk past have all been the village Post Office at one time or another. Location of the Milton Ernest Post Office is confusing, so Appendix 3 has been produced to try and clarify matters.

Fig 165 - The Old Post Office before it was a General Store or a Post Office.

The Old Post Office **23** (7 Rushden Road) is a former seventeenth century farmhouse. Again records are scarce relating to its time as a farm, but the 1851 census records William Low as the farmer and in 1881 William Henry Gibbins was the farmer at the 'Farm House, Kettering Road'. He farmed 390 acres and employed a servant, ten men and three boys.

The name 'Old Post Office' is a bit misleading as it suggests that this was the site of the first Milton Ernest Post Office. This isn't the case, as the oldest Post Office site was at Thurleigh Road. The Post Office was located there from circa 1847 to circa 1920. It then moved to what is now 5 Rushden Road, near the crossing. 'The Old Post Office' at this time was a General Store, meaning that Milton Ernest had a grocery store and a separate Post Office alongside each other on the A6.

Fig 166 – A post card of The Old Post Office, post marked 1924. Notice how sedate the A6 was at the time of the photograph! The advertising signs are 'Continental Tyres', 'Stocked by Pytchley Autocar Co Ltd Kettering' and 'Lyons Tea'.

Fig 167 – A close up section of Fig 166.

192

Fig 168 – Post Office Stores. Note the red telephone box to the left of the picture.

Fig 169 – The Old Post Office, 25th November 2004.

The Village Store was run by the Bonham family for a number of years. It was known as the 'Top Shop' by the villagers to distinguish it from the other store, Bob's Shop, which was known as the 'Bottom Shop'. George Willars remembers that when he and his fellow choirboys got paid each quarter in the 1930s, they would race down to the 'Top Shop'. Catherine

Bonham would then bring out a halfpenny tray covered with sweets. She would try to entice the choirboys to spend all of their money at once!

Fig 170 – Children standing on what is now the A6, circa 1910

Mabel Halgarth used to run the Post Office at 5 Rushden Road from 1920 until her retirement in 1940. She kept a parrot in a cage on her Post Office counter for many years. In 1939 Mrs Halgarth's Post Office contained the only public telephone in the village.

When Mrs Halgarth retired, the Post Office business moved into the 'Old Post Office' and was combined with the General Stores, run at this time by Mr Shiltoe. 5 Rushden Road became a residential property.

In 1975, the 'Old Post Office, then known as 'Mallaig Croft', was sold by Mr Welbourn. The area where the Post Office and General Store had been situated was converted into a garage. Mr Welbourn moved his business into the chalet style house, now known as 'Ambry House', which he'd specifically constructed for the purpose in 1974. Therefore, Milton Ernest Post Office slowly crept up Rushden Road, moving from number 5 to number 7 and finally to number 9.

The telephone kiosk near the Old Post Office first appeared in 1947. This was originally a red telephone box.

Cross the road at the traffic light controlled crossing which was introduced in 2003 and continue walking southwards along Rushden Road.

Fig 171 – Cottage that used to be sited where the bus shelter stands today. This 1906 photograph shows the Parrot family of thatchers. On the ladder is Ernest Parrot and his two sons Reg (aged 6) and Fred (aged 11). Standing from left to right are Samuel Hulatt, Ernest's assistant from Radwell and Mr Sabey, the village cobbler.

The bus shelter was originally provided in 1955 but had to be replaced at the start of the twenty-first century after being badly damaged in a traffic accident. The area of grass behind the shelter was known as Ball's Green. On the site where the bus shelter stands used to be an old stone thatched cottage. Alongside this was the site of the old smithy **24** and then Forge Cottage **25**.

The old smithy was attached to the eighteenth century 'Forge Cottage' where the village blacksmith used to live. Joseph Paris Covington was the blacksmith from circa 1836 to his death in 1866. His widow, Elizabeth, continued until her death five years later, and then Frederick Gamball took over the role until he passed away in 1917. Charles Clarke then became the final blacksmith to work in Milton Ernest.

The smithy used to have two wells and a water pump towards the front of the building. A row of red buckets with a metal ladder was kept by the side of the premises in case of a fire in the village. After Charles Clarke died in 1946 the smithy was bought by the village and was used as a village hall from November 1955. The village folk used the premises for whist drives and dances.

Fig 172 – The blacksmith, thought to be Charles Clarke, in front of the old smithy, circa 1920.

Fig 173 – The Old Forge and Forge Cottage.

George Willars tells an intriguing story that after the old forge was no longer used as a blacksmith's, he once looked inside and saw a pile of human skulls. The pile was so big that George estimates that there were between two and three hundred. Why they were there and where they came from remains a mystery.

When Milton Ernest Village Hall was opened in 1959, there was no longer a need for the old smithy and it was later demolished. This left just Forge Cottage which was formerly the home of a long line of blacksmiths who worked in the village. For a while it was known locally as 'Squatters Cottage' because it had been built on common land.

Fig 174 – The Smithy, 1965, just before it was demolished.

Fig 175 – An Eastern National Bus outside the Old Forge, 1939.

Fig 176 – The Old Forge, Forge cottage, and a whitewashed Queen's Head.

Fig 177 – Forge Cottage, 25th November 2004

A number of villagers state that Underhill Robinson, Bedfordshire's first printer, lived in what is now Forge Cottage. Unfortunately, no documents survive to prove whether this was the case. However, there is an inventory for Forge Cottage, dated 9th July 1707, which states that the blacksmith at the time was John Robinson. Could this blacksmith have been a relative of Underhill Robinson? If this was the case then maybe Underhill set up his printing press at the forge. Sadly, this is only conjecture and unless a document is found this theory cannot be proven.

After Forge Cottage turn left into Thurleigh Road.

Heritage Trail (Part VIII) – Thurleigh Road

On the immediate right is the local school.

Fig 178 – Milton Ernest Lower School, 25th November 2004.

Milton Ernest VC Lower School **26** was originally a Church of England (Diocese of St Albans) school. It is now voluntarily controlled by the Local Education Authority, which means that it is maintained and financed by the Bedfordshire Education Service. The Lower School is attended by boys and girls aged between four and nine years old. The Ofsted report of 1999 recorded eighteen boys and twenty-four girls, a total of just forty-two pupils. By 2006 the total number had risen to sixty-four. This is relatively high when you consider that the lowest number of pupils ever recorded at the school was twenty-one in 1977.

The school was built in 1872 with accommodation for 119 scholars and replaced the school house on Village Green. The land had been donated by Joseph Tucker of Pavenham in 1870, while Benjamin Helps Starey and the Reverend Beaty-Pownall contributed £250 towards the expenses of creating and furnishing the school. The blue engineering bricks within the structure were provided by railway workers who used these as a way of making payment for goods in the village.

Fig 179 – A thin glazed china 'bon-bon' dish depicting Milton Ernest School and Church. The dish is 7" in diameter and just over 1" deep. The picture would seem to be a transfer, not being glazed and feeling dry and dull to the touch.

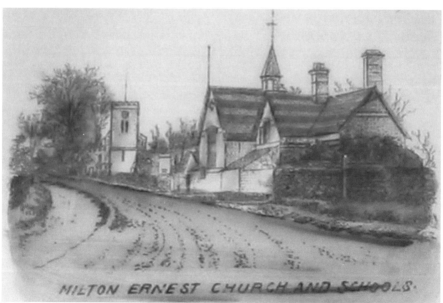

Fig 180 – A close up of the painting on the china dish. It was once a possession of George Barnett and therefore the scene could have been painted any time between 1882 and 1922.

Children were summoned to school by the ringing of a bell which was housed in a turret built on the roof. This bell tower was demolished on 21st February 1954. Monica Boielle recorded in the school log book at the time that "there had been some danger threatened because supports were quite rotten. Clapper and bell has been missing for years – to my knowledge ten years".

Fig 181 – 18 boys, 13 girls and 2 teachers of Milton Ernest School. The little boy in the front row is holding a board which has written in chalk "Milton Ernest School Group 1". On the far right is the headmaster, George Barnett, which means that the photograph dates between 1882 and 1922.

Lighting in the school used to be by oil light and heating was provided by a coal fire in each room. It could be so cold during the winter that children were known to cry with cold hands and feet. Reg Parrott, in his memoirs, recalled being made to stand at the front of class wearing a red conical shaped hat with the word 'Dunce' written on the front as a punishment.

With no church hall or village hall, until the old forge became available in 1955, the school was used for most village functions. These included whist drives, concerts, dances, jumble sales, political meetings and wedding receptions.

The earliest recorded school mistress at this building was Miss Mary Grant in 1877. Miss Margaret Rose, aged twenty-four, was recorded as 'certificated school mistress' in 1881. She was replaced by George Barnett who was school master for forty years (1882-1922).

Head Teacher	From-To	Years
Mary Grant	circa 1877	
Margaret Rose	circa 1881	
George Barnett	1882-1922	40
Amy Heritage	1922-1924	2
Gertrude Hazlett	1927-1935	8
Ivy Smith	1935-1944	9
Monica Boielle	1944-1965	21
Audrey Linford	1967-1972	7
Joan Carthy	1973-1982	9
Dennis Cloves	1983-1992	9
Barbara Levene	1992-1997	5
Sarah Lovett	1997-2003	6
Mary Harris	2004-	

Fig 182 – The Head Teachers of Milton Ernest Lower School since it opened in 1872. Where there are gaps in the years between head teachers there were various teachers temporarily in charge of the school. Only 2 (15%) of the 13 head teachers have been men.

Fig 183 – George Barnett, Head Teacher of Milton Ernest School from 1882 to 1922.

George Barnett, aged 25, commenced head teacher duties at Milton Ernest School on 28th September 1882. His wife Elizabeth taught needlework and cookery classes, receiving a supplementary teacher's wage. In 1901 their eldest daughter, Annie, helped out at the school and became a paid teacher in 1908 at the age of fifteen. Quite a family affair!

George Barnett played an important part in the life of Milton Ernest, where during his long period of activity he was held in great esteem. Apart from being Head Master he held the following positions:

Secretary and Treasurer of Milton Ernest Cricket Club (for 40 years),
Secretary and Treasurer of the Milton Ernest Horticultural Society (for 35 years),
Secretary of the local Friendly Society (for 32 years),
Chairman of Milton Ernest Committee of Beds National Health Insurance Society,
Secretary and Treasurer of the Milton Ernest Parochial Church Council,
Clerk of the Parish Council,
Assistant Overseer (for 26 years),
Collector of Taxes for Milton Ernest and Bletsoe (for 33 years),
Secretary and Treasurer of the Village Entertainments Committee,
Churchwarden,
Member of All Saints' Church Choir and occasional organist,
Warden of the Primrose League (Milton Ernest Branch),
Local correspondent for the Bedfordshire Standard.

That's an incredible eighteen different responsibilities within Milton Ernest. It's not surprising that when George came to leave the village, the Reverend Holmes stated "If ordinary persons were leaving everyone would wish them "God speed," but this departure left a great gap."

George Barnett's forty years will probably always remain as the longest period of service as head teacher at Milton Ernest School. The second highest period in charge was by Monica Boielle, who came to help out the school during the Second World War and ended up staying as headmistress until 1965.

Fig 184 – Milton Ernest School photograph, circa 1935. The arrow is pointing out Elmer John Willars (baptised 13th April 1919 at Milton Ernest All Saints'), father of Susan Sail who provided the photograph. The headmistress is believed to be Ivy Smith.

Mrs Boielle can remember the days during the War when the school was open half a day for the local children and half a day for the evacuees. She also recalls the harsh winter of 1947 when the school was closed due to the snow for an incredible six weeks! The school log book records that from 7th February there was heavy snow for seventeen days. The entry dated 28th March 1947 states "School has been closed for 6 weeks owing to lack of fuel". The school children must have been so disappointed!

Such was the lure of the Oakley Hunt meetings that children from the school used to run away from the playground to follow the hunters. Once gone they didn't return until the next day when they'd receive the cane across their hand as a punishment.

An entry in the school log book for 15th May 1958 records that "on the 16th the Education Committee would be informed that this school was being "taken over" from the Church and would become a controlled school. Lack of funds has troubled us for years. The Vicar the Rev. J L Turney has worked increasingly trying to obtain aid from the Diocesan authorities. At length he was told that no attempt would be made to keep the school".

The school swimming pool was opened on 13th July 1965. There was difficulty over its siting, as a covenant stated that there could be no building on the village green. The pool was therefore sited on the school playground. Almost three years later in June 1968, the swimming pool was re-located to its present site, a piece of land which used to be a garden belonging to one of the Thurleigh Road thatched cottages which stand opposite the swimming pool's present day position.

Fig 185 – Milton Ernest School photograph, circa 1940. Back row (left to right): Dick Denton, Don Willars, Gordon Brown, Bubbles Slatter, David Willett, Nigel Stanton, Les Goodman. Front row (left to right): Arthur Woodhams, Tony Marsh, Dorothy Peck, Greta Stanton, Eileen Slatter, Delcie Willars, Connie Stanton, Johnny Wrench, Tom Barrett.

In December 1962 notification was received that pupils aged 11+ were to be transferred to a new secondary modern school that was being built in Oakley and which would be called Lincroft. Previously, Milton Ernest School catered for pupils from when they started aged five to when they left for work aged fourteen. From 1963 the children were to complete their education at Lincroft. The school log book records on 8th January 1963 that "as from today this is to be a Junior and Infant School. It is exactly 32 years since a Headmistress of this school was notified that the Seniors (11+ group) were to be transferred to a new school which was to be built at Oakley". Today the pupils leave Milton Ernest Lower School aged 9 for

Lincroft Middle School and then move aged 13 to Sharnbrook Upper School.

On 7th October 1960 the Village Hall was first used by the school for physical education lessons. This arrangement is still in place. School uniform wasn't introduced at Milton Ernest School until 1968. School dinners used to be eaten in the school building but on 28th April 1970 the Village Hall was first used as a canteen. This arrangement is also still in place, with the pupils crossing Thurleigh Road each lunchtime to eat their school dinners.

Fig 186 – Milton Ernest Lower School badge which is based on the Erneys family's coat of arms (see Fig 4).

Mention should be made of Eve Racher who retired in 1973 after forty three years service as infant teacher of Milton Ernest Lower School.

The March 1977 school report states "Managers will have noticed that we have now replaced the word Primary in the name of the school and are now known as Milton Ernest Voluntary Controlled Lower School".

Thurleigh Road used to be a rough track used mainly for the delivery of coal. It was improved in the 1870s, around the time the school was built.

Fig 187 – Milton Ernest Village Hall, 1965.

Continue up Thurleigh Road and you will come to Milton Ernest Village Hall **27**. This was opened on 8th September 1959 by Sir Frederick Mander and paid for out of the proceeds of the annual gymkhana which had been instigated by Ernest Page. At last Milton Ernest had a proper community hall, replacing the school and old forge building which had been used for village functions up until this time. Today the Village Hall is used by Milton Ernest Lower School, Milton Ernest Youth Club, Milton Ernest Mother and Toddlers Group, Milton Ernest Brownies, Milton Ernest Parish Council, Milton Ernest Women's Institute and a Whist Drive amongst others. It is a real local community hall for local people of all ages. A Village Hall Committee exists to protect the interests of this valuable village asset.

Fig 188 – Milton Ernest Village Hall, 25th November 2004.

Next on the walk are two semi-detached thatched stone cottages **28** (1 & 3 Thurleigh Road) which date back to the seventeenth century.

This building was originally a row of four cottages. The first of these four cottages, as you walk towards Thurleigh used to be the location of Milton Ernest's first Post Office.

Fig 189 – Thurleigh Road Cottages at a time when they were split into four homes. Today it is just two homes.

William Solesbury was the first post master in Milton Ernest and was based in this Thurleigh Road cottage in 1847. By 1853 William Mortimer took over the role, as well as being school master, before being replaced by William Cowdall Solesbury in 1861. WC Solesbury remained as the village postmaster for fifteen years before the Mole family took on the job.

William Mole was a tailor and the sub postmaster, another example of a person in the village with two occupations. He was the postmaster living and working in this cottage for eighteen years from 1876 to his death at just 48 in 1894. William's widow, Emma Mole (nee Halgarth), then became postmistress and continued for twenty six years until her retirement in 1920 when Mabel Halgarth, her assistant and niece, took over. By then the Post Office had moved to Rushden Road. Emma Mole went on to reach the grand old age of 95 when she died in 1940.

Fig 190 – 1939 photograph of the Thurleigh Road cottages with the protruding extension which used to house the Post Office. Note there was a wooden fence in those days.

Fig 191 – The telegraph boy, Harold Smith (born 1893 in Woburn), outside Milton Ernest Post Office in 1909. The sign reads 'Milton Ernest Post Office. Telegraph Office. Money & Postal Orders'.

208

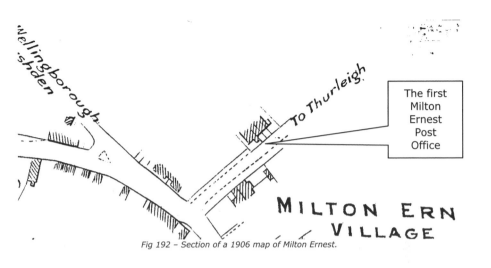

The first
Milton
Ernest
Post
Office

MILTON ERN

VILLAGE

Fig 192 – Section of a 1906 map of Milton Ernest.

Fig 193 – Thurleigh Road with the School to the left, Thurleigh Road cottages to the right.

On Wednesday 4th December 1889 a Telegraph Office was opened at this Post Office "for the collecting and delivering of telegrams". The Beds Mercury reported that "this will prove a boon for places around". A full time telegraph boy was employed to deliver the telegrams.

There are two other interesting facts about these cottages. The first being that when the floors were repaired it was discovered that the flooring was actually old tombstones laid face downwards! And secondly, it is reputed that the cottages were built on the site of a plague pit.

Fig 194 – Thurleigh Road as viewed from the top of All Saints' Church tower, circa 1960. Note the Chapel and the old Forge were still standing.

Just beyond the junction of Marsh Lane there used to be an old barn and workshop where Stephen Hooker, whose Radwell Road home you've already walked past, kept his steam threshing machines. Hooker had six threshing machines and employed ten men.

Now turn left into Marsh Lane.

Heritage Trail (Part IX) – Marsh Lane, Starey Close and Flewton End

The name 'Marsh Lane' seems to have been derived from the track which used to be in the locality. This track was known as 'Marshy Lane' by the villagers.

Walk along Marsh Lane, which is predominately homes for the elderly built in circa 1965, until you reach the junction of Starey Close, which is named after the Starey family who built and lived in Milton Ernest Hall. You will visit this gothic country house at the end of the heritage trail.

Fig 195 – Green Farm, 1919, after being re-thatched by Ernest Parrott and his son Reg. Note the two front doors which would suggest that Green Farm used to be two cottages.

Take a few steps along Starey Close, turn northwards and you will see an old farmhouse. This used to be Green Farm **29** and is now three separate homes.

On the left is a small seventeenth century stone outhouse which used to belong to Green Farm. This building was heightened in the nineteenth century. It was converted into a family home in 2003. Previously it was known as the Milton Rooms and could be hired for social functions.

211

The middle building is the seventeenth century farmhouse – Green Farm. There is a date stone which has been hidden by some renovation work but is thought to be inscribed 1660. Made from coursed limestone rubble with a thatched roof, it was known as Balls Farm in Victorian times after the occupiers James and Thomas Ball. In 1939 it was called Odell Farm and in more recent times it has been called Tamar Court and then Lindham Court. It is unknown where the name Green Farm came from. Records show it was called by this name when the farmers were Harry Ross (1903-1924) and Sydney Rowlatt (1928-1940). Presumably it was occupied by someone called Green sometime in its history and the name stuck.

A wind up air raid siren was situated at Green Farm during World War II to warn the villagers of any bombing raids.

To the right of the farmhouse is an old barn converted into a home which used to be part of Green Farm. This is known as 'Green Barns'.

Now re-trace your steps along Starey Close and turn left to continue your journey along Marsh Lane. In this area used to be sited another farm known as 'Fishpond Farm' named after the large pond which used to be within its grounds. Both the farm and the pond no longer exist.

Soon you will reach 'Green Barns' which you saw when viewing Green Farm.

The next part of your journey involves walking across a public right of way, so if the ground is wet or you are a wheelchair user, you may wish to follow the alternative route which is highlighted on the map at the end of the book.

Following the direction marked out by the public footpath sign, enter the field via the gate. Continue walking over the grassland. Aim for the stone cottage straight in front of you. This is appropriately called 'Stone Cottage!'

Stone Cottage **30** has a gable end date stone marked RTM 1669. RTM as mentioned in the Village Farm narrative, stands for Robert and Thomas Morris, the stonemasons who built the property. Little history since then is known about this building. Samuel Bass, a blacksmith, worked and lived in a house in this area in Victorian times and Stone Cottage would be the most likely location. For a period in the twentieth century it was split into two cottages and housed workers from Milton House Farm.

Stone Cottage was built in an area of Milton Ernest known as Flewton End. This name is thought to date back to Anglo Saxon times. Local knowledge passed down through time states that the meaning of Flewton End is 'watery meadow'. There seems to be some truth in this as the Old English word for a stream is *fleot*, while ton could be translated as a collection of dwellings and End is the outlying part of an estate. Flewton End could therefore be roughly translated as some houses near a stream on the edge of the village. Whatever the precise definition, the area was probably quite wet underfoot, as an old path in the area was known as 'Marshy Lane!'

Just past Stone Cottage, up the hill and over a style, is a hollow in the ground. This runs north west for 420 metres, is 10 metres wide and 1.5 metres deep. This hollow marks the extent of the medieval village. Pottery from this period has been ploughed up in this vicinity and to the east of this old roadway are the remains of medieval house platforms. This site hasn't been included in the heritage walk, as it needs to be reached by rougher ground, but if you're feeling energetic and have the time why not visit. Just walk past Stone Cottage and follow the public footpath sign.

Fig 196 – Stone Cottage at Flewton End, 25th November 2004.

To continue the walk turn right before Stone Cottage and head towards the gate in the field. This track will lead you back to Thurleigh Road.

Heritage Trail (Part X) – Thurleigh Road Revisited

Immediately on the left at the bottom of the track is a large house known as Woodlands.

Woodlands is the old vicarage **31**. It was built in 1694, as proven by the date stone on the north east elevation. John Hawkins was the vicar at the time of construction.

Fig 197 – The Vicarage, 1939. Note the croquet green in front of the house.

Records of the Milton Ernest rectory go back as far as 1291. By the sixteenth century Queen Elizabeth I granted the rectory to John Cotton. At the turn of the seventeenth century it became the property of the Franklin family of Bolnhurst who enjoyed it for the next forty years. The fact that the Franklins could buy the Rectory illustrates the laicisation *(withdrawal of ecclesiastical status from a building)* of church property in the sixteenth century. Sir Edmund Turnor was next to own the Rectory. He bought it sometime around 1693 and it would seem it was he who built the vicarage which you can see today. The assumption coming from the stone carved motto which reads 'QUOD DONAVI HABEO 1694 ET'. This translates as 'That I have given I have'. The initials 'ET' more than likely refer to Edmund Turnor and the date of 1694 highlights that after buying the Rectory he must have immediately started to build the new vicarage.

It would seem that the old vicarage that you see today was built on the site of the earlier vicarage. A survey undertaken in 1608 when Robert

215

Sutton was the vicar, entitled 'Terrier of Milton Ernest Vicarage', paints a good picture of the aforementioned earlier vicarage. Within its one acre of grounds was "one garden walled in with stone on the south west and another garden hedged on the south east and the yard and a grass yard with a long pool or pond on the north side". The vicarage house itself consisted of "five bays built of stone and covered with thatch". The five bays were the hall, two parlours, the buttery and the kitchen. All of which had a "boarded loft over" except for the kitchen. There was also a "barn of two bays built of timber and thatched and a stable built of stone and thatched". This parsonage barn is also shown in the 1635 deeds of the original rectory.

Its replacement, the Old Vicarage, still has many of its 1694 features, including a cellar which has a coal chute and two areas designed to hold many bottles of wine. The entrances to these wine cellars both have lockable metal gates.

In 1836 the building was extended. Again we know this from the date stone on the south east gable which has another motto: 'CCBP MDCCCXXXVI NON SIBI SOLUM'. This can be translated as 'Not for him alone'. The initials stand for Charles Colyear Beaty-Pownall, who was the vicar at the time of the extension. He'd only been vicar of Milton Ernest for one year when he employed Charles J Carter of Louth (Lincolnshire) as his architect to undertake the extension to the south of the building. The Reverend Beaty-Pownall is said to have come into money when he married his wife Catherine Hett, who was the daughter of the Reverend William Hett, prebendary of Lincoln. They married in Lincoln on 27th January 1835, so, if the stories are true, it didn't take long for Charles to start spending his new found wealth!

The 1836 alterations were very extensive. So much so that the Bedford Mercury reported that the old Vicarage was demolished. The newspaper also reports that the original stone carved with 'QUOD DONAVI HABEO 1694 ET' used to be situated at the front of the property but was carefully preserved during the alterations and repositioned on the back wall of the Vicarage house. Today it has been sited within the property, following recent renovation work, to protect it from the elements. A modern replacement has been sited in its former position.

Prior to the 1836 re-building, George Hurst, a Bedford Gent, who had been born in the Vicarage on 10th February 1800, described the Vicarage as a "rickety old dwelling".

To the rear of the building were stables with a hayloft. There was also a section where the trap was kept.

Throughout Victorian times the census records that the vicar employed on average four servants. In 1861 these were listed as a cook, a parlour maid, a house maid and a lady's maid (female servant responsible for the lady of the house's wardrobe, bathing needs and other personal services). There was a separate servants' quarters within the 23 bedroom house. The row of 13 bells, which were rung whenever the servants were required, still exist today.

In 1969 the Vicarage was bought from the Church and was converted into Woodlands Craft Centre. Ten years later Peter and Pamela Smith bought the property from where they ran Woodlands Tennis Centre and Woodlands Language Studio respectively. There were three grass tennis courts in the grounds of the house. Today one of these has been replaced by a croquet court. Among the many young people who were assisted in their tennis development at Woodlands was Marc Rosset, the Swiss player, who went on to win the men's singles gold medal at the 1992 Barcelona Olympic Games.

In 1988 an application was issued to convert the outbuildings and part of the house into four new self contained properties meaning that, including the old vicarage house, there are now five homes within the grounds of Woodlands.

Today the main part of Woodlands offers bed and breakfast and has four rooms for guests.

Now turn left and walk up Thurleigh Road a short distance before crossing the road where you can see East Manor Farm at the end of a shingle drive.

East Manor Farm **32**, which is now known as 'The Manor House', is built on the site of the Manor of Middeltone. At the time of the Domesday Book, 1086, the site belonged to Adeliza, wife of Hugh de Grandmesnil. Ivo, steward of Hugh de Grandmesnil, was the actual tenant. The land was valued at sixty shillings!

From the thirteenth century, East Manor Farm was owned by the powerful de Grey family (Sir Reynold de Grey who became Lord Grey in 1290, had a large estate including Wrest (Silsoe), Thurleigh and Brogborough) but it was the Erneys family who were the tenants and actually lived in the house. The first mention of Erneys is recorded in 1221 and Milton Ernest got its name from a combination of the original village name and this family – Middeltone Erneys.

At some stage it seems that the Erneys family became owners of the Manor of Middeltone. Records show the head of the Erneys household as being Robert (1221), John (1279), another John (1316), probably a further John (1346), Philip (1361), John (1428), Philip (1471), Edward, William (who had been insane for eighteen years before his death in 1528), John (who was just five years old in 1528) and finally Walter (1550). That's at least eleven generations of the Erneys family recorded as living at this manor.

Fig 198 – East Manor Farm.

When Sir Walter Erneys died in the mid sixteenth century (circa 1558), probably through the plague, the Manor of Milton Ernest was divided between his three daughters as the male line had failed. One daughter, Isabel, married Christopher Turnor who came from Haverhill in Suffolk. A further daughter gave her share to his son Edmund Turnor, and this meant that East Manor Farm became the property of the Turnor family.

Christopher Turnor married Isabel Erneys on 25th November 1542. They had six children, including the aforementioned Edmund who was baptised at Milton Ernest on 15th April 1548. Edmund married Alice Eastwick, of Milton Bryan, and together they had thirteen children between 1578 and 1595. One child was named Erneis, after the family connection. Edmund died in 1597.

The eldest son of Edmund and Alice, another Christopher Turnor, baptised 24th April 1580, married Ellen Samm on 17th February 1601. They had eleven children including Edmund who was born seven months before Christopher died aged just thirty-nine in 1619.

Fig 199 – The Turnor Coat of Arms.

The most notable child of Christopher and Ellen was Christopher Turnor (the third!) who was born in 1607. He became a barrister in 1633, aged 26, but a charge of delinquency (failed in his duty or committed an offence) was made and all his property, including East Manor Farm, was confiscated. Despite there being no evidence to support the claim, it took him fourteen years to clear his name, and his property was restored to him in 1647. On 16th July 1660 he was knighted and created third baron of the Exchequer. He became a member of the special court of summary jurisdiction and adjudicated on disputes between owners and occupiers of property ravaged by the Great Fire of London.

Unfortunately, when Sir Christopher Turnor, who had married Joyce Warwick, died in 1675, he was predeceased by his son and grandson, both called Edmund. Fortunately, the estate remained in the family as it was purchased by his brother Sir Edmund Turnor who had moved to Stoke Rochford, a village south of Grantham in Lincolnshire.

Edmund Turnor had been baptised at Milton Ernest on 14th May 1619. During the English Civil War he became a staunch royalist while his father was a parliamentarian! He married Margaret Harrison, was knighted in 1663 and was recorded as being "an eminent and excellent person". It was Edmund who provided the six almshouses, the site of which you will see later, for the poor of the village in 1694. It is likely that he also rebuilt the Vicarage in the same year. He died on 4th April 1707, not long after the Turnor family had left East Manor Farm, spreading far and wide to Bath, London and Stoke Rochford.

The Turnor family must have replaced the original manor building with the current East Manor Farm as this dates back to the seventeenth century. The West wing is the oldest part of the house with the south part being added in the nineteenth century.

Fig 200 – Edmund Turnor. An engraving by James Fittler in 1786 based on the 1693 painting by H. Verelit.

Sir Edmund Turnor left the manor to his grandson John, on whose death it passed to his elder brother Edmund, another grandson of Sir Edmund. Edmund passed the manor onto his cousin, Streynsham Master, in 1715. A Mrs Stuckley (nee Master) later owned East Manor and left it in her will to Withers Bramston. In 1799 it was sold by Arthur Bramston to Robert Gibbins.

Fig 201 – East Manor Farm, 1939.

Between 1841 and 1871, census records show East Manor Farm as being in the occupancy of William Pancras Gibbins. At this time his land consisted of over 600 acres and Gibbins, a maltster, brick maker and farmer, employed twenty five men, twelve boys, a cook and a house maid. During this period it was known as Church Farm.

William Feazey is shown as the next occupant in both the 1881 and 1891 census. Only working East Manor Farm, and having no connections to the brewery or brick making, the farmland was 304 acres and Feazey employed eight men and two boys to work the land.

Above what is now the entrance to The Manor House is an inscription carved into the stone. It reads M T 1878. This would suggest that this part of the house was an extension built in 1878. There is no conclusive proof of what the initials MT stand for, but an intelligent guess would point to Maria Tucker.

Joseph Tucker of nearby Pavenham Bury owned East Manor Farm. Records show him as being the owner in 1874. He died three years later on 17th February 1877 and left East Manor and other properties in his will to his wife. If the intelligent guess is correct then it would seem that Maria Tucker wasted no time in enlarging East Manor.

Inside 'The Manor House' is a stair case which originated in Odell Castle. It used to have an interesting feature – a trip stair. This was a step which was smaller than the rest of the steps and was designed to trip up burglars!

Heritage Trail (Part XI) – All Saints' Church

Now walk to the Church and enter the graveyard, which contains the graves of Lucy Starey (buried 12th December 1866) alongside William Butterfield (buried 1st December 1886), the father of the Victorian architect with the same name, and Bedfordshire's first printer, Underhill Robinson (buried 4th May 1719). The Starey and Butterfield graves are still identifiable (they are directly behind the chancel wall) but sadly the exact location of Underhill Robinson's final resting place is not known, despite books as recent as the 1960s stating that his gravestone is visible. The oldest still visible grave inscriptions are Thomas Boddington and William Stock who were buried in 1730 and 1766 respectively. There is also a fragment of a gravestone, clearly dated 1676, with three initials of which only the third, an "H", is easily decipherable. The burial register has five people recorded in that particular year, of which only John Hart has the correct surname initial.

Monica Boielle remembers the grave diggers unearthing a plague pit in the 1940s.

In medieval times All Saints' Church **33** used to be known as Allhallows and is the oldest surviving building in Milton Ernest. It is 73 feet (22 metres) long including the chancel and 45 feet (14 metres) in breadth. Including the steeple, All Saints is 75 feet high (23 metres).

There was a church, probably largely made of timber, before the present one was built some time shortly after the Norman Conquest. The story goes that All Saints' Church was going to be built higher up the hill near Lawn Wood, which no longer exists, in a field which has since been called Church Green Common. After each day's work of taking stones to the site, the stones were mysteriously removed at night and dumped on the present church site. The villagers, it is said, believed this to be the work of the devil and so built the church where directed.

It should be noted that originally All Saints' Church would have been a place of Roman Catholic worship until Henry VIII created the Church of England in the mid sixteenth century.

In the twelfth century Milton Ernest Church was granted to the nuns of Elstow Abbey. This advowson (the right to nominate the vicar of Milton Ernest) continued with the Albini family. Cecilia, mother of Robert de Albini, then granted it to the monks of the Priory of Beaulieu, Clophill, which had been founded by her son as a cell of the Abbey of St Albans. Cecilia's grandson reclaimed the church for the Albini family in 1220 but it was returned once again to Beaulieu Priory, this time by Bishop Gravesend in 1275. After the dissolution of the monasteries in 1539, Milton Ernest

Church became Crown property and remained that way until 1677, when it was granted to Sir Ralph Verney. From him it passed to the Rolt family and by 1775 All Saints' advowson was in the hands of the Turnor family, with whom it remained until the twentieth century.

Milton Ernest church possesses a fine chalice, inscribed 'Mylton Harnes', dated 1570 from the reign of Queen Elizabeth I. A Victorian communion plate, which was presented by Reverend Beaty-Pownall and his wife in 1844, is still used today.

Fig 202 – All Saints' Church, Milton Ernest, a watercolour dated 1815, painted by Thomas Fisher.

In 1730 a new pulpit and desk were provided during a period when the church was repaired and beautified throughout, funded by Thomas Rolt, Esquire.

William Butterfield turned his attention to Milton Ernest Church in 1858 after completing Milton Ernest Hall. He added an organ chamber on the north side of the chancel and created a fine High Victorian interior by use of good contemporary furnishings and decorative features. The scheme included stained glass by Alexander Gibbs, carved woodwork by Rattee of Cambridge, and metalwork by Hart of London. The altar service books have finely tooled leather covers designed by Butterfield, and the light iron chancel screen, the lectern, pulpit, wooden screens and oak pews all survive from the restoration of the church which was reopened on 30th November 1865. During this work, which was paid for by the Starey family from Milton Ernest Hall, Butterfield removed twenty five coats of whitewash from the church walls!

A new church clock from Cope of Nottingham was put up in 1882, but by the turn of the twentieth century it had to be raised higher up the tower as it was not deemed easy enough to see!

Vicar	From-To	Years
Johannes De Lega	1215-1239	24
Walter Percefoil	1239-1253	14
C. De wrastlingworth	1253-12??	26
John de Wakefend *	12??-1271	
Thomas De Irthlingburg	1271-1279	8
Matthew De Bedeford *	1279-1297	18
Robert De Connington	1297-1301	4
Fulk de Horsleya	1301-13??	49
Dom. Roger *	13??-1349	
John Roger	1349-1350	1
Hugh de Middleton	1350-1376	26
Dom. Peter	1376-13??	30
John Mason	13??-1406	
Roger Mapleton	1406-1409	3
William Fuller	1409-1447	38
Bartholomew Lovell	1447-1451	4
John Ffrankleyn	1451-1453	2
Thomas Marchall	1453-1462	9
Richard Jonysson *	1462-1464	2
William Gatys	1464-1472	8
William Conquest	1472-1479	7
Richard Bageley	1479-14??	9
John Capull *	14??-1488	
John Abraham	1488-1499	11
John Carre *	1499-1500	1
Roger Sharpe	1500-15??	19
William King *	15??-1519	
Richard Kene *	1519-1539	20
William Brasse	1539-1554	15
Robert Thorold *	1554-1572	18
Thomas Welles	1572-1574	2
Henry Leddisham	1574-1576	2

Vicar	From-To	Years
Robert Sutton *#	1576-1611	35
John Smith *#	1611-1636	25
Thomas Watson	1636-16??	21
John Hind *#	16??-1657	
Thomas Ceach	1657-1676	19
John Draper	1676-1676	1
Adam Haughton	1676-1677	1
John Hawkins *#	1684-1721	37
Samuel Shepeard *	1721-1723	2
Stephen Rolt *#	1723-1738	15
George Backhouse *	1738-1775	37
William Holmes	1775-1783	8
George Turnor *	1783-1825	42
Charles Turnor	1825-1832	7
Christopher Whichcote	1832-1834	2
Henry Foulis	1834-1835	1
Charles Beaty-Pownall *#	1835-1880	45
Henry Fuller	1880-1881	1
Edward Sutton-Dodd #	1881-1890	9
John Burton	1890-1896	6
Ernest Holmes	1896-1935	39
John Ingram Bryan #	1935-1946	11
W. Morgan	1946-1949	3
A. Ennis	1949-1954	5
J. Turney	1954-1959	5
James Daniels	1959-1964	5
Harold Jones	1964-1981	17
David Rees	1981-1984	3
Andrew Mottram	1984-1992	8
Chris Gonin	1992-1998	6
Victoria Raymer	1998-2002	4
Nicola & Ian McIntosh	2002-	

Fig 203 – The Vicars of Milton Ernest. The first five are shown as Rector rather than Vicar. * denotes that the vicar died whilst in office, while # denotes that the vicar is recorded in the All Saints' burial register.

Inside the church is a list of the incumbents of All Saints since 1215, the year that King John signed the Magna Carta. During a period of almost 800 years there have been 59 vicars and 5 rectors. The difference between the titles being that a rector received all of the tithes and had a deputy known as a vicar. The longest serving vicars have been Charles Colyear Beaty-Pownall (45 years, 1835-1880); George Turnor (42 years, 1783-1825); Ernest Holmes (39 years, 1896-1935); William Fuller (38 years, 1409-1447); John Hawkins (37 years, 1684-1721); George Backhouse (37 years, 1738-1775); and Robert Sutton (35 years, 1576-1611). In 1998 the Reverend Dr Victoria Raymer became the first woman vicar at Milton Ernest. She was followed in 2002 by Nicola and Ian McIntosh, the first job share vicars. Nicola has the legal title of vicar.

One vicar, Robert Sutton, seems to have been an especially interesting character. In 1578 during an archdeacon visit to the village, Thomas Jackson and John Church, Sutton's churchwardens, accused him of cutting down five ash trees in the churchyard, selling them and using the money to buy timber with which he repaired his house. The churchwardens were aggrieved that the money hadn't been used to repair the chancel. Then in 1584 a bishop visited Milton Ernest and the villagers informed on Robert Sutton, for quarrelling with his neighbours and for being in the alehouse at unlawful times of the night! Robert Sutton died on 27th March 1611, and although no evidence exists to prove he was related to the Milton Ernest Suttons who were tried and executed as witches a year later, is it just coincidence that as soon as the vicar called Sutton, who seemed to be unpopular, was dead, the villagers accused two women called Sutton of being witches?

Fig 204 – Note the clock was placed lower on the tower in those days.

During January and February 1695 tragedy twice struck Vicar John Hawkins as both his sons, Francis and John, died of smallpox.

The following section of the heritage trail gives you the opportunity to explore the interior of All Saints'. The church plan has been provided to help locate the main points of interest. These are highlighted with a letter of the alphabet which can also be found within the forthcoming text.

Enter the church via the fifteenth century porch. This originally had an upper storey which formed quarters for the incumbent. Once inside the church look up and you can see the blocked entrance **(A)** to this place. Access would presumably have been via wooden stairs of which nothing remains.

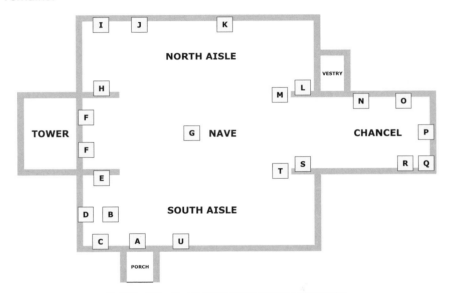

Fig 205 – Milton Ernest All Saints' Church Plan (not to scale).

Now that you're inside the church you will find yourself standing in the south aisle. This part of the church dates back to the fourteenth century and was rebuilt a century later. The font **(B)** dates back to the fifteenth century and replaces an earlier one. It is made from a soft stone, known as clunch, which came from Totternhoe, near Dunstable. The church registers show that in the period 1538 to 1991, there have been 3,836 baptisms performed in this very font!

In the area around the font are three memorials, two of which are stone tablets and the other a stained glass window. The first is a carved tablet to Christopher Turnor **(C)**, dated 1675. You walked past his home, East Manor Farm, just before the church. Sir Christopher was buried on 22nd May 1675. Next is a stained glass window **(D)**. This is a memorial to Lucy Starey, who was a resident of Milton Ernest Hall, which you will visit at the end of the trail. Lucy died, aged just 22, on 12th December 1866, after a lingering illness, and her death is commemorated in a privately printed account of her last days entitled 'In Memory of Lucy Starey'. The final memorial in this area is another stone tablet **(E)** on which the name is now indecipherable but the date 1615 can just be seen. Burial records suggest that the memorial is to a 'Mr Bartewe' who was annotated as being a 'Gent' and was buried on 2nd June 1615. Research of the shield with four quarters above the tablet prove the case, as this coat of arms is of Francis Barty, Esquire, who lived in the neighbouring village of Oakley. Why his memorial is in All Saints' Church, Milton Ernest, rather than in St. Mary's, Oakley, is unclear.

Moving further into the church you'll reach the door to the tower on the left and on your right is the nave.

The walls of the tower include the aforementioned lists of the rectors and vicars of All Saints' Church **(F)** from 1215 to the present day.

This thirteenth century west tower has a peal of six bells. Three of the bells date back to the early seventeenth century and have the inscription 'Newcome Leicester made me 1611' (the Newcome family traded in Leicester from about 1506). Two other bells are inscribed with 'Richard Chandler 1679' and 'George Backhouse Vicar, Henry Bull, James Hartwell Churchwardens 1765' respectively. The biggest bell at All Saints' has a diameter of 3 feet 2 inches (1 metre).

In 1893 under William Butterfield's direction the west tower was restored and the bells re-hung. More recent work to the tower saw the erection of a ringing platform and an organ gallery in 1970. At the back of the gallery is a small lancet window with a stained glass of St. George.

The nave was originally the main body of the church with the tower and chancel at each end. It was only in the fourteenth century that the north and south aisle were added to considerably extend the overall floor space.

The arches in the nave are Early English dating back to the early fourteenth century. Almost a century later the nave was heightened by the addition of a clerestory which is the windowed part of the aisle roof. There are eight windows in total.

The roof of the nave is fifteenth century with moulded timbers and has a number of bosses carved with foliage at the intersections of the beams. It is from this roof that hangs a fine sixteen branch brass chandelier **(G)** which Thomas Rolt gave to the church in 1729. Unfortunately, in 1956, the chain from which it was suspended broke and this two ton chandelier crashed to the floor. The damage was so bad that it was at first feared beyond repair. However the British Oxygen Company fully restored the chandelier and it once again graces the church.

Walk past the tower and you will come to the North Aisle. On the wall, immediately to your left, is a stone tablet memorial to Samuel Rolt **(H)**, who was buried on 10th October 1717, aged 46. He was twice MP for Bedford and lived at Milton Ernest Hall.

Fig 206 – The bread cupboard / dole board provided by Susanna Rolt in 1726.

As stated earlier the North Aisle was added in the fourteenth century. Housed on the north wall is another stone tablet **(I)** dedicated to Susanna Rolt who was the wife of Samuel Rolt, the Bedford MP. As the memorial states, Susanna was the third daughter of Richard Poulter, a merchant from London. She died on 30th August and was buried on 7th September

1726. The memorial was erected by her son, Thomas, in 1733. To the right of her memorial is the bread cupboard or dole board **(J)** which was provided by Susanna Rolt in her will of 1726. It has pigeon holes for twelve loaves which were to be delivered to the poor of the village weekly "for ever". The exact words in the will being "….. and in remembrance of me, I give five pounds in money to the poor of the parish, besides Twelve pennyworth of bread in little loaves to Twelve poor persons every Sunday for ever, taking it by turns, them that had it one day, to Twelve others the next…..". Each Sunday the choir boys delivered the loaves, which were baked at the village bakery and paid for by the owner of Milton Ernest Hall, to elderly people who couldn't attend church. George Willars, who was a choirboy in the 1930s, recalls that there was always a squabble as to which choirboy delivered the loaves to which person, as the rewards for the delivery varied between a halfpenny and a penny. Obviously it was better to deliver a loaf to someone who paid a penny! The 'dole' was discontinued in 1956 when the Milton Ernest bakery closed down. The Rolt money meant for the loaves was then incorporated with the Turnor charity.

Fig 207 – Ernest Holmes, Vicar of All Saints' Church, Milton Ernest, distributing free bread. The oldest village inhabitant is receiving a loaf.

The Turnor Rolt Charity still operates today with the aim of benefiting residents in the Parish of Milton Ernest. Its objective being to benefit persons who are (a) sick, infirm or convalescent and (b) those seeking employment. Aid for the sick could include gifts such as bedding, clothing, food, fuel and furniture; money to relieve the sickness, infirmity or distress; grants to assist in the cost of recuperative holidays or for domestic help; and payment of travelling expenses of those people or relatives visiting hospital. The employment side of the Charity aims to assist people who are preparing to enter any trade, occupation or profession with the provision of tools or books and the payment of examination fees. The objective being to help enable the parishioner to earn their own living or advance them in life.

The North Aisle also has an ogee-headed crocketed tomb recess, under which is laid a worn marble grave slab **(K)** with a Calvary cross which dates back to circa 1340.

Behind the medieval wooden screen at the end of the North Aisle is a wall tablet **(L)** dedicated to Stephen Rolt, who was vicar of Milton Ernest for fifteen years from 1723. Stephen died on 12th March 1738, aged 75, and was buried three days later. The tablet also mentions Elizabeth, his wife, who died eight years later on 19th August 1746, aged 80.

Next you will come across the pulpit **(M)** which is Victorian and used for preaching.

The pews that you have been walking past are Victorian and were designed by William Butterfield. Previously, in 1822, it was noted that there were private pews which were kept in repair by the parties to whom they belonged; common pews maintained by the Parish; and chancel pews which the vicar looked after. In the 1630s there were references to a private pew belonging to "the house called Weedons". This was almost certainly West Manor Farm, as it stands on a piece of land which was once called Weedons Close.

Enter the Chancel via the gate in the wrought iron screen. This screen was installed by William Butterfield in the nineteenth century and replaced the wooden medieval version which now stands at the end of the North Aisle. Immediately on your left is the vestry. This was home to the organ until it was moved to the balcony of the tower in 1970.

There used to be a painting hanging in the vestry called 'The Scourging of Christ'. This oil painting, which dates back to 1400, depicts Christ bound to a pillar being whipped by two men. A third man crouching on the ground is tightening the rope which binds Christ's feet to the pillar. Curiously Christ is painted as having five fingers and a thumb on his right hand!

Fig 208 – The Scourging of Christ, the fourteenth century German painting which mysteriously appeared at Milton Ernest Church. Note Christ's five fingers and thumb on his right hand!

Fig 209 – A close up of the unusual hand.

The painting originally formed a portion of one of the panels of a great altar piece in the Neustadter Marienkirche at Bielefeld in Westphalia, Germany. It disappeared in 1838 when that Church was restored. By 1850 it was in the hands of a German collector and four years later was purchased from him by the National Gallery, who then sold it at Christies in 1857. The painting wasn't heard of again until Boxing Day 1923 when Mr & Mrs Hockliffe from London discovered it hanging in the vestry of Milton Ernest Church while on a visit to the village. No-one knew how it ended up in All Saints' or where it had been for almost seventy years. However, Milton Ernest Church was to benefit from the find, as it was given permission to auction the painting, which it did in 1950, and £262 was raised at Christies from the sale to an American collector.

The Chancel is the oldest part of the church with the walls being built within half a century of William the Conqueror's victory in 1066. The west part dates back to this period and is the oldest unchanged part of the church, while the east end was added in the fourteenth century. The furthest end from the altar steps was added by William Butterfield in the nineteenth century.

Fig 210 – Milton Ernest Choir, 1908. Back row left to right: William Horn, Edgar Smith, Harold Chesney, Alfred Parrott. Middle row left to right: William Jacquest (who was killed in WWI), George Mitchell, Henry Cooper, Charlie Peck, Ernest Cooper, Gordon Cotton, Walter Taylor, Sidney Jacquest, Harold Smith. Front row left to right: Frank Salisbury (who was also killed in WWI), George Barnett (school headmaster), Rev E L Holmes, Mr Jacquest, Walter Cooper.

As you walk up the Chancel you will see two stained glass windows on your left. The first small window **(N)** is dedicated to Milton Ernest choir. Next is a much larger stained glass window depicting St. Matthew and St. Mark **(O)**. The text inscribed at the bottom of the window is a tribute from the children of Charles Colyear Beaty-Pownall who was the vicar from 1835 to his death in 1880. He was instrumental in making a number of improvements to the Church including the work undertaken by William Butterfield.

Under St. Matthew are the words 'In Gloriam Dei Parentvm' which roughly translates as 'Glory of God of Parents', followed by the names 'Kath-Amy', 'Editha L' and 'Georgivs A'. The text under St. Mark states 'Q Honorem', which means 'with honour', followed by three more names, 'Maria F', 'Carolvs E', and 'Gvi Thos Beaty-Pownall'. These six names are the children of Charles Colyear Beaty-Pownall and Catherine Beaty-Pownall (nee Hett). From the church baptism registers their full names and dates of birth are as follows: Mary Fanny (24th May 1836), Charles Ernest (13th May 1837), Catherine Amy (7th May 1839), Edith Louisa (18th November 1840), George Albert (6th March 1842) and William Thomas (9th December 1844). The window was a gift from them to the Church.

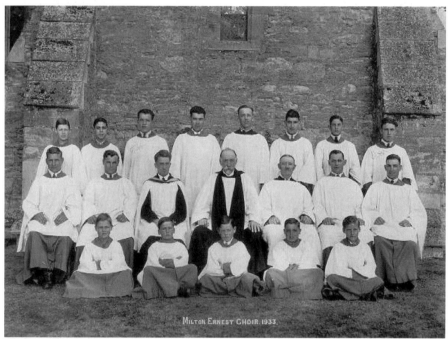

Fig 211 – Milton Ernest Choir, 1933. Ernest Holmes, in the centre, was the Vicar of Milton Ernest from 1896 to 1935.

At the end of the Chancel is another stained glass window which depicts the birth of Jesus **(P)** and has the words 'Peace on Earth'. This was designed by William Butterfield. At the bottom of the window is text in honour of 'Caroli Beatty', 'C C Beaty-Pownall', 'Georgii Pownall' and 'Catherinae'. These names include the aforementioned vicar Charles Colyear Beaty-Pownall and his wife Catherine.

While still facing the 'Peace on Earth' stained glass window you'll see to your right a piscina recess **(Q)**. This dates back to the fourteenth century and was incorporated into the wall in its current position by William Butterfield in the late nineteenth century. The piscina is used for the washing of the communion vessels.

Fig 212 – The 'Peace on Earth' stained glass window of All Saints' Church, Milton Ernest.

Next is another stained glass window with St. Luke and St. John **(R)**, which complements the St. Matthew and St. John window. The window has the names 'Caroli Hvrst' and 'Georgivs Hvrst' and was the gift of George Hurst, esquire of Bedford.

Rt Hon. Lord AMPTHILL	Albert HORNE	Henry ROBINSON
Matthew ANDREW (Wounded)	Daniel HORNE	O.H. RODDIS
Robert ANDREW	Ernest HORNE	Sydney ROWLATT
James BAILEY (Killed)	George HORNE	Hon. Guy RUSSELL (RN)
A.J. BILLINGHAM	Thomas HORNE (Killed)	Hon. John RUSSELL (RN)
Alfred BONHAM (Killed)	William HORNE	Thomas SMART
William BRATCHER	Ernest JACQUEST	Cecil Edgar SMITH
George BULL (Wounded)	Sydney JACQUEST	Edgar SMITH (Wounded)
Harry CHILDS	Walter JACQUEST (Wounded)	Harold SMITH
Percy CHILDS	William JACQUEST (Killed)	Cyril SOLESBURY (Killed)
Percy CLARKE (Wounded)	Berton KINCH	Edward SOLESBURY (Wounded)
Gordon COTTON	Robert KINCH	Frank SOLESBURY (Killed)
Thomas COTTON	George KNIGHT	Herbert SOLESBURY
William COTTON	William LINGER	Leonard SOLESBURY
James CURTIS	Charles LOWINGS (Wounded)	Ralph SOLESBURY
William CURTIS	Herbert MARSH	Herbert STANTON
G. DENTON	William MARSH	Arthur TAYLOR
Joseph FARRER (Killed)	A. MATTHEWS	Harry TAYLOR (Killed)
Percy GAMBRELL	George MITCHELL	Walter TAYLOR
Charles GARDENER	Alfred PARROTT (Wounded)	Arthur WOODHAMS
Charles GRAHAM	Albert William PAYNE	Fred WOODHAMS
Jesse GRAHAM	Charles PERKINS	Charles WOODS
Christopher HAYCOCK	J. PERKINS	Fred WOODS
H. Christopher HOLMES (RN)	J.S. PERKINS	William WOODS
Edmund HERITAGE (Killed)	John PURSER (Killed)	

Fig 213 – The Milton Ernest Roll of Honour depicts all of those people from the village who fought in the First World War. James Bailey is not listed on the roll but is on the war memorial, hence his inclusion. Edmund Heritage is not denoted as killed on the roll of honour but is named on the war memorial. RN is assumed to be 'Royal Navy'. Of the 74 men listed, 10 were killed and 8 were wounded.

George Hurst was a prominent Bedford figure, a councillor, alderman, mayor and a fellow of the Royal History Society. Such was his standing that when he died six weeks short of his 99th birthday, in December 1898, the Bedford Mercury printed a full page obituary with his photograph. George Hurst was born at Milton Ernest Vicarage on February 10th 1800. He was the son of the Reverend Isaac Hurst, clerk of All Saints'. Despite having such an active role in Bedford, George obviously never forgot his roots as he gifted the stained glass window to Milton Ernest Church. Interestingly, there are two Hurst tombs in the graveyard directly behind this window. The burial register records Sarah Hurst being buried in 1826, aged 19 and Elizabeth Hurst, buried 1834 aged 35. Both were living in Bedford at the time of their death. Sarah was George Hurst's sister while Elizabeth (nee Negus) was his wife. The latter's young death meant that George Hurst was a widower for sixty-four years.

Upon leaving the Chancel, immediately on your left is a wall memorial **(S)** dedicated to Alfred Chapman and his wife, Madeline. They resided at Milton Ernest Hall from 1885 until their deaths. Madeline died at the Hall on 8th June 1900 and Alfred followed her two years later, at Combe, near Dulverton, Somerset, on 21st October 1902.

Enter the South Aisle and you'll immediately come across the Victorian lectern **(T)** from where the Scriptures are read. Walk alongside the South wall and just before the door there is the Milton Ernest Roll of Honour **(U)** which lists all those people from the village who fought in the First World War.

Fig 214 – Milton Ernest War Memorial, 25th November 2004. The Manor House, formerly East Manor Farm, can be seen in the background.

Having completed your tour of the interior of All Saints', leave through the porch door where you originally entered the church. Immediately in front of you is the War Memorial **34** which was erected in 1920. This lists the ten men from Milton Ernest who died in the First World War and the three soldiers from the village who were killed in the Second World War. Brief details of these men who lost their lives in the line of duty are listed over the next few pages.

Located directly behind the war memorial is the stump of the old churchyard cross. It was the custom before the Reformation to erect a large cross in the centre of the churchyard. Few survive today.

IN MEMORY OF MEN FROM THIS VILLAGE WHO GAVE THEIR LIVES IN THE GREAT WAR 1914-1918

John Harold Farrar
(shown as Joseph Farrar on the memorial)

Rank & Regiment (R&R): Captain, 3rd Battalion attached 1st Battalion, Northamptonshire Regiment.

Milton Ernest Connection (MEC): Son of Captain J. P. Farrar, D.S.O. and Mrs A. Mary Farrar, whose addresses are listed as 110, Elm Park Gardens, Chelsea, London and Milton Ernest House, Milton Ernest.

War Details (WD): Gazetted in June 1906. John Farrar was the last of the original officers that was still with the battalion, from the 27 that sailed to France in August 1914. He was killed in action, aged 27, at Aubers Ridge on 9th May 1915. John Farrar is commemorated on Le Touret Memorial, Pas de Calais, France.

Harry Taylor

R&R: Private (23006) 1st/5th Bedfordshire Regiment and then Private (51049) 1st/8th Battalion, The King's (Liverpool) Regiment. Shown as Corporal on the War Memorial.

MEC: Harry was born in Cotton End, Bedfordshire, in 1889. He married Laura Childs of Milton Ernest at All Saints' Church on 21st February 1916.

WD: He volunteered in November 1915. Retained on important duties in England for two years. In August 1917 he went to Western Front and took part in many engagements. Killed in action, aged 28, Tuesday 20th November 1917. No grave. Commemorated on Thiepval memorial, Somme, France.

Alfred George Bonham

R&R: Rifleman (392471) 9th Battalion, London Regiment, Queen Victoria's Rifles.

MEC: Alfred George Bonham was born to Alfred and Catherine Bonham in Bedford in 1898. The 1901 census shows his parents as being Butcher and Grocer in Milton Ernest. Their shop was in Radwell Road. They later ran the village stores on Rushden Road, now known as 'The Old Post Office'.

WD: AG Bonham enlisted in April 1916. At this time he was a resident of Brixton, London. By December of that year he had completed his training and was drafted to France. Here he was involved in heavy fighting before being killed in action, aged 19, whilst on patrol near Arras, France on 14th April 1917.

238

Edmund Heritage

The war records do not include an Edmund Heritage but do include E Heritage and EA Heritage, either of which could be Edmund. As it is impossible to distinguish between them, details of both soldiers have been included. To add to the confusion Edmund is the only Heritage listed in the Roll of Honour in the church which depicts those that fought in the two World Wars but there is a gravestone in the churchyard for William Edward Heritage. He was Private 30233, an engineer, of the Northamptonshire Regiment and died in Kempston Military Hospital, aged 21, on 22nd March 1919 of tuberculous peritonitis and toxaemia. There must be a good possibility that both Edmund and William were related. Meaning that their parents lost two sons.

R&R: EA Heritage was a Private (16912) in the 1st Battalion of the Grenadier Guards. E Heritage was also a Private (43841) but in the 7th/8th Battalion, Royal Inniskilling Fusiliers.

MEC: William and Lavinia Heritage ran the Queen's Head public house from circa 1914 to 1930. Whether they are the parents of Edmund and/or William Edward is not known.

WD: EA Heritage died on Wednesday 2nd December 1914 and is buried in "Y" Farm Military Cemetery, Bois Grenier, Nord, France. E Heritage was killed on Saturday 23rd November 1918 and is buried in Poznan Old Garrison Cemetery, Poland.

Thomas Horne

R&R: Private (10557) 2nd Battalion, Bedfordshire Regiment.

MEC: Baptised 15th May 1893 in Milton Ernest All Saints' Church. Son of William, an agricultural labourer, and Mary Ann Horne of River Lane, Milton Ernest.

WD: Thomas volunteered in August 1914 and was drafted to Western Front in July 1915. After much severe fighting was wounded in action in the Somme in July 1916 and returned home due to his injuries. Thomas returned to France in January 1917 but was again wounded, this time at Arras, and again sent back to England in April of the same year. A year later, in May 1918, he rejoined his unit but was killed in action, aged 25, on Thursday 22nd August 1918. He is buried in Warloy-Baillon Cemetery, Somme, France.

William Hilson Jacquest

R&R: Private (271118) 4th/1st Battalion, Hertfordshire Regiment.

MEC: Born and baptised on 11th September 1898 in Milton Ernest to George and Elizabeth Jacquest. William was the ninth child of eleven. The family lived in the Flewton End part of the village. George was a groom and labourer. William's mother's maiden name was Hilson, hence his middle name.

WD: Volunteered in May 1915 and was sent to France in March 1916. Fought at Albert and on the Somme before being injured and sent home in November 1916. William was treated at Sheffield Military Hospital but died, aged 19, on Saturday 28th July 1917, from pneumonia and pleurisy. Buried All Saints' Church, Milton Ernest on 31st July 1917.

John Purser

R&R: Private (25576) Northamptonshire Regiment and then Private (31868) 6th Battalion, York and Lancaster Regiment.

MEC: John Purser was born in 1879 at Islip, Northants. He married Maud Ruth. Her surname and the place of marriage is unknown. At some stage they moved to Milton Ernest. On 24th November 1916 they baptised their five sons at All Saints' Church and a week later, on 31st November, they also baptised their two daughters.

WD: John died of wounds on Monday 18th June 1917, aged 38 and is buried in Dranoutre Military Cemetery, Heuvelland, West-Vlaanderen, Belgium.

Cyril Ernest Solesbury

R&R: Lance Corporal (PLY/2223(S)) 1st RM Battalion, Royal Naval Division, Royal Marine Light Infantry. Shown as Private on the War Memorial.

MEC: Born 14th November 1887 in Milton Ernest to Alfred and Agnes Solesbury. Alfred was a shoemaker. Agnes Mary Garratt had been a domestic servant before her marriage to Alfred at All Saints' on 24th September 1872. The family lived just south of the village green. Cyril was married to Florence, who came from Hawley in Hampshire.

WD: Died, aged 30, on Sunday 26th May 1918. Buried in Berlin South Western Cemetery, Berlin, Brandenburg, Germany.

Frank Solesbury

R&R: Private (25171) 6th Battalion, Bedfordshire Regiment.

MEC: Born 1891 in Milton Ernest to Robert and Phoebe Solesbury. Robert, a labourer, married Phoebe Cox, a lace maker, at All Saints' on 11th October 1872. They have eight children recorded in the Milton Ernest baptism records of which Frank was the final child. He is unrelated to Cyril Ernest. The family lived at Flewton End, Milton Ernest.

WD: Killed in action on Thursday 12th April 1917, aged 27, during very heavy fighting in which Wancourt village was captured. Buried in Wancourt British Cemetery, Pas de Calais, France.

James Bailey

R&R: Private. No other information.

MEC: No information.

WD: No information.

1939-1945

John Michael Bryan, DFC and Bar

R&R: Wing Commander (102570), Pilot, Royal Air Force Volunteer Reserve.

MEC: Son of the Reverend John Ingram Bryan, vicar of Milton Ernest 1935-1946, and Lucy Silver Bryan.

WD: John was killed in action, aged 22, on Saturday 10th June 1944 and is buried in Bretteville-Sur-Laize Canadian Cemetery, Calvados, France. His war record is detailed in an earlier section of this book.

(Christopher) Jack Haycock

R&R: Sergeant (1874077), Air Gunner, Royal Air Force Volunteer Reserve.

MEC: Born 12 January 1924 in Milton Ernest to Christopher and Mary Haycock. His father was the village grocer. Robert Haycock, the proprietor of 'Bob's Shop' on Radwell Road, is Christopher Jack's elder brother.

WD: Christopher Jack Haycock was killed in a plane accident in Scotland, aged 19, on Wednesday 6th October 1943. The plane had engine trouble and all of the crew bailed out. Tragically there wasn't time for the parachutes to open and the entire crew fell to their deaths. Jack Haycock, as he was known, was buried at All Saints' Church, Milton Ernest on 12th October 1943.

John William Hunt

R&R: Sapper (1921012), 121 Road Construction Company, Royal Engineers.

MEC: John William Hunt was the son of Cuthbert and Florence Ada Hunt. On 27th October 1938, a baby girl, Roslina was born to John William and Florence Lilian Hunt. She was baptised at All Saints' Church on 4th December 1938.

WD: JW Hunt died on Tuesday 6th February 1940, aged 24. He is buried in St Mary Magdelene Churchyard, Roxton.

Fig 215 – The wedding of Wilfred Matthew Lumley and Ethel Mary Barnett, both aged 29, at All Saints' Church on 6th September 1921. Ethel Mary (baptised 12th June 1892 at All Saints') was the daughter of George Barnett, headmaster of Milton Ernest School.

As you walk down the churchyard path, look towards the left and you'll see some old stone barns. These three East Manor Farm outbuildings **35** were converted into two private dwellings in 1979. 'The Barn' used to be a threshing barn, while 'Church Barn' has been converted from a stables block and a thatched barn. Immediately in front of 'Church Barn' used to stand a large Dutch barn which was used to store hay.

At the end of the churchyard path you'll come to a lych-gate, which derives its name from the Anglo-Saxon name *lich*, which means corpse. This is because a lych-gate is the roofed gateway at the entrance to the churchyard through which the coffin is carried.

Fig 216 – An aerial view of All Saint's Church, Milton Ernest, 1962.

Fig 217 – The Dutch Barn which used to be part of East Manor Farm.

Fig 218 – The East Manor barns and stables, 1961, before they were converted into houses.

Fig 219 – The former East Manor Farm outbuildings, now converted into two homes, 25th November 2004..

Heritage Trail (Part XII) – Church Green

Once out of the churchyard, immediately in front of you is the village green. It is here that there used to be a pound.

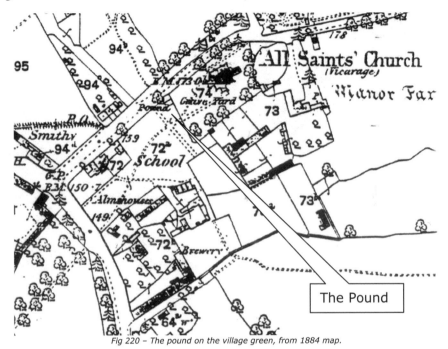

Fig 220 – The pound on the village green, from 1884 map.

The village pound **36** was maintained either by manor or vestry and used to hold stray animals. A fine had to be paid to retrieve them. It is not known how long there was a pound in Milton Ernest, although it is depicted on a map of the village dated 1884. Also, a document dated 1741 states "Indictment of Thomas Serjeant for rescuing certain sheep found doing damage in a field called Lynch Furlong, in the parish of Milton Ernest, in the occupation of John Sturges and which were being driven to the pound". Thomas Serjeant faced the Bedfordshire Quarter Sessions for a pound breach after 100 sheep and 100 lambs had been impounded by John Bassett, servant of John Sturges. Unfortunately, the outcome of the case is not recorded.

The pound is now part of the village green **37** which was conveyed to Milton Ernest Parish Council on 11th July 1963. Previously it belonged to East Manor Farm before being bought and later kindly given to the village by the Starey family. The Lower School's log book entry for 9th September 1963 records "The Green has been "handed over" to the village by Captain

245

Starey. It was ploughed and levelled last winter, is now being "dressed" and mown. Seeded in spring, thought it might be too late, but change in weather has meant amazing growth of grass". It went on to state "Church Green let to Education Committee for 21 years. Parish Council to act as holders. Green to be used by village if required for village functions – must make good any damage". Today the green is used primarily by the Milton Ernest Lower School and hosts the annual village fete.

Milton Ernest No:3705
All Saints' Church Fabric Fund and Playing Fields Association

VILLAGE FETE GRAND DRAW

1st Prize — £150 CASH

2nd Prize — £75 Cash
PLUS OTHER GREAT PRIZES

Draw to take place on Saturday, July 2, 2005 at the Village Fete

Registered under the Lotteries and Amusement Act, 1976 with Bedford Borough Council
Promoter: Neil Roy, Pyghtle, Thurleigh Road, Milton Ernest
Digitally printed by: LG Digital, 70 Singer Way, Kempston, Beds. 01234 843900

TICKETS
50p
EACH

Fig 221 – The winning raffle ticket from the 2005 Village Fete held on the Village Green. The author being the lucky winner!

During World War Two, in 1943, references were made in the local press as to how unsightly Milton Ernest Green had become. This was due to the dumping of large quantities of barbed wire on the village green and the unsatisfactory condition of three Air Raid Precaution shelters on the same piece of land. The barbed wire had been placed in front of the Church lych gate to represent military stores as part of a command exercise, while the ARP shelters had been built by private enterprise for the benefit of the schoolchildren and the old people at the time of Dunkirk (1940). Extreme weather conditions the following winter had caused them to collapse. The shelters were removed as they no longer served a useful purpose and were deemed dangerous, but the barbed wire dump stayed until 1946.

At one stage the Hooker family, who owned the garage which used to be on the A6 as you head towards Rushden, wanted to build a petrol station on what is now the village green. Fortunately, the Starey family, who owned the land were opposed to the idea and the plans never came to fruition.

Milton Ernest Lower School provided and maintained a football pitch with goalposts on the village green for a number of years.

Fig 222 – The football pitch which used to be on the Village Green

Fig 223– Path which used to run through the Village Green. The grass was a bit longer in those days!

Fig 224 – Haycocks on the village green, circa 1967.

Fig 225 – Milton Ernest Village Green, 25th November 2004.

Now walk along Church Green until you reach the almshouses. The aforementioned air raid shelters were dug into the village green at this spot.

Fig 226 – The Almshouses with the gated entrance to East Manor Farm in the background.

The almshouses **38** that you see before you were erected in 1965 by the Bedford Rural District Council (BRDC). They are replacements for the original red brick almshouses which were built in 1695 and funded by Sir Edmund Turnor of East Manor Farm.

Fig 227 – The original almshouses. Note the pigs on the village green!

Sir Edmund Turnor provided the six almshouses with thirty-one acres of land as a refuge for the aged of the village. He felt impelled to help the less fortunate people of Milton Ernest. A stone plaque was built into the original almshouse with the Latin phrase 'Amore et Exemplo 1695 Dona Dei Deo', which can be roughly translated as 'Love and to Serve as an Example 1695 Gift of God to God'. A replacement plaque has been added to the new almshouses with part of the original inscription plus the words 'Rebuilt BRDC 1965'. BRDC being Bedford Rural District Council. Bizarrely the same four numbers are on each date with just the 6 and the 9 transposed.

Fig 228 – Almshouses, 4th August 1957.

Monica Boielle recalls the almshouses as being known to the villagers as 'Scotland Yard' because "you couldn't do anything without them (the inhabitants) looking out".

Next to the almshouses is the old school **39** (1 Church Green).

In 1846 a church school inquiry stated that although there was a Sunday School, attended by 50 boys and 47 girls, a daily school was needed. There were many children in the village that would gladly go to a good daily school, if there was one in the parish. Five years later, the wishes of the village were granted when the Reverend Beaty-Pownall gifted a National School to Milton Ernest.

The Bedfordshire Times of 11th January 1851 reported that a neat and capacious building had been erected. There was a festival to celebrate the opening on Thursday 2nd January 1851. 140 people gathered at the new school room and a procession to All Saints' Church was formed by the children and teachers of the Sunday and National Schools and several visitors. The new master of the school was Mr D. Hanlon from the Westminster Training School.

Fig 229 – The Old School, 25th November 2004..

Milton Ernest National School was a 'Dame School', an elementary school charging 3d per week. There were 45 scholars here in 1854 when the teachers were William and Mary Mortimer. In the 1861 census Jeremiah Mays was the school master and ten years later, in 1871, Amelia Holloway was the school mistress at just twenty-two years of age. Amelia's younger sister, Annie, who was fifteen, was recorded as the school monitor.

When what is now Milton Ernest Lower School opened in the village this school became a private dwelling. The Bedfordshire Mercury newspaper, dated 11th September 1880, reported the sale as follows: 'MILTON ERNEST SALE OF PROPERTY. – The old school house and room in the village, the property of the late Rev. C. C. Beaty-Pownall, was disposed of by public auction at the Swan Inn on Tuesday last by Mr Pulley, of

Bedford. The bidding, commencing at £100 by Mr E. Bale, of St. John-street, Bedford, ran very quickly up to £160, which price was bid by Mr Henry John Staff, brewer and maltster; the property was knocked down to that gentleman. A year later and the building had been converted into a cottage and occupied by James Betts, a drayman, who worked for Mr Staff.

Fig 230 – Milton Ernest Brownies on the Village Green, 1952. Note in the background what was an East Manor Farm barn.

Walk to the bottom of Church Green turn left and you'll reach Bedford Road which is a section of the A6.

Heritage Trail (Part XIII) – Bedford Road

The house on the corner of Church Green and Bedford Road (1 Bedford Road) has been built on the site of an old thatched cottage.

Fig 231 – A long gone cottage on the corner of Church Green and Bedford Road. Note the green had gated access in those days.

Fig 232 –All Saints' and Village Green as viewed from the entrance to Milton Ernest Hall.

The main road through Milton Ernest is named Rushden Road and Bedford Road after the two towns which are linked by this part of the A6. This thoroughfare was originally used for driving animals to market and has been an important communications corridor ever since.

In the mid seventeenth century John Ogilby described a direct road from London to Oakham (in Rutland) passing through Milton Ernest. In 1727 the Bedford to Rushden section was turnpiked. The nearest toll gate to Milton Ernest was at the south end of Clapham. By the nineteenth century Royal Mail coaches travelled this route to Leeds and Manchester.

Walk along Bedford Road and you'll come to a large Victorian house. 3 Bedford Road was built for William Gibbins a farmer and maltster. In 1871, aged 37, he employed a house maid and a cook on the premises. It is now called 'Mulberry House'. Records show that he owned the brewery and malting next door in 1878, which is the next building to be viewed on the trail.

The 1881 census names a house as 'The Old School House, Bedford Road'. At first glance this would seem that there has been some confusion with the two recorded schools in the village. However, the same census also records the 'Old School, Village Green' and the 'New School House, Village Green'. This suggests that there must have been three school locations in the village. As the 1881 owner of the 'Old School House, Bedford Road' was James Mimms, a maltster, it would suggest that children were taught at what is now known as 'Mulberry House'. However, as no other evidence exists it can be assumed that schooling did not take place there for very long.

The old brewery building, known as 'The Maltings' **40** is a nineteenth century red brick malthouse on stone footings. Trade directories and census records show a number of people in Milton Ernest as being brewers or maltsters throughout the nineteenth century. These include the aforementioned Gibbins family shown as brewers from 1839; William Randall, 1841; and Edward Coe, 1861. Whether Randall and Coe owned or worked at this brewery is unclear, although the 1881 census records are more definite, showing Henry Staff as being brewer, maltster and coal merchant at the Milton Ernest Brewery on Bedford Road. He employed a servant and five men, one of whom was probably James Betts, a brewer's drayman who lived at the old school house on Village Green.

In 1881 the Milton Ernest brewery was known as the Steam Brewery. A map of the village dated 1884 shows the brewery as being located in a building attached to the rear of the Maltings. It is easy to imagine beer brewed in Milton Ernest being drunk in the Swan and across the road at the Queen's Head.

Fig 233 – Bedford Road looking south. The Maltings is on the left. The Photo was taken before the work commenced to straighten the road, dating it pre 1957. The sign reads 'Work In Progress'.

Fig 234 – The Maltings, 25th November 2004.

There are no records available to show when the brewery closed down or which businesses used the premises in the early twentieth century. The last record of a brewery on the site relates to 1900.

During the First World War when the Veterinary Corps were based in Milton Ernest they used stables at the Maltings for their Horse Re-mount Depot. After that all that is known is that it was used as a factory in World War II, where many of the female villagers worked. Monica Boielle remembers a sewing business operating there. It is thought that 100 sewing machines operated on the top floor. For the last fifty years R. Fairbrother Associates have used the premises to sell new and used office equipment.

Fig 235 – A drawing of Chestnut Cottage dated 17th October 1860. An oast house looking building, which would have been part of the Maltings, can be seen to the extreme left of the picture.

Just after the Maltings is Chestnut Cottage. This was designed and built in 1857 by William Butterfield as a home for the gardener of Milton Ernest Hall. Butterfield also provided homes for the coachman and gamekeeper of the Hall. These homes have since been converted into a single residence, now known as Meadow End House, which is located just past the entrance to Milton Ernest Hall as you head south on Bedford Road.

Fig 236 – February 1957 and work has been started to straighten Bedford Road. The photograph clearly shows the old route which ran alongside the Milton Ernest Hall wall.

Chestnut Cottage could have been built on the site of a Roman potter as vast amounts of Roman pottery have been unearthed in the garden. The cottage itself used to have two wells and two pigsties. It housed the gardener of Milton Ernest Hall and his family. The earliest known residents of Chestnut Cottage are recorded in the 1861 census as Joshua and Harriette Deuett. Joshua, aged 27, was the gardener while Harriette, 29, was a laundress, both assumingly employed at Milton Ernest Hall.

From the entrance to Chestnut Cottage carefully cross the road. There is no crossing here and the traffic can speed past despite a speed limit of thirty miles per hour and an electronic sign which flashes 'slow down' to drivers entering the village. The sign was erected in 2003 and has been successful in reducing car speeds but don't be lulled into a false sense of security, the A6 is still a dangerous road to cross.

Once safely over the road, walk along the path as if you were leaving the village. You'll walk past the wooden village gates which were installed in 1999. On your right hand side is a wall which marks the boundary of the former Milton Ernest Hall estate. The A6 used to run alongside this wall until safety work was undertaken to straighten this section of Bedford Road.

The Milton Ernest Hall estate wall was designed by the architect Sir Albert Richardson and built by local craftsmen. It took ten years to build in the 1920s/1930s and now has grade II listed status. Alf Hall from Kempston was the main craftsman who built the wall using, mainly, stone from local demolished buildings. He had taken a job with the Starey family, who owned the Hall, so that he could be available to undertake work for Professor Richardson.

Keep following the wall until you come to the entrance to Milton Ernest Hall. You are about to enter private land, so please consider the privacy of the people who live in this area and note the following:

<u>PERMISSIVE PATH</u>

The landowner has agreed to allow the public to use this path for the time being. There is no intention to dedicate this path as a right of way.

Milton Ernest Parish Council

Heritage Trail (Part XIV) – Milton Ernest Hall

Follow the private road and you'll walk past some metal gates which marked the entrance to Milton Ernest Garden Centre before it moved to Radwell Road. The Garden Centre was located on this site for twenty years between 1973 and 1993.

Fig 237 – Milton Ernest Garden Centre in Milton Ernest Hall Gardens, 1975.

Once you come to the 'T' junction, stop and turn to the left. In front of you is Stable Cottage **41**. As the name suggests, this building was originally a stable block which was converted into a private residence. Stable Cottage dates back to the 17th Century and was therefore constructed as stables for an earlier manor house that once existed where Milton Ernest Hall stands today.

Fig 238 – The stable building, circa 1910, viewed from Milton Ernest Hall looking towards what is now the A6.

Fig 239 – Stable Cottage, 25th November 2004.

You've now reached the last, but not least and probably the best, building on your tour of the village. Milton Ernest Hall **42** is built on a site which was the Manor of Bassets. In the Domesday Book of 1086 Hugh de Beauchamp owned the manor and William Basset was his tenant. The manor stayed in the hands of the Basset family for three centuries. Heads of the Basset family included Robert (1252), William (1278), Sibyl (1302) and John. When John Basset died in Brittany in 1372 his property consisted of 120 acres of arable land, 8 acres of meadow and 4 acres of pasture. His son and heir, John, died in Brittany the following year (1373).

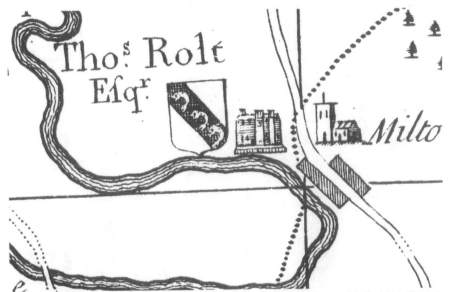

Fig 240 – Bassets Manor and the Rolt coat of arms from William Gordon's 1736 map of Bedfordshire. This is the earliest surviving drawing of a house on the site of Milton Ernest Hall. Note how different it is to the house owned by Philip Booth (Fig 243) and the present day Hall.

John Basset's sister Alianor, wife of John Barle, inherited Bassets Manor and held it until 1414. After that date the Manor was divided and many different people held parts of the Manor. That was until the mid sixteenth century when Thomas Rolt of Bolnhurst bought land in Milton Ernest. Between 1562 and 1578 he managed to buy the four divided parts, after which he owned all of Bassets Manor.

The Rolt family line in Milton Ernest went as follows: the aforementioned Thomas handed over his Milton Ernest land to John Rolt who married Judith the widow of George FitzGeffrey from Great Barford. John and Judith had five children. Their only son, Thomas Rolt, was born in Milton Ernest in 1587. When John died in 1627, the Milton Ernest estate passed to Thomas. He was a Justice of Peace for Bedfordshire in 1634 and was the Burgess of Bedford in 1647 and 1648. A burgess was someone either elected by a borough to represent them in Parliament or a citizen with full municipal rights.

Thomas Rolt married Catherine Staveley and together they had eleven children. Their second child and first boy was born in 1615 and named John Rolt. During the English Civil War Thomas Rolt sided with Oliver Cromwell while his son, John, was a Royalist. John Rolt, who was knighted in 1641 for his services to Charles I, inherited Bassets Manor on the death of his father in 1649. He was married to Ann Barnardiston and they had four children. Tragically, Sir John Rolt died in 1651 aged just thirty six years old. At the time his wife was three months pregnant with their fourth child.

Fig 241 – The Rolt Coat of Arms depicts three dolphins.

The only son of Sir John Rolt and Ann was called Thomas. Having been born in 1641, Thomas Rolt was just ten years old when he succeeded his father at Milton Ernest. He married Mary Coxe who was the daughter of Dr Thomas Coxe, the physician to Charles II. However, like his father before him, Thomas Rolt died at a relatively young age on 26th September 1672 aged just thirty one. His widow, Mary, then bizarrely married another Thomas Rolt, this time, Sir Thomas Rolt of Sacombe Park (Hertfordshire).

Thomas and Mary, from the first marriage, had a son called Samuel Rolt who went on to become the Member of Parliament for Bedford in 1700 and 1713. However, his political activities were to be his downfall as he lost two contested elections in the early eighteenth century and with them his fortune. Samuel and his wife Susannah (nee Poulter) had three children, the oldest of whom, Thomas, took over Bassets Manor on the death of his father in 1717.

Mary Rolt's seventeenth century cookery book survived until the twentieth century but unfortunately can no longer be found. One recipe survives – Warden Pie, which uses pears that originated in the orchards of the industrious monks of Warden Abbey.

Mary Rolt's Recipe for Warden Pie
(Note: Mary Rolt's spelling has not been corrected)

Firs pare your wardens and then bake them in an earthen pot in the oven with a little water and a good quantity of sugar. Lett your pot be close covered with a piece of corse past. Let them not be fully baked by a quarter of a hour. When they are cold, make a high coffin of past and put them in whole, adding to them some cloves, whole cinamon, sugar, with some of the liquor they were baked in. So close up the pye and bake it.

As already mentioned in the Church part of the heritage trail, Susannah Rolt left a bequest that loaves be given to the poor, for ever, in her will when she died in 1726.

Fig 242 – Mary Rolt, wife of John Orlebar

Thomas Rolt presented the chandelier to Milton Ernest Church before moving to Northampton, while his sister, Mary, at the age of 29, married John Orlebar of Poddington who was at the time MP for Bedford. Having no son, Thomas Rolt, in 1746, conveyed his Milton Ernest estate to the Orlebar family and so the Rolt family connection with Milton Ernest came to an end.

Bassets Manor was the property of Francis Anthony Herman in 1785. By the start of the nineteenth century Mrs Boyden was lady of the manor. She passed it on to John and Dinah Donne circa 1820.

Fig 243 – Milton Ernest Hall before it was demolished and replaced by the current country house. Philip Booth owned the house at the time of the drawing, dating it as circa 1840.

Although reference to Bassets disappears from records around the early nineteenth century, the next known owners of Milton Ernest Hall were the Booth family. The 1841 census records Fanny Booth, aged 25, "of independent means", with three servants. Ten years later, in 1851, Philip Booth was shown as the head of the household. The servants had increased to seven. As mentioned earlier, the Queen's Head was renamed the Booth's Arms at this time.

An advert in the Times on Friday 8th April 1853, which presumably caught the eye of the next owner, Benjamin Starey, described the estate as follows:

...an attractive freehold residential estate, with the family mansion distinguished as Milton Hall, approached by fine avenues of stately timber, and surrounded by highly decorated pleasure grounds and gardens, delightfully situate on the banks of the river Ouse, with an extensive privilege of excellent fishing, highly preserved, only four miles from Bedford, on the high turnpike road to Kettering and Melton Mowbray, in a fine agricultural and sporting part of the county of Bedford, 55 miles from London in point of distance, and little more than two hours, with reference to time, by the railway, in the centre of the domains of his Grace the Duke of Bedford, Lady Bridgwater, and Lord St. John, and other noblemen and great landed proprietors, comprising, with the adjacent farms, 600 acres, or thereabouts, of highly cultivated arable, meadow, pasture, and wood land, nearly all tithe-free, with suitable farm-houses, homesteads, and buildings, in the occupation of very respectable tenants, together with a water corn-mill, public houses, numerous cottages, and tenements, in the village of Milton Ernest, at low rents, and (including the mansion) of the estimated value of nearly £1,000 per annum. The Manor or the reputed Manor of Bassets, and Milton Ernys, with the right of fishing in the river Ouse (by which the estate is bounded for a considerable distance), will be included in the purchase of the property, which also possesses the further advantages of an excellent neighbourhood and good roads diverging in every direction. The mansion contains accommodation for a numerous family and domestic establishment; with coach-houses, harness rooms, most complete stabling and loose boxes for 20 horses, brood mares etc, several first-rate race horses having been bred on this property by the present owner (Philip Booth Esq). To sporting gentlemen the property offers superior attractions. The Oakley hounds are kennelled in the village, within a quarter of a mile of the mansion; Lord Fitzwilliam's, the Pytchley, Lord Southampton's, Mr Lowndon, and the Cambridgeshire Hunts also within easy distance. The field sports in all their variety are liberally sustained, there is also a rookery, and a most excellent dove house. The temperature of the atmosphere is dry and salubrious. Two spacious pews in the parish church are appropriated to the family. The above property presents altogether one of the most desirable opportunities for occupation or investment that has been offered to the public for a considerable period.

In 1853, Benjamin Helps Starey used his inheritance and money from the sale of both his business, Prices's Candles, and the patented wick, to buy the 590 acre estate for £22,000. His diary entry for September 28th 1853 reads "I took Mr Butterfield to see the house and garden which was desolate. The house thoroughly bad irreparable". William Butterfield was Benjamin Starey's brother-in-law and an eminent Victorian architect.

The house was in such a state that in February 1854 work was started to take down the building, and the materials were stacked away to be re-used in the construction of the new property. The new Milton Ernest Hall took four years to build using local materials whenever possible. It was built under different contracts all co-ordinated by William Butterfield. The materials of the old house were almost entirely used for the foundations; stonework was laid by London stonemasons; most of the stone was quarried from a bank on the Pavenham side of the river, about a quarter of a mile beyond the railway arches, and transported down the Ouse by barge; sand and gravel were dug in the grounds; oak was taken from Lawn Wood, which used to be near Yarl's Wood but no longer exists; and the joiners' work was done by Reynolds, a Bedford builder.

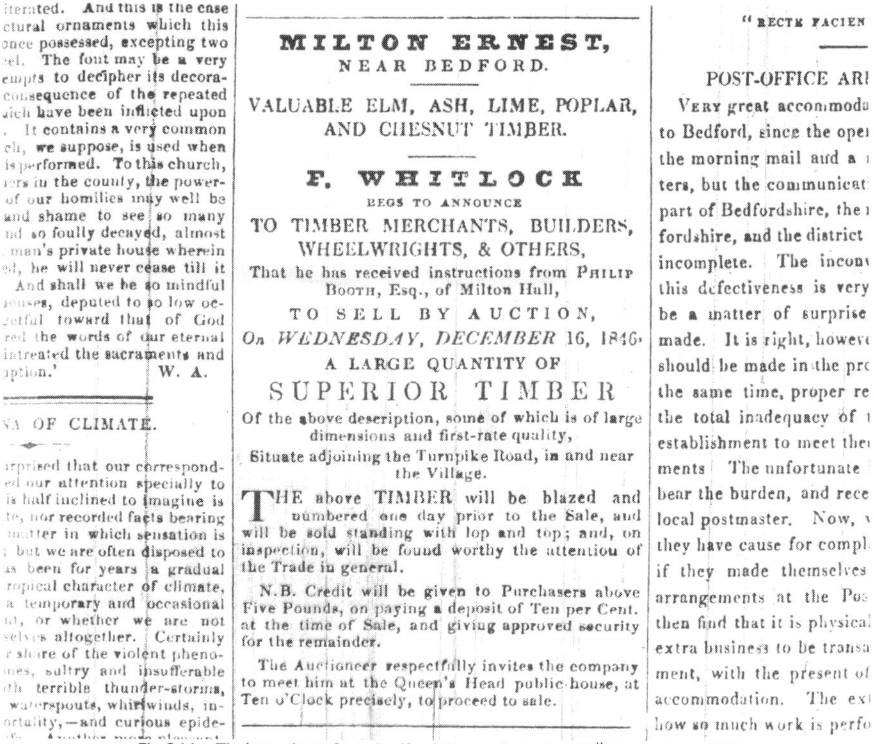

MILTON ERNEST,

NEAR BEDFORD.

VALUABLE ELM, ASH, LIME, POPLAR, AND CHESNUT TIMBER.

F. WHITLOCK

BEGS TO ANNOUNCE

TO TIMBER MERCHANTS, BUILDERS, WHEELWRIGHTS, & OTHERS,

That he has received instructions from PHILIP BOOTH, Esq., of Milton Hall,

TO SELL BY AUCTION,

On WEDNESDAY, DECEMBER 16, 1846,

A LARGE QUANTITY OF

SUPERIOR TIMBER

Of the above description, some of which is of large dimensions and first-rate quality,

Situate adjoining the Turnpike Road, in and near the Village.

THE above TIMBER will be blazed and numbered one day prior to the Sale, and will be sold standing with lop and top; and, on inspection, will be found worthy the attention of the Trade in general.

N.B. Credit will be given to Purchasers above Five Pounds, on paying a deposit of Ten per Cent. at the time of Sale, and giving approved security for the remainder.

The Auctioneer respectfully invites the company to meet him at the Queen's Head public-house, at Ten o'Clock precisely, to proceed to sale.

Fig 244 – Timber advert from Bedford Times, Saturday 12th December 1846.

A letter dated September 26th 1906, from William Starey (Benjamin Helps Starey's eldest son and a clergyman) to Lord Ampthill, describes the landscaping that took place as follows: "In January 1854 a plantation from the entrance gate to the river was made and planted at a cost of £250. At the same time the walnut trees at the back of the stable, and other places in the park were planted. In 1856 dead trees in the plantations and avenue were replaced, 60 elms and a few oaks being planted. The date of planting the elm avenue (in the place of an older one still) was about 1760. When we went to the Hall there was an old gardener named Abbott, who had worked there from 1815, and who said that he had heard a man say that the avenue was planted on his wedding day – circa 1760. Other trees again were planted in 1859, the gardens were completed, and the gravel pit by the river filled in and levelled, and also one of the three fish ponds filled in."

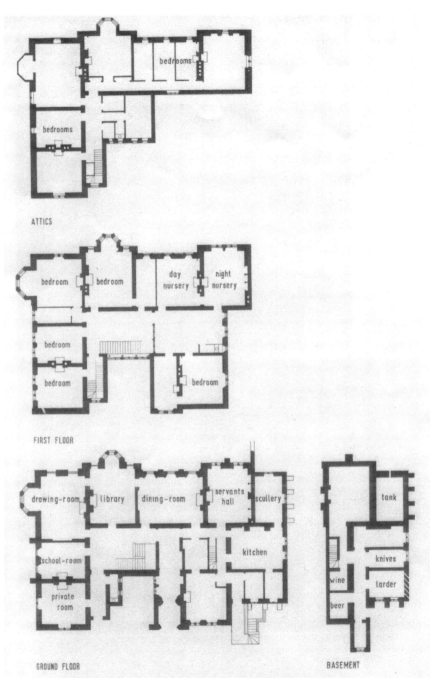

ATTICS

FIRST FLOOR

GROUND FLOOR

BASEMENT

Fig 245 – William Butterfield's plans of Milton Ernest Hall.

267

In 1856 the shell of the new house was in place and by 1858 Milton Ernest Hall became the only complete country house designed by William Butterfield. Benjamin Helps Starey had spent a further £12,167 on building his gothic country home. In July of that year the Starey family took up residence.

Fig 246 – Gardeners working at Milton Ernest Hall, circa 1910.

The census of 1861 records that Benjamin Helps Starey, aged 53, was the head of Milton Ernest Hall and employed six servants. These was a cook; a parlour maid; a nurse maid; a kitchen maid; a house maid; and a groom. However, this wealthy lifestyle was short lived, as in 1872, after a number of disasters on the stock market, Starey was forced to sell the Hall to Thomas Bagnall. To make matters worse he only received a third of the money that he had put into the estate. Two years later, on 6th April 1874, Benjamin Helps Starey was dead.

The sale particulars for the freehold estate of Milton Ernest Hall and lands, which was auctioned on 26th June 1871 at the Mart, Tokenhouse Yard, London, described the residence as follows:

THE RESIDENCE CONTAINS ON THE -

UPPER STOREY – Large Dormitory for female servants, Seven Bed Rooms, Bath Room, Sink with hot and cold water supply, Housemaids' Closet etc.

FIRST FLOOR – Five principal bedrooms, varying from 18ft by 21ft to 18ft by 14ft, Three Dressing Rooms, Nursery, Ladies' Morning Room, Closets, Linen Stores etc.

GROUND FLOOR – Drawing Room, 16ft by 25ft, Library 21ft by 17ft 6in, Dining Room 18ft by 25ft, Private Sitting Room 18ft by 16ft, School Room 18ft by 14ft, Inner Hall 17ft by 16ft, Grand Marble Staircase, Entrance Hall.

The Domestic Offices are judiciously arranged for the service of the house, and comprise Servant's Hall, Spacious Kitchen, Scullery, Cook's Pantry, Store Closet, Butler's Pantry, Still Room, Closets, and Lobby.

The Drawing Room is richly decorated in exquisite taste; the Dining Room is handsomely panelled in solid oak, and the Grand Staircase is of Marble, rich in design, and admirably lighted.

BASEMENT – A Boarded Room for men servants, Wine, Beer, and Coal Cellars, Larder, Dairy, Knife Room, Large Store Tank for rain water, and force pump to supply the cisterns in roof etc.

THE EXTERNAL OFFICES – Substantial Stone, Brick, and Tiled Erections, in complete repair, comprise Coachhouse for Carriages, Stalls, and Loose Boxes for seven horses, Harness Room, Corn Bins, Hay and Straw Lofts, Barn, Cow Houses, Piggeries, Hen Houses, Sheep Yard, Sheds, Cart Shed, Brick-built Dove Cote, Root House, and Apple Room, and an Oak and Tiled Boat House.

Over the next fifty years the ownership of Milton Ernest Hall changed hands four times. The owners included Thomas Bagnall (1872-1884), Alfred Chapman (1884-1901), Mrs Robinson (1901-1906), and Lord Ampthill (1906-1919). Mortgage records show that Thomas Bagnall, "the younger, late of Rushden", took out a mortgage on 9th September 1873 for £7,524 at 4.25%. Madeline Chapman, wife of Alfred, borrowed £7,000 at 4.00% on 30th October 1884, while Isabella Robinson of Knill Court, Herefordshire, paid £10,000 to buy the property on 20th May 1901.

During the First World War, King George V and Queen Mary evacuated some of their family from Buckingham Palace. Two young princes came to Milton Ernest Hall to live with Arthur Oliver Villiers Russell and Margaret Russell, otherwise known as Lord and Lady Ampthill. This was kept very secret at the time but locals recalled them rushing around the Hall grounds on their bicycles. The two princes were thought to be Edward and Albert, who became King Edward VIII and King George VI respectively.

Fig 247 – Milton Ernest Hall, circa 1910.

Throughout this period, John Helps Starey, the youngest son of Benjamin Helps Starey, built up a successful tea planting business in Ceylon. He was there for thirty years from 1871 and developed other business interests in rubber plantations in Malaya. His success enabled him to re-purchase Milton Ernest Hall from Lord and Lady Ampthill in 1919.

John Helps Starey resided at the Hall for eight years until his death in 1927. His widow, Grace, continued to live there with family and friends until her death in 1941.

Fig 248 – Bing Crosby and officers in front of the operations room at Milton Ernest Hall, 1944. Note the boarded up windows, designed to stop people from seeing what was being undertaken in that room.

With Grace's death coinciding with the Second World War, Milton Ernest Hall was promptly requisitioned. Some of the family moved into Home Farm from where Stephen Starey, youngest son of John Helps Starey, had run the estate and lived with his family since 1928.

In the late Spring of 1943 the headquarters of the US Eighth Air Force Service Command was set up at the Hall and the premises was named Station 506. An extensive camp of huts was built in the grounds. It is believed that important activities were undertaken at the Hall during the war, but their exact nature has remained classified.

Milton Ernest Hall played host to Glenn Miller during this period. It also provided sleeping accommodation for two famous visiting singers. Dinah Shore stayed two nights in early August 1944 and Bing Crosby slept there on the night of Tuesday 29th August 1944. Two years earlier he had recorded White Christmas, which topped the American music chart in 1942, 1944, 1945 and 1946, and went onto sell an estimated 32 million copies of the song. Having a star as big as Bing Crosby stay at Milton Ernest Hall must have been a huge thrill for everyone based there.

Fig 249 – Officers of VIII AF CC pose on the rear steps of Milton Ernest Hall, 10th June 1945, just a few days after the death of Adolf Hitler.

Once the army had vacated the premises the Hall remained unoccupied for over twenty years and the poor state of the roof placed its future in jeopardy.

In 1968 Mr Dobrzanski bought the Hall from the Starey family for £15,000 and planned to renovate his "Gothic House". However, in September 1971, he in turn sold the property to Mr Francis Harmer-Brown. This time it cost £21,000. With the help of a fifty percent grant (£5,000) from the Historic Buildings Council towards the cost of structural repairs, Harmer-Brown was able to convert the Hall into a hotel and restaurant.

After ten years in which it built a high reputation for its cooking, Milton Ernest Hall Hotel closed in July 1982. Mr Ledson bought the property for a reputed £200,000 and planned to revert the building to a family home. The cost of maintaining this forty two room house was probably the reason for this plan not coming to fruition. By 1984 the Hall had been converted into a nursing home.

Today Milton Ernest Hall, a Grade I listed building, is still a nursing home, although it is now under new ownership. Majesticare, who run luxury care homes, bought the Hall in October 2003. There are twenty-five bedrooms, some being doubles, enabling nursing care for up to twenty-nine older people and specialist nursing care for up to six younger people. Forty people work at the Hall to ensure that there is twenty-four hour cover every day of the year.

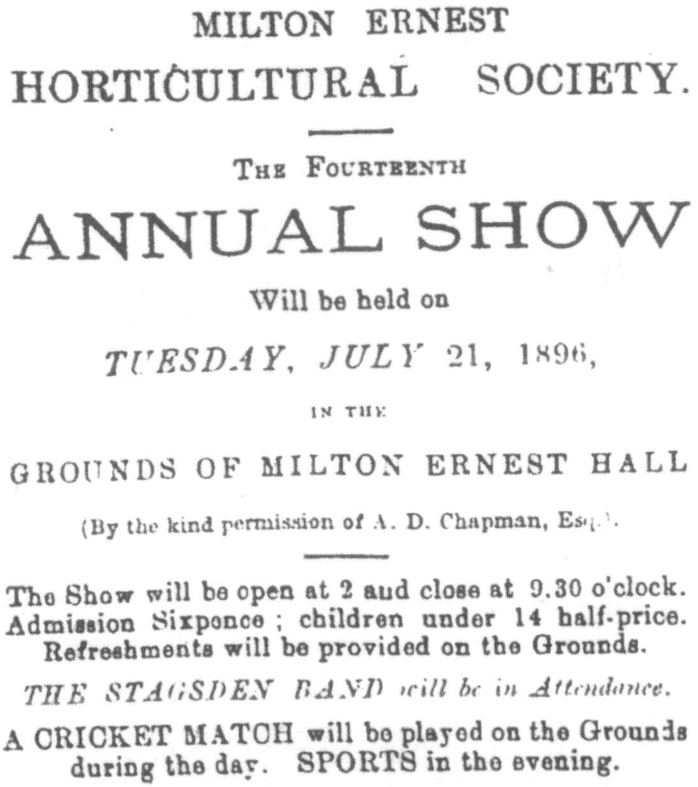

MILTON ERNEST

HORTICULTURAL SOCIETY.

THE FOURTEENTH

ANNUAL SHOW

Will be held on

TUESDAY, JULY 21, 1896,

IN THE

GROUNDS OF MILTON ERNEST HALL

(By the kind permission of A. D. Chapman, Esq.).

The Show will be open at 2 and close at 9.30 o'clock.
Admission Sixpence ; children under 14 half-price.
Refreshments will be provided on the Grounds.

THE STAGSDEN BAND will be in Attendance.

A CRICKET MATCH will be played on the Grounds
during the day. SPORTS in the evening.

Fig 250 – An advertisement in the Bedfordshire Mercury, dated 11th July 1896, for the annual show held at Milton Ernest Hall. Note that this is the 14th event which means that it probably started in 1883.

The grounds of the Hall were used regularly in past times. The annual flower show was usually held on August bank holidays. There was a large marquee; a cricket match; athletics competitions; cycle races; and a brass band. Competitions included flowers, fruit, vegetables, pillow lace and sewing. Dancing sometimes went on until midnight and the Hall grounds were lit up by nightlights in multicoloured glass containers tied around the trees.

A programme survives for the 1913 Milton Ernest Horticultural Society Flower Show and the cover is reproduced in this book along with the timetable for the athletics. The Bedfordshire Times reported on the show the following week. It noted "very pleasant weather" and that "the 'buses took a fair number of people out of Bedford, and visitors found the park an ideal place for a half-holiday on a summer's day". "Great interest was taken in a cricket match between the Rev. A. H. Moss's XI and Mr Stileman Gibbard's XI", although there is no record of who won.

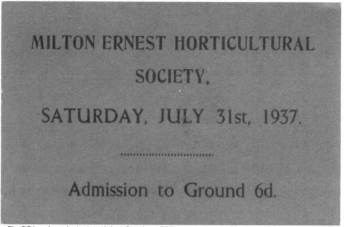

MILTON ERNEST HORTICULTURAL

SOCIETY,

SATURDAY, JULY 31st, 1937.

Admission to Ground 6d.

Fig 251 – An admission ticket for the 1937 Horticultural Show at Milton Ernest Hall.

There were 45 prizes issued to different people, as no one was allowed to win twice, in the categories of vegetables, fruit, flowers, plants in pots, cut flowers and bouquets.

Milton Ernest had cricket and football teams which used the Hall grounds to play their matches. Facing the A6 from Milton Ernest Hall, the football pitch used to be in the field to the left and the cricket ground was to the right of what was the Elm Avenue entrance. Stephen Starey invested heavily in the cricket team. He bought a pavilion, paid for the cricket gear and even employed a cricket tutor to teach the players. George Willars remembers that the wicket was so good that Northamptonshire County Cricket Club enquired about hiring the pitch.

One of the earliest reports of a Milton Ernest cricket match, at the time of Stephen Starey's grandfather, was a game against Sharnbrook on 12th August 1869. Milton Ernest, having scored 32 and 51 in their two innings, set Sharnbrook 28 to win and promptly bowled them out for 14! Football came along a bit later with a meeting recorded in 1896.

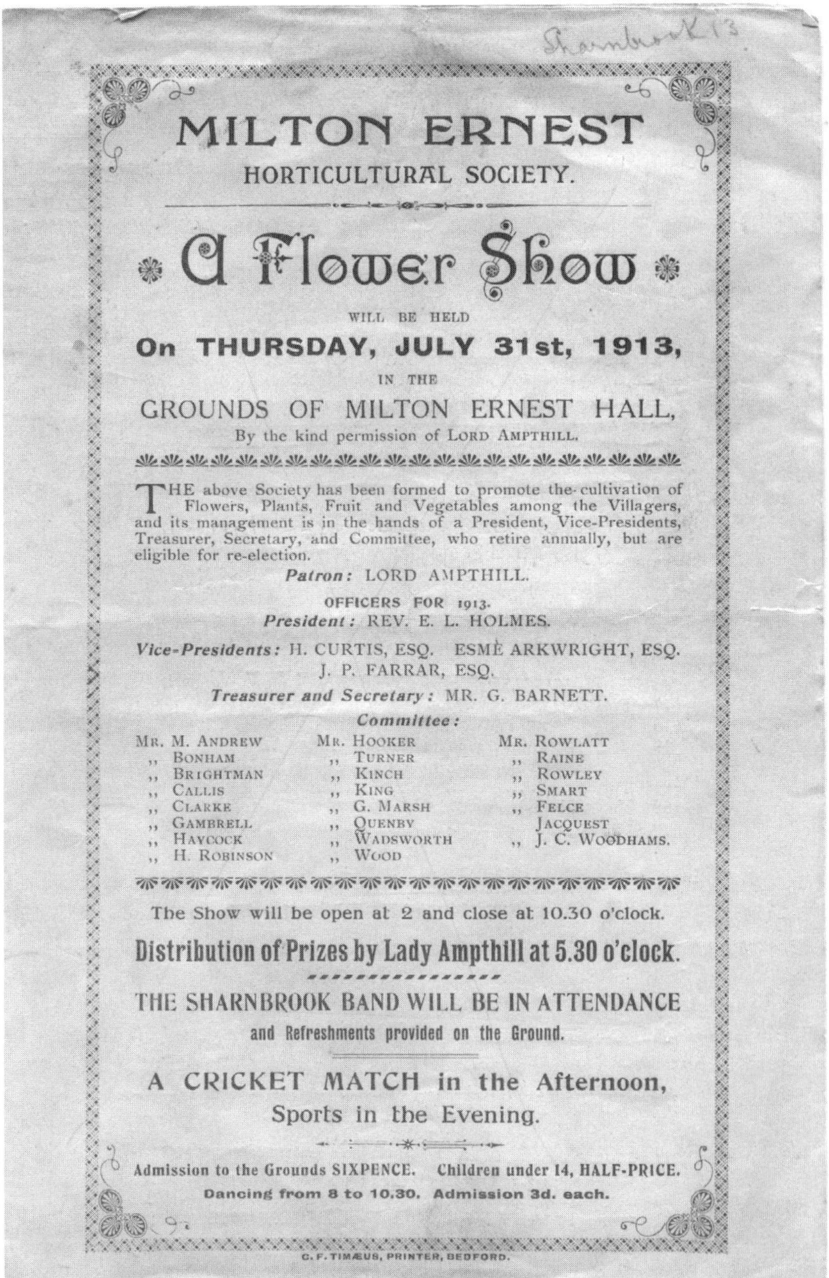

MILTON ERNEST
HORTICULTURAL SOCIETY.

A Flower Show

WILL BE HELD

On THURSDAY, JULY 31st, 1913,

IN THE

GROUNDS OF MILTON ERNEST HALL,

By the kind permission of LORD AMPTHILL.

THE above Society has been formed to promote the cultivation of Flowers, Plants, Fruit and Vegetables among the Villagers, and its management is in the hands of a President, Vice-Presidents, Treasurer, Secretary, and Committee, who retire annually, but are eligible for re-election.

Patron: LORD AMPTHILL.

OFFICERS FOR 1913.

President: REV. E. L. HOLMES.

Vice-Presidents: H. CURTIS, ESQ. ESMÈ ARKWRIGHT, ESQ.
J. P. FARRAR, ESQ.

Treasurer and Secretary: MR. G. BARNETT.

Committee:

MR. M. ANDREW	MR. HOOKER	MR. ROWLATT
,, BONHAM	,, TURNER	,, RAINE
,, BRIGHTMAN	,, KINCH	,, ROWLEY
,, CALLIS	,, KING	,, SMART
,, CLARKE	,, G. MARSH	,, FELCE
,, GAMBRELL	,, QUENBY	JACQUEST
,, HAYCOCK	,, WADSWORTH	,, J. C. WOODHAMS.
,, H. ROBINSON	,, WOOD	

The Show will be open at 2 and close at 10.30 o'clock.

Distribution of Prizes by Lady Ampthill at 5.30 o'clock.

THE SHARNBROOK BAND WILL BE IN ATTENDANCE
and Refreshments provided on the Ground.

A CRICKET MATCH in the Afternoon,
Sports in the Evening.

Admission to the Grounds SIXPENCE. Children under 14, HALF-PRICE.
Dancing from 8 to 10.30. Admission 3d. each.

Fig 252 – Front page of the four page programme for the 1913 Flower Show. Note the top right hand corner scribbled telephone number for Milton Ernest Hall – Sharnbrook 13.

ATHLETIC SPORTS

IN CONNECTION WITH THE

Milton Ernest Horticultural Society,

THURSDAY, JULY 31st, 1913.

1. at 6.0.—100 Yards Flat Race, for Boys under 13.
   Two Prizes.

2. ,, 6.10.—100 Yards Flat Race, for Girls under 13.
   Two Prizes.

3. ,, 6.15.—One Mile Handicap Flat Race for Men.
   Three Prizes.

4. ,, 6.30.—Quarter-mile Flat Race for Boys under 16.
   Two Prizes.

5. ,, 6.40.—220 Yards Flat Race for Girls under 16.
   Two Prizes.

6. ,, 6.50.—One Mile Bicycle Race in Heats.
   Two Prizes.

7. ,, 7.15.—Egg and Spoon Race for Married Women.
   Two Prizes.

8. ,, 7.25.—Stepping a Chain for Men over 30.
   Two Prizes.

9. ,, 7.40.—Bicycle Race, Final.

10. ,, 7.45.—Two Mile Race, open.
    Three Prizes.
    Entrance Fee for this Race, 6d. each.

U. F TIMÆUS, PRINTER, BEDFORD.

Fig 253 – The Sports events at the 1913 Flower Show. This was an insert in the Horticultural Show's programme. Note that only married women were allowed to compete in the egg and spoon race!

In 1926 the Milton Ernest Football Club entered Division IV of the Bedford & District Football League. Their home ground was known as 'Milton Park'. The team competed for six seasons and always finished in the top five of whatever division they played in. The highest position being runners-up of Division II in 1930-1931. The following season was to be their last. There are no records of the team after 1932.

Fig 254 – Milton Ernest Football Club (1927-1928) who used to play at the grounds of Milton Ernest Hall. The cup pictured is the Division IV Championship. Key members from the title winning team, and probably in this photograph, were E Green, C Smith, P Surridge, J Pevling, W Marsh, A Fairey (goalkeeper), Chester, G Church, J Perkins, W Linger, T Bonham, and B Cox.

	Pld	W	D	L	F	A	Pts
Milton Ernest	26	24	0	2	120	28	48
Kempston Stars	26	19	2	5	120	38	40
Riseley Stars	26	18	3	5	78	46	39
Lidlington United	26	18	2	6	108	52	38
Marston Shelton	26	15	5	6	101	40	35
Meltis Sports	26	13	5	8	108	70	31
Cryselco	26	10	4	12	77	92	24
Pavenham United	26	11	2	13	68	91	24
Queen's Park Excelsior	26	10	2	14	55	75	22
Queen's Juniors	26	8	4	14	74	86	20
Stevington	26	7	3	16	56	104	17
Blunham Athletic	26	7	2	17	44	87	16
Bromham Rovers	26	4	1	21	36	84	9
Oakley Hounds	26	0	1	25	22	174	1

Fig 255 – Bedford & District League Division IV League Table, 1927-1928

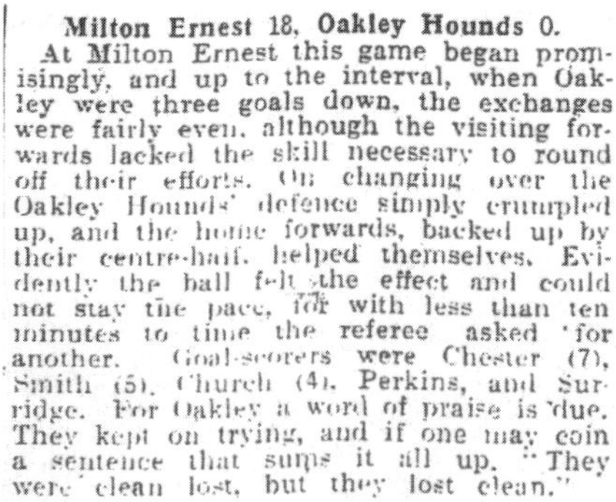

Milton Ernest 18. Oakley Hounds 0.

At Milton Ernest this game began promisingly, and up to the interval, when Oakley were three goals down, the exchanges were fairly even, although the visiting forwards lacked the skill necessary to round off their efforts. On changing over the Oakley Hounds' defence simply crumpled up, and the home forwards, backed up by their centre-half, helped themselves. Evidently the ball felt the effect and could not stay the pace, for with less than ten minutes to time the referee asked 'for another. Goal-scorers were Chester (7), Smith (5), Church (4), Perkins, and Surridge. For Oakley a word of praise is due. They kept on trying, and if one may coin a sentence that sums it all up. "They were clean lost, but they lost clean."

Fig 256 – Report of match played on 12th Nov 1927, from Bedfordshire Times dated 18th Nov 1927.

The greatest achievement by Milton Ernest FC during those six seasons was the Division IV championship which they won in 1927-1928. Of the 26 games played, Milton Ernest won 24 of them, scored 120 goals and only lost two matches (Riseley Stars 2-3 and Cryselco 0-3). The biggest victories, all at Milton Park, being 18-0 v Oakley Hounds; 11-0 v Pavenham United; 11-3 v Cryselco; and 9-0 v Stevington. After losing to Cryselco on 26th November 1927, Milton Ernest didn't look back and won the next fourteen consecutive matches! From the few match reports from that season it is apparent that C. Smith, the centre-forward, scored in the majority of the games.

Fig 257 – Programme cover of the 1965 Horse Show and Gymkhana.

The Milton Ernest Horse Show and Gymkhana was started in the grounds of Milton Ernest Hall in 1947 with the sole purpose of raising funds for a village hall. This annual event was so successful that Milton Ernest Village Hall opened twelve years later. Such was the popularity of the show it continued for a number of years after its objective had been met.

Fig 258 – Milton Ernest Horse Show and Gymkhana.

Fig 259 – Action from the 1965 Milton Ernest Horse Show and Gymkhana.

The local scouts troop also used the Hall grounds as the following pictures demonstrate.

Fig 260 – Scouts stand around the flag pole in the grounds of Milton Ernest Hall.

Fig 261 – Milton Ernest Scouts, circa 1940.
Back row (left to right): Clifford Willett, Stanley Darnell, Jack Haycock (died in WWII), Bob Haycock (of 'Bob's Shop') , Fred Willett, Tom Bradshaw, Frank Woods, George Willars.
Front row (left to right): Nigel Stanton, Gerald Willars, Unknown, Don Willars, Ray Bradshaw, Gordon Brown, Fred Murray, David Willett, Jim Smith (son of the head mistress, Ivy Smith).

In the grounds of Milton Ernest Hall are farm buildings which cost William Butterfield £940 to build in 1859. He also designed a boathouse, which has sadly disappeared, and an attractive pyramid roofed dovecote. This has a wrought iron sundial on top of the hexagonal bird entry on the roof. It was originally used to house pigeons as a source of meat in the winter.

Fig 262 – The dovecote at Milton Ernest Hall, circa 1910.

Fig 263 – The Milton Ernest Boathouse.

Fig 264 – The Milton Ernest Boathouse, 1939.

A tall iron windmill structure stands near the river which was used to supply Milton Ernest Hall, stables and outbuildings with water. It forced water up into the Hall where the water overflowed, filling pipes that ran down to the stables, so that every shed and stall had an adequate running water supply.

The walk is now almost over. Head back towards the A6 using the old track which used to be known as the Elm Avenue. With a row of Elm trees on each side, this track used to be the only entrance to the Hall. This entrance was used by the army in the Second World War and was the exit that Glenn Miller used on that fateful day in 1944 when he set off to catch his plane at Twinwoods.

Fig 265 – The Elm Avenue looking from Milton Ernest Hall towards what is now the A6.

Unfortunately the trenching for water and electricity was carried out too close to the trees during the Second World War. Weakened by this work the trees became an easier target for the elm bark beetle and had to be felled in the late 1970s.

Local legend speaks of a coach and four horses driven by a headless coachman which has been seen driving down this track and turning into Bedford Road. This phantom coach is said to pay a yearly visit to the village. Maybe today is that day!

Fig 266 – The gates and Elm Tree Avenue leading to Milton Ernest Hall, circa 1910.

Turn left at the gate and walk along Bedford Road. Soon you will come to Home Farm and immediately afterwards you're back at The Queen's Head where you started the Heritage Trail.

You have now reached the end of the Importance of Milton Ernest Heritage Trail. Hopefully you enjoyed your walk and learnt something about the history of the village at the same time. Now go and have that well earned drink!

Fig 267 – Interior of The Queen's Head, 2005. The ideal place to visit at the end of the Heritage Trail!

Information derived and extracts taken from the following sources. Sincerest apologies for any references that I might have missed. There is also the possibility that references already acknowledged earlier in this book may have also been used in this Heritage Trail section. Please note that the abbreviation BLARS stands for Bedfordshire and Luton Archives and Records Service (followed by their reference). QUEEN'S HEAD: Mortgage, BLARS (CC6); Conveyance, BLARS (CC44); Photograph with information of the Newport Pagnell Brewery, courtesy of Bev Plumbley of the Queen's Head. COOK'S ALLEY: Maps at BLARS (Z951/3/5 & Z951/3/8). HOME FARM: 'The Architectural Work of Sir Albert Richardson in Bedfordshire, 191-1964', Simon Houfe, Bedfordshire Magazine, Volume 13 Number 100, Spring 1972; 'Scouting in Bedfordshire', Robert W. Turner, Bedfordshire Magazine, Volume 18, Number 141, Summer 1982. CHAPEL: 'Non Parochial Register (Methodists) held at BLARS; Methodist records at BLARS (MB series); 'Bedfordshire Ecclesiastical Census, 1851', edited by D. W. Bushby, Bedfordshire Historical Record Society, Volume 54, 1975; 'Bedfordshire Chapels & Meeting Houses Official Registration 1672-1902', edited by Edwin Welch, Bedfordshire Historical Record Society, Volume 75, 1996. STRAWBERRY TREE: 'The Strawberry Tree Restaurant', pamphlet, courtesy of John Bona. BARRACKS: Milton Ernest Lower School Log Books 1912-1989; WORKHOUSE: List of paupers in the workhouse, BLARS (P80/12/2). RIVER GREAT OUSE: Bedford Mercury, 9th February 1895, Bedford central Library; 'Bygone Water Supplies', J. Steele Elliott, Ancient Buildings Survey II, Bedfordshire Historical Record Society. SWAN: Printed sale catalogue from the Greene King archive, BLARS (GK140/4); Deeds, BLARS (GK140/1). WEST MANOR FARM: Bedfordshire County Council Sites and Monuments Record, number 5777; Letter from C. J. Pickford, Assistant Archivist at County Record Office, to Mrs Heather Morris, dated 2nd May 1985, regarding research into West Manor Farm. WILD FLOWER MEADOW: Bedford Herald advertisements, 1996-1998, for Holmes Estate Agents. GARDEN CENTRE: 'The Garden Centre that's different!', local newspaper advertisement for the opening on 20th April 1973, provided by Maureen Catlin. PLAYING FIELD: Bedford Borough Council planning records (75/674CC, 77/98, 77/2078, 79/678, 79/678A). KENNELS: 'The Oakley Hunt', edited by Joyce Godber, Bedfordshire Historical Record Society, Volume 44, 1965, at BLARS; 'Fire at Oakley Hunt Kennels. Staff Escape: Hounds and Horses Saved', Bedfordshire Times, April 1933; Various advertisements from Bedfordshire Times, 1976-1978, for Shanley Homes by Newman & Partners estate agents; 'The Oakley Hunt', Eric Rayner, Bedfordshire Magazine, Volume 9, Number 66, Autumn 1963. OLD POST OFFICE: Bedford Borough Council planning records (73/844, 73/844A, 75/884); BLACKSMITH'S SHOP: 'The Old Smithy May Become Village Hall', Bedfordshire Times, circa 1955, Local Studies, Bedford Central Library. SCHOOL: Conveyance, 28th December 1871, BLARS (CRT 130 MIL 11); Milton Ernest Lower School Log Books 1912-1989; Vestry minute book, BLARS (P80/8/1); 'The Bedfordshire Schoolchild Elementary Education Before 1902', edited by David Bushby, Bedfordshire Historical Record Society, Volume 67, 1988; 'Milton Ernest Lower School Prospectus', 1996.

VILLAGE HALL: Milton Ernest Lower School Log Books 1912-1989: *THURLEIGH ROAD COTTAGES:* Bedfordshire Mercury, 7th December 1889, opening of a telegraph office. *OLD VICARAGE:* Notes written by Paul Beaty-Pownall on his visit to Milton Ernest on 6th September 2004; Guided tour of Woodlands with historical information by Peter Smith, the owner; Latin translations by James Collet-White of BLARS; 'Copy A.B.E 1/2/11. Terrier of Milton Ernest Vicarage, 1608' courtesy of David Purser; 'Woodlands Language Studio' brochure from Pamela Smith; 'Tennis Coaching International' brochure from Peter Smith; 'The Francklins of Thurleigh and Bolnhurst', David Kennett, Bedfordshire Magazine, Volume 20, Number 153, Summer 1985. *EAST MANOR FARM:* 'The Orlebar Chronicles' by Frederica St. John Orlebar, 1930; 'Burke's Landed Gentry', 1871, at BLARS; Turnor family tree, BLARS (X694); 'A Calendar of the Feet of Fines for Bedfordshire', Part II, edited by G. Herbert Fowler, Bedfordshire Historical Record Society, Volume 6, 1919. *CHURCH:* 'Welcome to All Saints'' pamphlet by Roger Lewis; 'Our Roll of Honour' listing the Milton Ernest villagers who fought in WWI, which hangs inside the church; 'A List of Rectors and Vicars of All Saints' Milton Ernest, which also hangs inside the church; 'All Saints' Grave Yard List' kindly provided by the vicar, Nicola McIntosh; 'The Scourging of Christ' – BLARS (P80/28/2); Details of vicars - BLARS (Fasti/1/MiltonE); Details of wall tablets etc – David Newman visit to the church; 'Bedfordshire Notes & Queries' edited by Frederick Augustus Blaydes, Volume III, 1893 - monumental inscriptions; Turnor Rolt Charity, 14th May 1965, details provided by Rolt family; Repair of Rolt chandelier, Bedfordshire Magazine, Volume 5, Number 37, Summer 1956; 'Archdeacons' Visitations and Churchwardens' Tribulations in 1578, Isobel F. Thompson, Bedfordshire Magazine, Volume 16, Number 124, Spring 1978; 'Hundreds, Manors, Parishes & the Church', edited by John S. Thompson, Bedfordshire Historical Record Society, Volume 69; 'Bedfordshire Churches in the Nineteenth Century', edited by Chris Pickford, Bedfordshire Historical Record Society, Volume 77, 1998. *WAR MEMORIAL:* Commonwealth War Graves Commission, www,cwgc.org; Bedfordshire Family History Society, Milton Ernest Roll of Honour, compiled by Martin Edwards, www.roll-of-honour.com. *VILLAGE POUND:* 'The Pounds of Bedfordshire', J. Steele Elliott, Ancient Buildings Survey III, Bedfordshire Historical Record Society. *VILLAGE GREEN:* Bedford Rural District Council letters, BLARS (PC Milton Ernest 24/8). *ALMSHOUSES:* Latin inscriptions translated by James Collett-White of BLARS; *OLD SCHOOL:* 'Opening of New National School', Bedfordshire Times, 11th January 1851; 'Milton Ernest – sale of Property', Bedford Mercury, 11th September 1880. *BREWERY:* Vestry minute book, BLARS (P80/8/1); Bedfordshire Mercury, 24th February, 1883. *MILTON ERNEST HALL:* 'Glenn Miller in Britain Then and Now' by Chris Way, 1996; 'William Butterfield' by Paul Thompson, 1971; 'Milton Ernest Flower Show', Bedfordshire Times, August 1913; Letter from Lilian Thornhill of Croydon Natural History and Scientific Society Limited, December 1985; Milton Ernest Hall, Bedfordshire, The Property of Mr L Dobrzanski' by Mark Girouard, Country Life, 23rd October 1969; 'Milton Ernest Hall', magazine article source unknown, Bedford Central Library Local Studies; Nursing Home details from Fritha Irwin of Majesticare Luxury Care Homes; Mortgage details, BLARS (Z951/8/3,5,7 & 10); 'A Bedfordshire Armorial, LXXI – Rolt of Milton Ernest, Thurleigh etc', F. W. Kuhlicke, Bedfordshire Magazine, Volume 12, Number 90, Autumn 1969. *GENERAL VILLAGE HISTORY* which contained references to many of the buildings on the Heritage Trail: Memories of John Starey, Monica Boielle, Tony Marsh and Bill Dunham, interviewed by David Newman and Jane Green; Memories of David Purser, George Willars and Roger Harris, interviewed by David Newman; The notes of J.B. Purser compiled whilst researching an article on Milton Ernest for the North Bedfordshire Preservation Society's 'Not Another Guide Book – Cameo Studies of North Bedfordshire'; 'Kelly's Directories', BLARS and Bedford Central Library, 1853, 1847, 1853, 1854, 1861, 1862, 1864, 1869, 1871, 1876, 1877, 1885, 1890, 1894, 1898, 1903, 1906, 1910, 1914, 1920, 1924, 1928, 1931, 1936, 1940; 'Pigott's Commercial Directory', BLARS, 1839; Schedule of Listed Buildings in Milton Ernest, BLARS; Milton Ernest Parish Council minutes, 1894-2005; Milton Ernest Census, 1841, 1851, 1861, 1871, 1881, 1891, 1901; 'Scheduled Monument', English Heritage, monument number SM13613, Bedfordshire County Council; Milton Ernest Parish Registers, Baptisms 1538-1991, Marriages 1538-1982, Burials 1539-1984, all held at BLARS; 'A History of the County of Bedford', edited by William Page, 1912; Various editions of the Bedfordshire Times, Bedford Central Library; Various editions of the Bedfordshire Mercury, Bedford Central Library; 'Milton Ernest Parish Survey', Bedfordshire County Council; 'The Bedfordshire Village Book', Bedfordshire Federation of Women's Institutes; 'Bedfordshire Within Living Memory', Bedfordshire Federation of Women's Institutes; 'Not Another Guide Book – Cameo Studies of North Bedfordshire', North Bedfordshire Preservation Society; 'Milton Ernest Down Your Way', Dennis Bidwell, Bedfordshire County Life, Summer 2003; 'Bedfordshire', Laurence Meynell; 'Village Scrapbook', Charlotte Mackay Brown, Bedfordshire Times, 26th October 1979; 'A Regional Survey of Milton Ernest, Beatrice Gillam, 1939, BLARS (Z1057/2); 'Memories of Milton Ernest', Edward Newell, Bedfordshire Times article 3rd May 1942, BLARS (Z158/7); 'Bedfordshire's Yesteryears, Volume 1, The Family Childhood and Schooldays', Brenda Fraser-Newstead; 'Sixty Years A Thatcher', W. R. (Reg) Parrott; CRT 130 MIL 1-13, BLARS; 'Milton Ernest', Eric Rayner, Bedfordshire Magazine, Volume 8, Number 58, Autumn 1961; Milton Ernest building records at conservation section of the planning department of Bedfordshire County Council. *GENERAL BOOKS:* 'A Dictionary of Old Trades, Titles and Occupations', Colin Waters; 'The Local Historian's Encyclopaedia', John Richardson.

Appendix 1: Milton Ernest Poems

The following poem was written by Frederick Payne of 62, Leigh Street, Attercliffe, Sheffield. It was basically a letter written in poem form regarding his stay back at his childhood home. It is entitled 'A Few Verses Suggested by A Summer Holiday in Bedfordshire, August 1903'. Frederick Payne was born in Roxton in 1850. His parents were William (born Roxton, circa 1826) and Sarah Payne (born Thurleigh, circa 1826). Frederick had six brothers – Jabez, Walter, William, Lewis, John and Charles. They were all agricultural labourers while his father was a shepherd. The family moved from Roxton to Thurleigh and by 1861 were in Milton Ernest. The 1901 census, which is the closest to the date of the poem, records William and Sarah Payne as living in one of the Thurleigh Road thatched cottages, next door to the Post Office. This is where Frederick would have spent his holiday in 1903. It is interesting to note his feelings towards his new industrial life compared to his previous rural existence.

My train I rode a hundred miles,
My kith and kin to see,
Whence they regaled me with good fare,
And gave me lodgings free.

Then in that smokeless land of light,
I breathed the finest air,
And hailed with evanescent joy,
The flowers so sweet and fair.

There I had olfactory pleasure,
Among the verdant trees,
And many optical delights,
Which tend the mind to please.

Once more I saw my aged sire,
Who looked quite hale and hearty,
Though he's the village veteran,
Among the Shepherd party.

With pride and pleasure once again,
I saw my kind old mother,
Who will attain to eighty years,
If she lives to see another.

I also saw my brother four,
With many sons and daughters,
Who seem to thrive on common food,
And drink the crystal waters.

I met some old acquaintances,
And had a friendly greeting,
Thus absence from our friend awhile,
Implies a happy meeting.

I listened to the district news,
With all attentive mind,
For men and women told me tales,
Of a homely village kind.

They told of recent births and deaths,
Of marriages and matches,
Of new arrivals in the place,
And outward going batches.

They told me of the clubs finance,
Which had a welcome sound,
And of the Parish Councils work,
Upon the village ground.

They told me that the times were hard,
With some men in the place,
That some had gone to the workhouse,
And thought it no disgrace.

They told me of torrential rains,
Which came with woeful rage,
They like of which they never saw,
Though eighty years of age.

Then I rambled about the fields,
There natural sights to see,
Yea gathered fungus from the grass,
And then went home to tea.

For in that rusticating sphere,
I roamed with hearts content,
And found a refreshing welcome,
In every house I went.

I viewed the scenes of former years,
Where oft I ate my rations,
And mused upon the altered times,
In rural situations.

I saw some fields of waving corn,
In rather backward state,
Foe heavy rains and sunless days,
Had kept the harvest late.

The brambles were with berries strewn,
With signs of an excellent yield,
And are the most delicious fruit,
We find in the harvest field.

I saw the nuts upon the boughs,
Did not in number lack,
But ere one gets into the wood,
The keepers on his back.

So they have cost a privilege,
Foe many years employed,
For gathering nuts inside the wood,
Is by the law denied.

I mused among those hills and dales,
Of rustic occupation,
And seemed to live old scenes again,
In my imagination.

I viewed with joy the village clock,
And heard its hourly ring,
I saw for once the surpliced choir,
And heard them chant and sing.

I rode behind the panting steed,
And tramped the "shanks" mare,
I saw the genial rains descend,
And the heavens bright and fair.

I saw bare fields where corn once grew,
For daily food and brewing,
And houses where plebeians dwelt,
All gone to rank and ruin.

I missed some faces once I knew,
And forms I used to see,
I missed the juicy autumn fruit,
From plum and apple tree.

I missed some trees from grassy Bab's,
And the hedge from Hibury Hill,
I missed a bank from Thurleigh Road,
And the noise of Milton Mill.

I saw once more the grand old church,
Refreshed with paint and stain,
And read the epitaphs of men,
Who sleep beside the fane.

Five times I crossed the flowing Ouse,
Famed for summons bends,
And saw the beautiful landscape,
In which the river blends.

I saw a few improvements made,
In different parts of places,
And still I hope to see some more,
To better the human race.

For social pleasure by the way,
In seeing old chums and friends,
I paid a neighbourly visit,
To "London" and Flewton Ends.

Thus I ended my summer tour,
Amid salubrious scenes,
And homeward heed to earn my bread,
Among hydraulic machines.

A poem first published in 'Sixty Years A Thatcher' by W.R. Parrott has been replicated here. The poem was written by an unknown resident of Milton Ernest in the nineteenth century. There are two marriages mentioned in the text of which one can be traced in the parish records to a ceremony at All Saints' Church, Milton Ernest, on 8th May 1865 between Joseph Crow and Emma Parrott. The Dove/Hawk marriage did not take place in Milton Ernest.

There is beside the river Ouse,
Upon its left hand bank;
A village for convenience set,
That will with many rank.

Upon the high road it abuts,
That leads both North and South;
And in the parish food is found,
To feed the mud and mouth.

For centuries the Church has stood,
A landmark in the place;
It is a fane where Christian men,
Discourse on faith and grace.

Contiguous to the high-way,
The school for children stands;
Where education's freely taught,
With tutor'd voice and hands.

Suspended high upon the fane,
Is seen the parish clock;
Daily showing the flight of time,
To all the pastor's flock.

And as the river runs close by,
Which is a limpid stream;
Should any have an angling mind,
They there can fish for bream.

Should any like a rural bath,
Or, a refreshing swim;
They there may doff their outer 'duds',
And take a header in.

So here we have a lovely park,
And spacious mansion fair;
A gentleman both good and kind,
Doth keep them with much care.

In the village are many things,
For people to talk about;
Commencing with useful tradesman,
And ending with horny lout.

A man once wooed a pretty maid,
Which caused some people to talk;
For when the nuptial knot was tied,
A Dove was changed to a Hawk.

Once there was billing and cooing,
By a pair I used to know;
And when it came to a climax,
A Parrott married to a Crow.

Of course I've missed a lot of things,
And purposely left them out;
As telling all the village sights,
Would put the writer about.

Appendix 2: The Manors of Milton Ernest

Time Period	Milton Ernest Manor (East Manor Farm)		Bassets Manor (Milton Ernest Hall)		Babs Manor (Unclear)
	Land #1 — 390 acres	Land #2 — 330 acres	Land #3 — 210 acres	Land #4 — 240 acres	Land #5 — unknown acres
11th Century / 12th Century	Domesday Book (1086). Owner: Adeliza, wife of Hugh de Grandmesnil. Tenant: Ivo, steward of Hugh de Grandmesnil.	Domesday Book (1086). Owner: Nigel d'Aubigny. Tenant: Turgis.	Domesday Book (1086). Owner: Hugh de Beauchamp. Tenant: William Basset.	Domesday Book (1086). Owner: Walter the Fleming. Tenant: Rainald.	No records pre 1544
13th Century	1200-1528. Owner: de Grey. Tenant: Erneys.	1227-1279. Owner: Knights Hospitallers. Tenant: John de Hertewell	1086-1373. Basset	1279: William de Lega	
14th Century			1373-1414. John Barle.	1371: Peter Hulier.	
15th Century			1414-1578: Martyn; Sampson; FitzRobert; Babyngton; Stanley; Penythorn; Anable; Ryggley; Styrop; Rosewell; Dawson; Crispe		
16th Century	1528-1550. Owner: Erneys			1511-1578: FitzGeffrey	1544. Greyves / 1557. Astrey
	Turnor	Keale	Strange		
17th Century	1575-1715. Turnor		1578-1746. Owner: Rolt. Tenant (1662-1692) Barnardiston.		
18th Century	1715. Streynsham Master / circa 1750. Mrs Stuckley / 1799. Bramston		1746. John Orlebar of Hinwick Hall. / 1785. Francis Herman.		1711. Faldoe / 1718. Haselden / 1746. Huskey
19th Century	1803. Gibbins		1803. Mrs Boyden / 1821. Donne		1803. Fisher, Shipley & Wyatt

By 1853, although East Manor Farm was owned by different people, Philip Booth, the owner of Milton Ernest Hall, laid claim to "The Manor, or the reputed Manor of Bassets, and Milton Ernys". It is probably safe to say that by the mid nineteenth century all of the manors had been combined into the one manor centred at Milton Ernest Hall.

Fig 268 – The owners and tenants of the three Milton Ernest Manors. Note that Rolt combined a third share of the Manor of Milton Ernest with the Manor of Bassets. He kept the name 'Bassets' for this combined manor. It is not known where Babs Manor was situated. Two possibilities are West Manor Farm and the land south of East Manor Farm.

Appendix 3: Milton Ernest Post Office

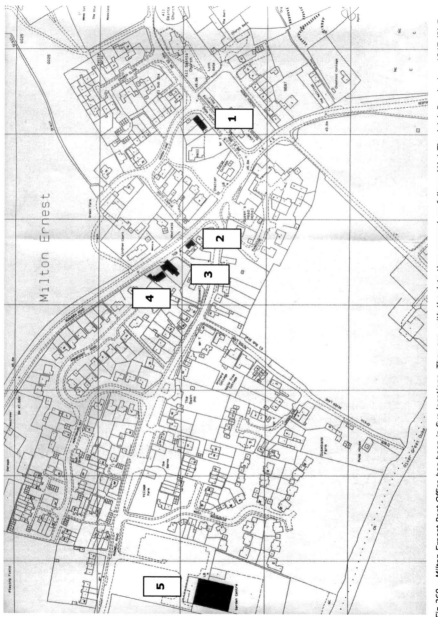

Fig 269 – Milton Ernest Post Office has been in five locations. They are, with the date they opened, as follows (1) 1 Thurleigh Road, circa 1847 (2) 5 Rushden Road, circa 1920 (3) The Old Post Office, 7 Rushden Road, circa 1940 (4) Ambry House, 9 Rushden Road, 1975 (5) Milton Ernest Garden Centre, 1993.

Fig 270 – Milton Ernest Post Office Location #1 (from 1847) - 1 Thurleigh Road. Photo taken 15th January 2006

Fig 271 – Milton Ernest Post Office Location #2 (from 1920) – 5 Rushden Road. Photo taken 15th January 2006.

Fig 272 – Milton Ernest Post Office Location #3 (from 1940) – The Old Post Office, 7 Rushden Road. Photograph taken 15th January 2006.

Fig 273 – Milton Ernest Post Office Location #4 (from 1975) – Ambry House, 9 Rushden Road. Photograph taken 15th January 2006.

Fig 274 – Milton Ernest Post Office Location #5 (from 1993) – Milton Ernest Garden Centre, Radwell Road. Photo taken 25ᵗʰ November 2004.

Fig 275 – Milton Ernest Post Office Location #5 (from 1993) –Inside Milton Ernest Garden Centre. Photo taken 15ᵗʰ January 2006.

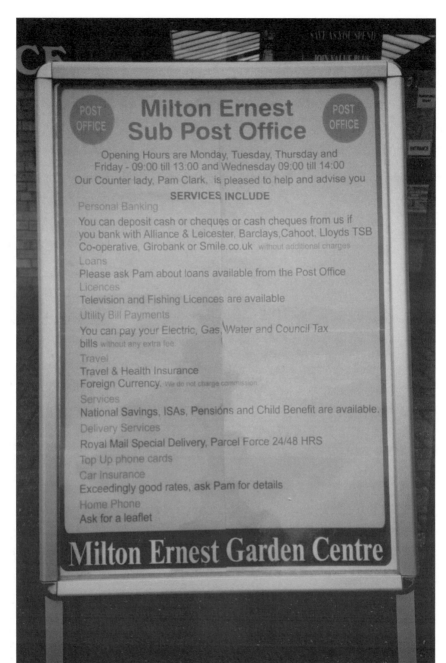

Fig 276 – Sign outside Milton Ernest Garden Centre advertising Milton Ernest Post Office, 15th January 2006.

Figures

Please note that every effort has been taken to obtain permission to publish the photographs within this book. However, in some instances the source of the photograph has been lost through time. These pictures have still been included as not to do so would prevent them from being seen and enjoyed by this and future generations. There has been no intention to breach copyright in these cases. Any amendments will be made to future re-issues of the book.

Fig 1	Children playing on Bedford Road. Courtesy of Bill Dunham.
Fig 2	Radwell Road. From a postcard produced by Midland View Company, 47 Kings Road, Market Harborough. Courtesy of Monica Boielle/Milton Ernest Lower School.
Fig 3	Parish map of Milton Ernest. Source: 'Provisional Map of Registered Common Land & Open Country". Courtesy of The Countryside Agency. Reproduced by permission of Ordnance Survey on behalf of HMSO. © Crown copyright 2006. All rights reserved. Ordnance Survey Licence number 100045207.
Fig 4	Erneys family coat of arms. Source: 'A History of the County of Bedford' edited by William Page, 1912. Reproduced from the Victoria County History, Bedford, Volume III, page 144, by permission of the Executive Editor.
Fig 5	Hermitage archaeological excavation. Source: Bedfordshire Magazine, Volume 8, Number 63, Winter 1962. Published and printed by White Crescent Press Ltd, Luton.
Fig 6	Heraldic pendant shield. Source: Bedfordshire Magazine, Volume 8, Number 63, Winter 1962. Published and printed by White Crescent Press Ltd, Luton.
Fig 7	Thomas Fisher's painting of 'Milton Ernest Church and Parsonage, Bedfordshire' circa 1820. Ref Z50/82/16. Courtesy of Bedfordshire & Luton Archives & Records Service.
Fig 8	Map of possible Windmill location. Reproduced by permission of Ordnance Survey on behalf of HMSO. © Crown copyright 2006. All rights reserved. Ordnance Survey Licence number 100045207.
Fig 9	East Manor Farm in the snow. Courtesy of David Purser.
Fig 10	Thomas Fisher's painting of the Almshouses at Milton Ernest. Source: 'History of Bedfordshire' by Joyce Godber. Bedfordshire County Council, 1984.
Fig 11	John Peck clock which was made in Milton Ernest. Courtesy of Melvyn Parrott.
Fig 12	John Peck clock face. Courtesy of Melvyn Parrott.
Fig 13	Rushden Road. Source: 'Sixty Years A Thatcher' by W.R.Parrott. Courtesy of Gillian Winser.
Fig 14	Policeman and George Robinson, circa 1940. Courtesy of Connie Richards.
Fig 15	Police House, 1965. Digital photograph taken by David Newman of original photograph. Source: Bedfordshire & Luton Archives & Records Service (ref X351/9). Courtesy of Milton Ernest Women's Institute.
Fig 16	Policeman outside the Police House, 1965. Digital photograph taken by David Newman of original photograph. Source: Bedfordshire & Luton Archives & Records Service (ref X351/9). Courtesy of Milton Ernest Women's Institute.
Fig 17	Milton Mill. Courtesy of Old English Inns/Bev Plumbley of the The Queen's Head.
Fig 18	Milton Ernest Parish Council chairmen. Created in Microsoft Excel by David Newman.
Fig 19	German Zeppelin over Milton Ernest, circa WWI. Photograph taken by George Barnett and courtesy of Kate Jones, his great grand-daughter.
Fig 20	Milton Ernest Women's Institute, 1923. Courtesy of Kathleen Willars.
Fig 21	Thurleigh Road, 1939. Courtesy of David Purser.
Fig 22	Telephone numbers. Created in Microsoft Excel by David Newman.
Fig 23	Population chart. Created in Microsoft Excel by David Newman.
Fig 24	Properties by Street. Created in Microsoft Excel by David Newman.
Fig 25	Public water tap. Courtesy of Bill Dunham.
Fig 26	Coronation Parade reaches Bedford Road, 1953. Courtesy of Connie Richards.
Fig 27	Milton Ernest Good Companions Club, 1956. Courtesy of David Purser.
Fig 28	Aerial photograph of Yarl's Wood, 15th February 2002. Courtesy of Ian Miles, Flashpoint Pictures.
Fig 29	Aerial photograph of Yarl's Wood, 15th February 2002. Courtesy of Ian Miles, Flashpoint Pictures.
Fig 30	Milton Ernest Mill. Courtesy of Old English Inns/Bev Plumbley of The Queen's Head.
Fig 31	Underhill Robinson's book. Permission British Library (4255.A.24/1007628.571).
Fig 32	John Turner letter dated March 16th 1835. Courtesy of Bedfordshire & Luton Archives & Records Service (ref Z629/15).

Fig 33	Enclosure Act map of Milton Ernest, 1803. Courtesy of Bedfordshire & Luton Archives & Records Service (ref MA16/2).
Fig 34	Robert Arkwright. Source: 'A Short History of the Oakley Hunt' by Ralph Greaves. Published by Reid-Hamilton Limited. Courtesy of the Oakley Hunt.
Fig 35	The Oakley Hunt by Stephen Pearce, 1850. Inventory number 1501. In the collection at Woburn Abbey, Woburn, Bedfordshire. By kind permission of His Grace the Duke of Bedford and the Trustees of the Bedford Estates.
Fig 36	Robert Arkwright. Source: 'Villages of the Ouse' by Peter Grey. Barracuda Books, Buckingham.
Fig 37	Oakley Hunt. Source: 'Villages of the Ouse' by Peter Grey. Barracuda Books, Buckingham. Courtesy of Gladys Clark.
Fig 38	Oakley Hounds postcard dated 1904. Courtesy of Bedfordshire & Luton Archives & Records Service (The Swain Collection, ref Z1130).
Fig 39	Reproduced from the 1884 Ordnance Survey map. Courtesy of Bedfordshire & Luton Archives & Records Service and Ordnance Survey.
Fig 40	William Butterfield, from a drawing by Lady Coleridge at Ottery St Mary. Source: 'William Butterfield' by Paul Thompson, 1971. Originally published by Routledge & Kegan Paul, London.
Fig 41	Oil painting of Benjamin Helps Starey. Source: Croydon Natural History Proc Vol 17 'From Palace to Washhouse' by Lilian Thornhill, Bedfordshire & Luton Archives & Records Service (ref 180 STA). Courtesy of the Trustees of Mrs G.C. Starey Deceased.
Fig 42	Map of Milton Ernest Hall, 10 August 1906. Courtesy of Bedfordshire & Luton Archives & Records Service (ref Z951/8/10).
Fig 43	Milton Ernest Hall. Courtesy of Bill Dunham.
Fig 44	Lucy Starey circa 1866. From 'In Memory of Lucy Starey'. Courtesy of the Trustees of Mrs G.C. Starey Deceased.
Fig 45	Dedication from 'In Memory of Lucy Starey'. Courtesy of the Trustees of Mrs G.C. Starey Deceased.
Fig 46	Lucy Starey's grave, 1868. From 'In Memory of Lucy Starey'. Courtesy of the Trustees of Mrs G.C. Starey Deceased.
Fig 47	Milton Ernest School Log Book. Courtesy of Milton Ernest Lower School.
Fig 48	Children of Milton Ernest School. Photograph taken by George Barnett. Courtesy of Kate Jones.
Fig 49	Milton Ernest School. Courtesy of Milton Ernest Lower School.
Fig 50	Opening Meet of the Oakley Hunt at the Mill, Milton Ernest, on the first Monday in November, about 1908. Source: 'Sixty Years A Thatcher' by W.R. Parrott. Courtesy of Gillian Winser.
Fig 51	Oakley Hunt Meet. Courtesy of Old English Inns/Bev Plumbley of The Queen's Head.
Fig 52	School group photograph, circa 1935. Courtesy of Connie Richards.
Fig 53	School children on Milton Ernest Green, circa 1935. Courtesy of Connie Richards.
Fig 54	Mrs Boielle and some of her scholars, 1951. Courtesy of Milton Ernest Lower School.
Fig 55	Milton Ernest Hall during WWII. Courtesy of Connie Richards.
Fig 56	Nissen hut in the grounds of Milton Ernest Hall. Courtesy of Connie Richards.
Fig 57	Construction of the bailey bridge. Courtesy of Connie Richards.
Fig 58	Bailey bridge. Courtesy of Connie Richards.
Fig 59	USAF envelope, 1944. Courtesy of Rachel Atkinson.
Fig 60	Westland Whirlwind Mark I. Source: 'www.cbrnp.com'. Courtesy of Bob Pearson.
Fig 61	Hawker Typhoon Mark 1b. Source: 'www.raf.mod.uk'. © Crown Copyright/MOD. Reproduced with the permission of the Controller of Her Majesty's Stationery Office.
Fig 62	Obituary of John Michael Bryan. Source: The Times/The Gale Group.
Fig 63	Glenn Miller and Joe Luck outside Milton Ernest Hall, 1944. Courtesy of Connie Richards
Fig 64	Glen Miller's band departing a bus outside what is thought to be the entrance to Milton Ernest Hall, 1944. Courtesy of Connie Richards.
Fig 65	Glenn Miller and band at Milton Ernest Hall, 1944. Courtesy of Connie Richards.
Fig 66	Glenn Miller in grounds of Milton Ernest Hall. Courtesy of Connie Richards.
Fig 67	Glenn Miller at Milton Ernest Hall. Source: 'Glenn Miller In Britain Then and Now' by Chris Way. Courtesy of Chris Way/After the Battle.
Fig 68	Plan of the Water Tower move, 1952. Courtesy of Molly Foster of Clapham Historical Society.
Fig 69	Water Tower move. Courtesy of Jewell-Harrison Studios/Molly Foster of Clapham Historical Society.
Fig 70	Water Tower base. Courtesy of Jewell-Harrison Studios/Molly Foster of Clapham Historical Society.
Fig 71	Ball bearings. Courtesy of Jewell-Harrison Studios/Molly Foster of Clapham Historical Society.
Fig 72	Water Tower workers. Courtesy of Jewell-Harrison Studios/Molly Foster of Clapham Historical Society.
Fig 73	Tractor cables. Courtesy of Jewell-Harrison Studios/Molly Foster of Clapham Historical Society.
Fig 74	Water Tower move. Courtesy of Jewell-Harrison Studios/Molly Foster of Clapham Historical Society.
Fig 75	Water Tower newspaper report. Courtesy of Bedfordshire Times/Molly Foster of Clapham Historical Society.

Fig 76	Cover of the Milton Glebe proposal pamphlet. Source: Bedfordshire & Luton Archives & Records Service (ref PC Melchbourne/Yelden 18/4). Courtesy of Phillips Planning Services/Bedfordia.
Fig 77	Site of the proposed Milton Glebe development. Source: Bedfordshire & Luton Archives & Records Service (ref PC Melchbourne/Yelden 18/3). Courtesy of Phillips Planning Services/Clifton Ibett.
Fig 78	Artist's impression of Milton Glebe Railway Station. Source: Bedfordshire & Luton Archives & Records Service (ref PC Melchbourne/Yelden 18/4). Courtesy of Phillips Planning Services/Clifton Ibbett.
Fig 79	Map of Milton Glebe. Source: Bedfordshire & Luton Archives & Records Service (ref PC Melchbourne/Yelden 18/4). Courtesy of Phillips Planning Services/Bedfordia.
Fig 80	David Green's painting of Radwell Road, Milton Ernest (owned by David Newman). Also used for the cover, at the start of each section and the abridged version's cover. Courtesy of David Green.
Fig 81	Queen's Head. Photographed by David Newman on 25th November 2004.
Fig 82	Queen's Head circa 1930. Courtesy of Connie Richards.
Fig 83	Queen's Head circa 1910. Courtesy of Old English Inns/Bev Plumbley of The Queen's Head.
Fig 84	Queen's Head circa 1915. Courtesy of Old English Inns/Bev Plumbley of The Queen's Head.
Fig 85	Queen's Head circa 1925. Courtesy of Charles Wells and Bedfordshire & Luton Archives & Records Service (ref WL 800/4 p10).
Fig 86	Mr Bradley outside Queen's Head, 1951. Source: 'Riverside Taverns', by Page Woodcock, Bedfordshire Magazine, Vol 3 No. 17, Summer 1951. Photograph taken by Tom Sheen. Published and printed by White Crescent Press Ltd, Luton.
Fig 87	Bedford Road. From a postcard produced by Midland View Company, 47 Kings Road, Market Harborough. Courtesy of Monica Boielle/Milton Ernest Lower School.
Fig 88	Queen's Head, 1961. Source: 'Milton Ernest' by Eric Rayner, Bedfordshire Magazine, Volume 8 Number 58, Autumn 1961. Published and printed by White Crescent Press Ltd, Luton.
Fig 89	Whitewashed Queen's Head, 1975. Courtesy of Bedfordshire County Council.
Fig 90	Whitewashed Queen's Head, 1975. Courtesy of Bedfordshire County Council.
Fig 91	Cook's Alley map. Courtesy of Bedfordshire & Luton Archives & Records Service (ref Z951/3/6).
Fig 92	Home Farm pre-renovation. Courtesy of Bill Dunham.
Fig 93	Home Farm. Photographed by David Newman on 25th November 2004.
Fig 94	Old Home Farm outbuildings. Photographed by David Newman on 25th November 2004.
Fig 95	Aerial shot of Milton Ernest Chapel. Courtesy of Simmons Aerofilms.
Fig 96	Milton Ernest Chapel, 1939. Source: 'A Regional Survey of Milton Ernest' by Beatrice Gillam. Courtesy of Beatrice Gillam and Bedfordshire & Luton Archives & Records Service (ref Z1057/2).
Fig 97	Chapel interior, 26th July 1973. Courtesy of North Bedfordshire Archaeological Society/Bedfordshire County Council.
Fig 98	Chapel interior, 26th July 1973. Courtesy of North Bedfordshire Archaeological Society/Bedfordshire County Council.
Fig 99	Chapel, 26th July 1973. Courtesy of North Bedfordshire Archaeological Society/Bedfordshire County Council.
Fig 100	Strawberry Tree. Photographed by David Newman on 25th November 2004.
Fig 101	Radwell Road circa 1910. Source: The Swain Collection. Courtesy of Bedfordshire & Luton Archives & Records Service (ref Z1130).
Fig 102	Close up of swing from figure 101.
Fig 103	Close up of Forge Cottage from figure 101.
Fig 104	Ernest Milton. Photograph taken by David Newman on 25th November 2004.
Fig 105	Radwell Road. Courtesy of Susan Sail.
Fig 106	The Barracks. Courtesy of Bill Dunham.
Fig 107	The Barracks. Courtesy of Bill Dunham.
Fig 108	Bob's Shop. Photographed by David Newman on 25th November 2004.
Fig 109	Butterfield's Cottage. Photographed by David Newman on 25th November 2004.
Fig 110	Rose Cottages, 1910. Courtesy of Bedfordshire & Luton Archives & Records Service (ref Slide 6621).
Fig 111	Workhouse viewed from River Lane, circa 1940. Courtesy of Connie Richards.
Fig 112	Public tap in River Lane. Source: 'A Regional Survey of Milton Ernest' by Beatrice Gillam. Courtesy of Beatrice Gillam and Bedfordshire & Luton Archives & Records Service (ref Z1057/2).
Fig 113	The Spring in River Lane. Source: 'A Regional Survey of Milton Ernest' by Beatrice Gillam. Courtesy of Beatrice Gillam and Bedfordshire & Luton Archives & Records Service (ref Z1057/2).
Fig 114	Punts. Source: 'A Regional Survey of Milton Ernest' by Beatrice Gillam. Courtesy of Beatrice Gillam and Bedfordshire & Luton Archives & Records Service (ref Z1057/2).
Fig 115	Punting on the Ouse. Courtesy of Bill Dunham.
Fig 116	George Barnett fishing at Milton Ernest, circa 1910. Courtesy of Kate Jones.
Fig 117	The River Ouse at Milton Ernest. Courtesy Monica Boielle/Milton Ernest Lower School.
Fig 118	River Lane, 1961. Source: 'Milton Ernest' by Eric Rayner, Bedfordshire Magazine, Volume 8 Number 58, Autumn 1961. Published and printed by White Crescent Press Ltd, Luton.

Fig 164	Puppy show at Milton Ernest Kennels, 1949. Source: 'A Short History of the Oakley Hunt' by Ralph Greaves. Published by Reid-Hamilton Limited. Courtesy of The Oakley Hunt.
Fig 165	The Old Post Office before it was a Post Office. Courtesy of Bill Dunham.
Fig 166	Bletsoe Road (now Rushden Road) circa 1910. Source: The Swain Collection. Courtesy of Bedfordshire & Luton Archives & Records Service (ref Z1130).
Fig 167	Close up of figure 166.
Fig 168	Post Office Stores. Source: Postcard produced by Midland View Company, 47 Kings Road, Market Harborough. Courtesy of Monica Boielle/Milton Ernest Lower School.
Fig 169	Old Post Office. Photographed by David Newman on 25th November 2004.
Fig 170	Bletsoe Road (now Rushden Road) circa 1910. Courtesy of Bill Dunham.
Fig 171	Old thatched cottage. Photograph courtesy of Kathleen Willars.
Fig 172	Charles Clark outside the Smithy. Courtesy of Bedfordshire & Luton Archives & Records Service (ref Z50/82/1). Original hangs in Milton Ernest Village Hall.
Fig 173	The Old Forge and Forge Cottage. Courtesy of Connie Richards.
Fig 174	Forge Hall. Digital photograph taken by David Newman of original photograph. Source: Bedfordshire & Luton Archives & Records Service (ref X351/9). Courtesy of Milton Ernest Women's Institute.
Fig 175	Eastern National Bus. Source: 'A Regional Survey of Milton Ernest' by Beatrice Gillam. Courtesy of Beatrice Gillam and Bedfordshire & Luton Archives & Records Service (ref Z1057/2).
Fig 176	Forge Cottage and the Old Forge. Courtesy of Susan Sail.
Fig 177	Forge Cottage. Photographed by David Newman on 25th November 2004.
Fig 178	Milton Ernest VC Lower School. Photographed by David Newman on 25th November 2004.
Fig 179	China dish. Courtesy of Kate Jones.
Fig 180	Close up of Milton Ernest School picture on the china dish. Courtesy of Kate Jones.
Fig 181	Milton Ernest School group photograph. Courtesy of Susan Sail. Original photograph taken by K.A. Martin of Bedford.
Fig 182	The Head Teachers of Milton Ernest Lower School. Created in Microsoft Excel by David Newman.
Fig 183	George Barnett, Headmaster of Milton Ernest School. Courtesy of Kate Jones.
Fig 184	Milton Ernest School photograph, circa 1930. Courtesy of Susan Sail. Original photograph owned by Frank Hull.
Fig 185	Milton Ernest School photograph. circa 1940. Courtesy of Connie Richards.
Fig 186	Milton Ernest Lower School badge. Courtesy of Susan Newman.
Fig 187	Milton Ernest Village Hall. Digital photograph taken by David Newman of original photograph. Source: Bedfordshire & Luton Archives & Records Service (X351/9). Courtesy of Milton Ernest Women's Institute.
Fig 188	Milton Ernest Village Hall. Photographed by David Newman on 25th November 2004.
Fig 189	Thurleigh Road cottages. Photograph courtesy of Kathleen Willars.
Fig 190	Thurleigh Road Cottages, 1939. Source: 'A Regional Survey of Milton Ernest' by Beatrice Gillam. Courtesy of Beatrice Gillam and Bedfordshire & Luton Archives & Records Service (ref Z1057/2).
Fig 191	Telegraph boy outside Milton Ernest Post Office. Source: 'Sixty Years A Thatcher' by W.R.Parrott. Courtesy of Gillian Winser.
Fig 192	Section of 1906 map. Courtesy of Bedfordshire & Luton Archives & Records Service (ref Z951/8/10).
Fig 193	Thurleigh Road. Courtesy of Susan Sail.
Fig 194	Aerial view of Thurleigh Road from All Saints' Tower, circa 1960. Courtesy of Bill Dunham.
Fig 195	Green Farm, 1919. Photo taken by Martin of Bedford. Commissioned by Ernest Parrot. Courtesy of Rosalind & Graham Tucker.
Fig 196	Stone Cottage. Photographed by David Newman on 25th November 2004.
Fig 197	Vicarage, 1939. Source: 'A Regional Survey of Milton Ernest' by Beatrice Gillam. Courtesy of Beatrice Gillam and Bedfordshire & Luton Archives & Records Service (ref Z1057/2).
Fig 198	East Manor Farm. Courtesy of Rob and Kathy Robson.
Fig 199	Turnor family coat of arms. Source: 'A History of the County of Bedford' edited by William Page, 1912. Reproduced from the Victoria County History, Bedford, Volume III, page 145, by permission of the Executive Editor.
Fig 200	Edmund Turnor. 1786 engraving by James Fittler based on 1693 painting by H. Verelit. Courtesy of Bedfordshire & Luton Archives & Records Service (ref X254/88/365).
Fig 201	East Manor Farm, 1939. Source: 'A Regional Survey of Milton Ernest' by Beatrice Gillam. Courtesy of Beatrice Gillam and Bedfordshire & Luton Archives & Records Service (ref Z1057/2).
Fig 202	Thomas Fisher's painting of All Saints' Church, 1815. Courtesy of Bedfordshire & Luton Archives & Records Service.
Fig 203	The Vicars of Milton Ernest. Created in Microsoft Excel by David Newman.
Fig 204	All Saints' Church. Courtesy of Bill Dunham.
Fig 205	Plan of All Saints' Church (not to scale). Created in Microsoft Excel by David Newman based on a plan drawn by Roger Lewis in the 'Welcome to All Saints' pamphlet.
Fig 206	Bread cupboard in All Saints' Church. Source: 'The County Books – Bedfordshire' by Laurence Meynell, 1950. Courtesy of Robert Hale Limited.

Fig 207	Ernest Holmes, vicar of All Saints' Church, distributing free bread. Photograph from a newspaper cutting. Courtesy of Kate Jones.
Fig 208	'Scourging of Christ' painting. Source: Burlington Magazine, 1920. Courtesy of Bedfordshire & Luton Archives & Records Service (ref P80/28/2).
Fig 209	A close up of figure 208.
Fig 210	Milton Ernest Choir, 1908. Photograph from newspaper cutting. Courtesy of Susan Sail. Original photograph owned by Walter Parrott.
Fig 211	Milton Ernest Choir, 1933. Courtesy of Kathleen Willars.
Fig 212	Stained glass window, All Saints' Church. Courtesy of Bill Dunham.
Fig 213	WWI Roll of Honour. Created in Microsoft Excel by David Newman.
Fig 214	War Memorial. Photographed by David Newman on 25th November 2004.
Fig 215	1921 wedding of Wilfred Lumley and Ethel Barnett at All Saints' Church. Courtesy of Kate Jones.
Fig 216	Aerial view of All Saints' Church, 1962. Courtesy of Mary Daniels Grimwood.
Fig 217	Dutch Barn in front of East Manor Farm. Courtesy of Rob and Kathy Robson.
Fig 218	East Manor Farm outbuildings, 1961. Source: 'Milton Ernest' by Eric Rayner, Bedfordshire Magazine, Vol 8 No 58, Autumn 1961. Published and printed by White Crescent Press Ltd, Luton.
Fig 219	Former East Manor Farm outbuildings. Photographed by David Newman on 25th November 2004.
Fig 220	The pound from extract of map of Milton Ernest. Source: Bedfordshire & Luton Archives & Records Service (Ordnance Survey Sheet VII.14 and VIII.15, 1st Edition). Reproduced from the 1884 Ordnance Survey map.
Fig 221	Winning raffle ticket from the 2005 Village Fete. Printed by LG Digital. Courtesy of David Newman!
Fig 222	School football pitch on the Village Green. Courtesy of Simmons Aerofilms.
Fig 223	Village Green with path. Courtesy of David Purser.
Fig 224	Haycocks on the village green. Source: 'Bedfordshire in Pictures', Bedfordshire Magazine, Vol 11 No. 82, Autumn 1967. Published and printed by White Crescent Press Ltd, Luton.
Fig 225	Village Green. Photographed by David Newman on 25th November 2004.
Fig 226	Almshouses. Courtesy of Bill Dunham.
Fig 227	Almshouses. Courtesy of Bill Dunham.
Fig 228	Almshouses. Source: 'Bedfordshire Then and Now' by Eric G. Meadows. Courtesy of S.B. Publications.
Fig 229	The Old School. Photographed by David Newman on 25th November 2004.
Fig 230	Milton Ernest brownies, 1952. Courtesy of Susan Sail.
Fig 231	Bedford Road Cottage. Courtesy of Bill Dunham.
Fig 232	Church and Village Green viewed from Hall gates. Source: 'Milton Ernest' by Eric Rayner, Bedfordshire Magazine, Volume 8 Number 58, Autumn 1961. Published and printed by White Crescent Press Ltd, Luton.
Fig 233	Bedford Road before straightening safety work. Courtesy of David Purser.
Fig 234	The Maltings. Photographed by David Newman on 25th November 2004.
Fig 235	Chestnut Cottage drawing dated 17th October 1860. From an unknown publication. Courtesy of Prue and John Harris Watson.
Fig 236	Bedford Road, 1957. Courtesy of David Purser.
Fig 237	Milton Ernest Garden Centre in Milton Ernest Hall Gardens, 1975. Courtesy of Maureen Catlin.
Fig 238	Stable buildings at Milton Ernest Hall, circa 1920. Courtesy of Milton Ernest Parish Council.
Fig 239	Stable Cottage. Photographed by David Newman on 25th November 2004.
Fig 240	Bassets Manor & Rolt coat of arms from William Gordon's 1736 Map of Bedfordshire. Courtesy of Bedfordshire & Luton Archives & Records Service (ref Z50/143/221).
Fig 241	Rolt Coat of Arms. Source: 'A Bedfordshire Armorial', by F. W. Kuhlicke, Bedfordshire Magazine, Vol 12 No. 90, Autumn 1971. Published and printed by White Crescent Press Ltd, Luton.
Fig 242	Mary Rolt painting. From the 'Orlebar Chronicles' by Frederica St.John Orlebar. Artist unknown. Courtesy of C.J.D. Orlebar.
Fig 243	Milton Ernest Hall, the seat of Philip Booth Esq. Lithograph by A. Butler and W. Gauci after a drawing by P. C. Auld. Courtesy of Bedfordshire & Luton Archives & Records Service (ref Z879/9).
Fig 244	Timber advert. Source: Bedford Times, Saturday 12th December 1846.
Fig 245	William Butterfield's plans of Milton Ernest Hall. Source: 'William Butterfield' by Paul Thompson, 1971. Originally published by Routledge & Kegan Paul, London. Courtesy of the Trustees of Mrs G.C. Starey Deceased.
Fig 246	Gardeners working at Milton Ernest Hall, circa 1910. Courtesy of Old English Inns/Bev Plumbley of the Queen's Head.
Fig 247	Milton Ernest Hall circa 1910. Courtesy of Milton Ernest Parish Council.
Fig 248	Bing Crosby at Milton Ernest Hall. Courtesy of Connie Richards.
Fig 249	Officers at Milton Ernest Hall at end of WWII. Courtesy of Connie Richards via Dale Titler.
Fig 250	Annual Show advertisement from the Bedfordshire Mercury dated 11th July 1896. Courtesy of Bedfordshire & Luton Archives & Records Service.
Fig 251	Admission ticket to 1937 Horticultural Show. Courtesy of Rachel Atkinson.

Fig 252	Programme for Milton Ernest Flower Show, 1913. Courtesy of David Purser.
Fig 253	Athletic Sports timetable, 1913. Courtesy of David Purser.
Fig 254	Milton Ernest FC 1927-28. Courtesy of Bedfordshire & Luton Archives & Records Service (ref Z50/142/768).
Fig 255	1927-28 Bedford & District League Division IV League table created in Microsoft Excel by David Newman. Compiled from results published in the Bedfordshire Times.
Fig 256	Football match report from Bedfordshire Times dated 18th November 1927. Courtesy of Bedfordshire & Luton Archives & Records Service.
Fig 257	Horse Show & Gymkhana programme, 1965. Digital photograph taken by David Newman of original programme. Source: Bedfordshire & Luton Archives & Records Service (ref X351/9). Courtesy of Milton Ernest Women's Institute.
Fig 258	Milton Ernest Horse Show and Gymkhana. Courtesy of Connie Richards.
Fig 259	Action from the 1965 Milton Ernest Horse Show & Gymkhana. Digital photograph taken by David Newman of original programme. Source: Bedfordshire & Luton Archives & Records Service (ref X351/9). Courtesy of Milton Ernest Women's Institute.
Fig 260	Scouts in the grounds of Milton Ernest Hall. Courtesy of Milton Ernest Parish Council.
Fig 261	Milton Ernest Scout Group. Courtesy of Connie Richards.
Fig 262	Milton Ernest Hall dovecote, circa 1910. Courtesy of Milton Ernest Parish Council.
Fig 263	Milton Ernest Boathouse. Source: 'William Butterfield' by Paul Thompson, 1971. Originally published by Routledge & Kegan Paul, London. Courtesy of the Trustees of Mrs G.C. Starey Deceased.
Fig 264	Milton Ernest Boathouse. Courtesy of Milton Ernest Parish Council.
Fig 265	Elm Avenue at Milton Ernest Hall. Courtesy of Bill Dunham. .
Fig 266	Elm Tree Avenue. Source: 'Sixty Years A Thatcher' by W.R.Parrott. Courtesy of Gillian Winser.
Fig 267	Inside the Queen's Head. Courtesy of Bev Plumbley/Ian Hulland Photography Ltd.
Fig 268	Manors of Milton Ernest. Created in Microsoft Excel by David Newman.
Fig 269	Map of Milton Ernest, 2000, annotated by David Newman with the five locations of Milton Ernest Post Office. Reproduced by permission of Ordnance Survey on behalf of HMSO. © Crown copyright 2006. All rights reserved. Ordnance Survey Licence number 100045207.
Fig 270	Post Office location #1 (1 Thurleigh Road). Photographed by David Newman on 15th January 2006.
Fig 271	Post Office location #2 (5 Rushden Road). Photographed by David Newman on 15th January 2006.
Fig 272	Post Office location #3 (7 Rushden Road). Photographed by David Newman on 15th January 2006.
Fig 273	Post Office location #4 (9 Rushden Road). Photographed by David Newman on 15th January 2006.
Fig 274	Post Office location #5 (Milton Ernest Garden Centre, Radwell Road). Photographed by David Newman on 25th November 2004.
Fig 275	Post Office inside the Garden Centre. Photographed by David Newman on 15th January 2006.
Fig 276	Sign outside Milton Ernest Post Office. Photographed by David Newman on 15th January 2006.
Fig 277	Heritage Walk map. Designed and produced by David Newman. © David Newman, 2006.
Fig 278	Fox button found in the garden of 11 Arkwright Road, 2003. Courtesy of David Newman.

The photographs in the abridged heritage walk section of the book were taken by David Newman on 25th November 2004. The only exceptions being the cover painting, the heritage trail map and buildings which no longer exist. These pictures have already been credited in the figures list.

Index of Milton Ernest People & Places

220, 221, 222, 227, 242, 243, 245, 249, 252, 293
East Manor Farm Outbuildings, 242, 244
Eastwick, 218
Emerye, 13, 157
Enger, 43, 44, 45
Ernest Milton, 149
Erneys, 9, 11, 24, 32, 205, 217, 218
Eyles, 52

F

Fairbrother Associates, 256
Fairey, 277
Farrar, 238
Farrer, 24, 32, 51, 55
Feazey, 221
Fisher, 9, 14, 176
Fishers Farm, 51, 54
Fishpond Farm, 212
Fishwick, 81
FitzGeffrey, 12, 261
Fitzwilliam, 190
Fletcher, 13
Flewton End, 11, 51, 54, 172, 212, 213, 239, 240, 290
Foot, 56
Forge Cottage, 47, 148, 195, 196, 198
Foster, 32, 52, 53
Franklin, 215
Fuller, 225

G

Gables, 37
Gamball, 195
Gambrell, 81
Gammons, 96
Garner, 96
Gawp Row, 151
Geaney, 154
Gentleman's Club, 151

Gibbard, 274
Gibbins, 51, 52, 53, 55, 144, 191, 221, 254
Godwin, 30
Good Companions Club, 36
Goodman, 103, 154, 204
Goodrich, 118
Goodwin, 103, 104
Gore, 52
Gower, 144
Grandmesnil, 8
Grange, 22, 110
Grant, 202
Green, 277
Green Barns, 212
Green Farm, 19, 211, 212
Green Lady, 178
Green's Close, 53
Griffin, 14
Griggs, 19, 21, 51, 172
Grimwood, 171

H

Hailey, 14
Haley, 103
Halgarth, 32, 36, 194, 207
Hall, 149, 154, 258
Hand, 154
Hanlon, 251
Hardiman, 59
Harmer-Brown, 272
Harris, 190
Harrison, 53, 219
Hart, 20, 32, 51, 52, 55, 144, 165, 223
Hartwell, 55, 228
Hawk, 291, 292
Hawkins, 215, 225, 226
Haycock, 30, 96, 110, 151, 158, 159, 241, 280
Haynes, 118, 119
Hazlett, 91, 93
Hebbes, 89
Herbert, 88, 91, 95
Herdman, 82, 92

Heritage, 87, 89, 236, 239
Herman, 264
Hermitage, 10, 19
Hertewell, 9
Hett, 216, 234
Higgins, 58
Hill, 109, 110
Hine, 20
Holloway, 251
Holmes, 82, 83, 89, 111, 225,
   230, 233, 234
Home Farm, 29, 49, 50, 54, 107,
   138, 141, 142, 143, 144, 284
Hooker, 25, 28, 95, 96, 165,
   166, 210, 246
Hooker's House, 166
Horn, 233
Horne, 25, 28, 239
Horse Croft, 56
Hovel, 143
Howe, 13
Hugh de Beauchamp, 261
Hugh de Grandmesnil, 24, 217
Hulatt, 195
Hulier, 10
Hunt, 47, 57, 89, 93, 190, 241
Huntsmans Way, 32, 60, 176,
   181, 182, 183, 184, 185, 190
Hurst, 51, 216, 236

I

Ibbett, 34, 35, 36, 127, 173
Ireland, 24
Ivo, 8, 217

J

Jackson, 16, 226
Jacquest, 233, 239

K

Keech, 93

Kennels, 22, 27, 56, 57, 59, 60,
   63, 96, 183, 184, 185, 186,
   187, 188, 190
Kettering Road, 191
Kinge, 13
Knight, 55, 96, 97, 154
Koch, 119

L

Lamb, 144, 176
Langhoe, 10
Larkins, 119, 170
Lawn Wood, 20, 223, 266
Layton, 52
Ledson, 272
Lilley, 52
Lindham Court, 212
Linger, 89, 277
Little, 19
Littlechild, 106
Littledale, 58
Loch, 104
London End, 16, 30, 37, 50, 51,
   54, 55, 63, 65, 158, 159, 254,
   290
Lord, 53, 55, 56
Low, 53, 191
Lucking, 105
Ludlow, 59
Luff, 89, 92
Luke, 190
Lukey, 51
Lumley, 242
Lynch Furlong, 245

M

Macan, 57
Maddoc, 51
Magenis, 58
Magniac, 58, 59
Makeham, 53, 138, 155
Mallaig Croft, 194
Maltby, 87

Parkside, 141, 144, 147
Parrott, 17, 20, 25, 31, 32, 52,
55, 56, 85, 141, 158, 195,
201, 211, 233, 291, 292
Parsonage, 52, 63, 216
Payne, 32, 287
Payton, 171
Peck, 17, 18, 30, 53, 55, 56,
142, 158, 204, 233
Perkins, 277
Perrott, 80
Perryman, 89
Pevling, 277
Phantom Coach, 283
Pink, 36
Pinnock, 98, 100, 101, 104, 105
Playing Field, 181, 182
Pointer, 55, 154
Police House, 21, 22
Pontet, 74
Poole, 51
Pope, 190
Post Office, 180, 191, 194, 207,
208, 287, 294, 295, 296, 297,
298
Poulter, 105, 229, 262
Pound, 245
Praed, 59
Prat, 154
Priddon, 31
Protech Food Systems Limited,
31
Purser, 36, 96, 240

T

313

The final section of this book is an abridged version. This was issued free in 2006 to all residents in the parish of Milton Ernest. It is the intention to ensure that a supply of free copies will always be available at All Saints' Church, The Queen's Head and Milton Ernest Garden Centre. These will be provided by Milton Ernest Parish Council to ensure that future generations can enjoy the heritage trail and learn about the importance of Milton Ernest. If you cannot find a copy of the abridged version of the heritage trail please contact a member of the Parish Council who will arrange for a copy to be made available to you.

The abridged version is, as it suggests, a précis of this book. It has been included within this book as it was felt that it would be an easier reference guide when undertaking the heritage trail. Modern day (25th November 2004) photographs have been included of each existing building to visually assist the walker in locating their exact whereabouts.

The
Importance
of
Milton Ernest

Heritage Trail
Abridged Version

ABOUT THE TRAIL

The Importance of Milton Ernest Heritage Trail is 3.2 miles (5.2 kilometres) long. The route has been designed to cater for all ages and abilities. The major part of the route covers the tarmac footpaths of the village making the trail accessible throughout the year. However, there are parts of the walk which cross grassed areas that could be difficult for wheelchair users or become muddy at certain times of the year. Bearing this in mind, alternative routes are shown on the map to ensure that everyone can complete the walk, no matter the weather conditions, without missing any of the historic buildings.

Please note that walkers must respect the privacy of householders and not enter their gardens or properties.

Directions are in italics. Green box = building exists. Grey box = building no longer exists.

1

THE QUEEN'S HEAD

Originally two 17th century cottages which were converted into a public house. Earliest record of the Queen's Head dates back to 1733. Always known as the Queen's Head except between 1851-1854 when called 'Booth's Arms' after Philip Booth, a local landowner who lived at Milton Ernest Hall. The Queen's Head was in private ownership until 1876 when it was bought by a brewery. In 1987 the public house expanded into a hotel. An adjoining threshing barn, with a date stone of 1666, was converted into bedrooms. Due to the low ceiling a trapdoor in the floor was required for people to play darts.

2

SITE OF

COOK'S ALLEY

In the vicinity of what is now the Queen's Head car park and 1 Radwell Road there used to be a small lane known as Cook's Alley. A map of 1857 (shown above) depicts that William Cook, a baker, owned a large barn, a pig sty, a bakehouse and a cottage in this area. It's therefore quite easy to discover how the alley got its name! Cook's Alley had three other cottages, a wood yard, a stable, a cart shed and a butcher's shop which was ran by Mr Mole. James Parrott, the local shepherd, lived in one of the cottages. Today there is no sign that Cook's Alley ever existed. *Now walk along Radwell Road.*

3

HOME FARM

Turn left into Parkside and walk to the end of this small close where you will find a late 16th / early 17th century building which was a farmhouse. Home Farm was renovated in the 1730s and then largely rebuilt in 1859 by the Victorian Gothic architect, William Butterfield. In 1871 the farm consisted of 228 acres providing employment for 12 men and 9 boys. The Starey family owned the property in the 20th century. They hired Sir Albert Richardson, who transformed Home Farm into a country residence. It was he who added the first floor balcony entrance. Today, Home Farm is two separate homes.

4
HOME FARM OUTBUILDINGS

Opposite Home Farm are a number of its former outbuildings which were converted into five homes circa 1985. These outbuildings would have had various uses for a working farm. The names of three of the dwellings sheds some light on their previous purpose - 'East Barn', 'West Barn' and 'The Old Stables'.

5
SITE OF
WESLEYAN CHAPEL

Retrace your steps back along Parkside and just before you reach Radwell Road is the site of the Wesleyan Chapel. This was built for the Methodists of the village in 1839. Previously the villagers had to obtain official registrations to worship at their own buildings or homes. At its peak 120 villagers attended the Sunday evening service, but the congregation dwindled and the chapel closed its doors in 1970. Six years later the chapel was demolished. One little known fact of its 157 year history is that Glenn Miller performed at a chapel service on 6th August 1944. *Now turn left and walk along Radwell Road.*

6
THE STRAWBERRY TREE

Dating back to the 17th Century, The Strawberry Tree was originally three cottages, a sweet shop at the front, a laundry in the middle and a small cottage at the back. In the first half of the 20th century it was a scrap merchant's business. An extension (the right hand side of the building) was added during the Second World War. It was known as 'The Old Cottage' until renamed 'Strawberry Tree' and converted into a tea shop (1982) and then a restaurant (1993). There are three strawberry trees (arbutus) in the garden. Did you see the face of 'Ernest Milton' carved into the wall?

7
SITE OF
THE BARRACKS

On the opposite side of the road is a small grassed area with a bench. Here used to stand a large three storey red brick building. Fronting Radwell Road with no back yard the building was given the nickname 'The Barracks' by the villagers due to its sheer size. It was also known as 'Gawp Row' as the inhabitants of the six homes used to peer out of their windows at anyone who passed! The Barracks was demolished in 1962. *Continue along Radwell Road.*

8

BOB'S SHOP

Milton Ernest used to be a self contained village. Victorian records show that there were as many as 30 different trades being undertaken in the village many of which had shops to sell their goods. 'Bob's Shop' is the last reminder of these old style shops and is named after the proprietor, Mr Robert Haycock. His father, Christopher Haycock, used to run this grocer's shop. Other members of the Haycock family, based in River Lane, used to be carpenters and undertakers as well as hire out punts. Prior to being a grocery store it is thought that the premises were a Gentleman's Club. *Continue along Radwell Road.*

9

BUTTERFIELD'S COTTAGE

Number 13 Radwell Road was designed and built by the eminent Victorian architect, William Butterfield. It was built in 1859 at a cost of £259. William Butterfield (1814-1900) designed many ecclesiastical buildings in Britain as well as two cathedrals in Australia. He was a decorative designer with an individual Gothic style. Butterfield married into the Starey family which meant that the village benefited from his skills. In Milton Ernest he built the Hall and Mill, restored All Saints' Church and built other cottages and farm buildings.

10

SITE OF
THE WORKHOUSE

Opposite the entrance to River Lane stand three cottages. Numbers 18, 20 and 22 Radwell Road, which along with two other cottages (on the site of number 24), long since demolished, used to be known as 'Rose Cottages'. Milton Ernest Workhouse was based in one of the demolished cottages. Here paupers were restricted to the building every day of the week except Sundays. They made lace to generate income for the person who ran the workhouse. Records show the workhouse as being in existence, at least, between 1783 and 1834. In 1812 it was described as 'the most filthy place I was ever in'.

11

RIVER GREAT OUSE

Turn left into River Lane and keep walking until you reach the river. This section of the River Great Ouse used to be a ford. Evidence (coins, slabs) suggests that it was used by the Romans. In bygone days people used to hire punts on this stretch of the river. It has also been used by villagers for fishing, rowing and swimming. However, where there's water, there's danger. The worst tragedy in the history of Milton Ernest occurred in July 1576 when four men from the village drowned 'by misadventure'. *Now retrace your steps and head back towards Radwell Road.*

12

THE OLD BAKERY

Walk past 'Ousebank Farm' home of the aforementioned Haycock family; continue past the entrance to the strangely named 'London End'; and turn left into Radwell Road. Formerly known as 'Nookery Corner', the Old Bakery dates back to the 15th century. The Newell family owned the business for 90 years (1847-1937). A steady stream of villagers used to take their Sunday roast to the bakery. Every Saturday 12 small loaves would be produced in the bakehouse and placed in a special box in All Saints' Church. These were distributed to the poor of the village but the practice stopped when the bakehouse closed in 1956.

13

HOOKER'S HOUSE

Continuing along Radwell Road and you'll come to a large pale brick building. 'Hooker's House' is not as shocking as it first seems, as this is the former home of Stephen Hooker. He ran an agricultural threshing business in and around Milton Ernest. His machinery was kept in a barn on Thurleigh Road which has long since been demolished. Stephen Hooker was a jack of all trades, with the 1891 census listing his profession as 'Agricultural engineer, machinist, cycle and motor manufacturer & threshing machine proprietor!' He also owned the village petrol station.

14

SWAN HOUSE

Next door to Hooker's House is a building with a white colour washed front. Swan House dates back to the 18th Century and was previously called 'North View'. It was renamed after the pub which used to be next door. A change of name would have been appropriate as the north view would have been blocked by the development of the housing estate across the road! *Walk a few steps and you will come to two detached houses (numbers 27 and 27a, Radwell Road) which have been built on the site of The Swan public house.*

15

SITE OF
THE SWAN

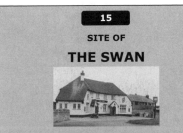

Deeds for the Swan exist from 1785 although it is thought that the original stone building was built sometime before then. Records of pubs in the village date back to 1584 when the vicar was accused of being in the alehouse. In Victorian times the Swan was also a butcher's shop! In 1934 the old stone building was demolished and replaced with a brick version, which was regularly frequented by Glenn Miller and his band ten years later. The Swan used to host the village feast in Victorian times and more recently the local pig roast. On 21st February 1999 last orders were called for the final time.

16 & 17

THE BARNS & VILLAGE FARM HOUSE

Further along Radwell Road are buildings which were part of Village Farm. In 1994 two homes were created from the stables and barn ('The Barns') and the farmhouse ('Village Farm House'). The Village Farm house has 'RTM 1670' carved into the stone which depicts the year that it was built. The initials RTM refer to Richard and Thomas Morris, the stonemasons who built the property. During the Second World War Italian and German prisoners of war were housed here. It was around this time that Claude Ibbett bought the farm which in time led to the creation of the Milton Ernest based Bedfordia company.

18

WEST MANOR FARM

Across the road stands a former manor farmhouse which has been converted into three properties. West Manor Farm dates back to the early 17th century and once farmed 329 acres. In 1861 the farmer employed 10 men and 3 boys as well as relying on 6 men who travelled from Ireland each year to help with the harvest. It was named West Manor Farm to distinguish it from the other Manor Farm in the village. In the 1940s and 1950s locals told stories of the ghost of the 'Green Lady' who appeared at the now blocked up window.

19

WILD FLOWER MEADOW

Continue along Radwell Road and turn left into Riverside View. This area used to house many barns and outbuildings belonging to Village Farm. *At the end of the road* you will come to a wild flower meadow which leads down to the River Great Ouse. If you have the time, wander down to the river, *before retracing your steps along Riverside View. Once you reach Radwell Road again, turn left and almost immediately you'll come to the entrance of Milton Ernest Garden Centre.*

20

MILTON ERNEST GARDEN CENTRE

This is the second site for Milton Ernest Garden Centre. It originally opened on Good Friday 20th April 1973 in the gardens of Milton Ernest Hall, before moving to Radwell Road on 26th August 1993. Milton Ernest Garden Centre sells much more than plants. There is a pet shop, art centre, coffee shop, book area, craft stalls and post office on the premises. *Walk back to Radwell Road, cross over and you now have a choice. Either turn left and go to the playing field, which will mean walking on grassland, or turn right and walk down the path with the sign which reads 'Radwell Road, Even No's. 58 to 64 & Huntsmans Way.'*

21

MILTON ERNEST
PLAYING FIELD

In 1980 Bedfordia provided the land from which Milton Ernest Playing Field was created. The annual peppercorn rent costs just 5p per year! The playing field is better equipped than many larger villages. There are swings, an adventure trail, a slide, a rocker, two climbing frames and a youth shelter. Add to this the basketball court, tarmac path, football pitch, seats and bin and you can see what a good job the Milton Ernest Playing Field Association have done over the last 25 years. *Follow the path and exit via the Huntsmans Way gate. Walk along Huntsmans Way and turn left into Arkwright Road.*

22

SITE OF

OAKLEY HUNT KENNELS

Huntsmans Way and Arkwright Road are so named because the housing development was built on land previously owned by the Oakley Hunt. Robert Arkwright being their most famous Master of the Hunt. It was he who bred the brown into the coats of hunt hounds which had previously been just black and white. The Kennels were built in 1834 on a 2.5 acre site known as Rabletts Close. In 1873 the site was extended. At its peak the Kennels site housed 100 hounds and 30 horses. In 1972 the Oakley Hunt moved its kennels to Melchbourne ending 138 years association with Milton Ernest.

23

THE
OLD POST OFFICE

Turn left down the Arkwright Road alleyway and then turn right into Rushden Road. You'll soon come to a 17th century former farm house, now known as 'The Old Post Office'. Records of the farm are scarce, but it is known that William Gibbins was the farmer at the 'Farm House, Kettering Road'. In 1881 he employed a servant, 10 men and 3 boys to cope with the 390 acres of land. It was converted into a village stores known locally as the 'Top Shop'. It later combined with a post office, before closing down in 1975. Milton Ernest Post Office was also situated in both neighbouring properties. *Cross the road at the pedestrian crossing.*

24

SITE OF

BLACKSMITH'S SHOP

Continue along Rushden Road until you get to the bus stop. This used to be the site of the blacksmith's shop. The blacksmith used to make and repair iron items for the villagers. One of the most important roles was to make and fit horseshoes. Milton Ernest Smithy used to have two wells and a water pump in front of the building. A row of red buckets and a metal ladder were kept by the side of the Smithy in case of a fire in the village. The old smithy was bought by the village and used from 1955 for whist drives and dances. This continued until the Village Hall was built.

25

FORGE COTTAGE

The next building on Rushden Road is Forge Cottage which dates back to the eighteenth century. This used to be attached to the smithy and was the home of the village blacksmith. Joseph Paris Covington was Milton Ernest's blacksmith from 1836 to his death in 1866. His widow, Elizabeth, continued until her death 5 years later and then Frederick Gamball took over the role. When he passed away in 1917 Charles Clark became the final blacksmith to work in Milton Ernest. He died in 1946. Underhill Robinson, Bedfordshire's first printer, may have lived here. *Turn left into Thurleigh Road.*

26

MILTON ERNEST LOWER SCHOOL

Across the road is the village school. Milton Ernest Voluntary Controlled Lower School was built in 1872, replacing the school on Village Green. The blue engineering bricks within the structure were provided by railway workers. They were working on widening the railway and used the bricks in exchange for goods in the village. The school was built to accommodate 119 scholars. They were summoned by the ringing of a bell which was housed in the turret on the roof. The School held jumble sales, political meetings, dances and wedding receptions, until the Old Smithy was used for this role instead.

27

MILTON ERNEST VILLAGE HALL

Continue along Thurleigh Road. In 1959 Milton Ernest Village Hall was built from the proceeds of the local gymkhana. It was a long overdue community hall, replacing the School and the Old Smithy, which had in turn been used for village events. Today, Milton Ernest Village Hall is well used by the local community. Mothers & Toddlers Group, Milton Ernest Lower School, Brownies, Milton Ernest Youth Club, Milton Ernest Women's Institute and a Whist Drive all use the Village Hall which goes to show that people of all ages benefit from the facility. As the name suggests it truly is a village hall for the villagers.

28

THURLEIGH ROAD COTTAGES

1-3, Thurleigh Road date back to the 17th century and were originally a row of four cottages. The first was the original Milton Ernest Post Office, ran by William Solsbury in 1847. By 1876 William Mole was Post Master and also ran a tailor business. The Post Office was to remain in the Mole family until 1920 when it moved to Rushden Road. A telegraph office was opened in 1889 which would 'prove a boon for places around'. When the floors of the cottages were replaced it was found that they were made from face down tombstones! It is also reputed that the cottages were built on a plague pit.

29

GREEN FARM

Turn left into Marsh Lane. Walk to the entrance to Starey Close and from here you can see what was Green Farm. This old farmhouse dates back to the 17th century. It was named Balls Farm in Victorian times after the occupiers James and Thomas Ball. More recently it has been known as Tamar Court and then Lindham Court. The derivation of the name Green Farm is unknown. On either side of the old farmhouse are two homes converted from farm buildings. A wind up air raid siren was situated at Green Farm during World War II to warn of any bombing raids. *You now have a choice of route.*

30

STONE COTTAGE

If you're in a position to walk across grassland, turn left and continue along Marsh Lane. You'll come to a public footpath on the right which leads to Stone Cottage. Otherwise, turn right, retrace your steps to Thurleigh Road and follow the map. Either way you'll eventually be able to see Stone Cottage which has a gable end stone inscription of 'RTM 1669'. This depicts that it was built a year before Village Farm and by the same stonemasons. This area of the village is known as Flewton End, which translates roughly as some houses near a stream on the edge of the village. Medieval Milton Ernest used to extend 500 metres up the hill. *Leave Flewton End via the track.*

31

THE OLD VICARAGE

On the left at the end of the track, just before Thurleigh Road, is a large house known as Woodlands. Built in 1694, probably using Edmund Turnor's money, this used to be the vicarage. Records of the Milton Ernest Rectory actually date back to 1291, but whether it was on the same site is likely, but unproven. In the 16th century Queen Elizabeth I granted Milton Ernest Rectory to John Cotton. In 1836 the Vicarage was extended and during Victorian times the vicar employed four servants. By the late 20th century it was called 'Woodlands' and was a craft centre before tennis and languages were taught here.

EAST MANOR FARM

Turn left, walk a short distance, cross the road and you're at the entrance to what was East Manor Farm *but is now called* The Manor House. This was the site of the Manor of Middeltone. Ivo was listed as tenant in the Domesday Book. Between 1221 and 1558, the Erneys family, from which the village name is derived, lived in a house on this site. East Manor Farm dates back to the 17th century and was probably built by the Turnor family who acquired the manor through marriage. In the mid 19th century East Manor Farm had 600 acres and employed 25 men, 12 boys and 2 servants.

33 (a)

ALL SAINTS' CHURCH

Walk a short distance back towards the village and turn left into the churchyard. All Saints' Church, previously known as Allhallows, dates back to the 11th century. Previously a wooden church stood on this site. It is said that the stone church was being built up the hill but the stones kept being dumped on the present site. Seeing this as a sign of the devil, the church was built where directed! William Butterfield restored the church between 1858 and 1865. The clock dates back to 1882. The 13th century, 23 metres (75 feet) high, tower has 6 bells, 3 of which are inscribed 'Newcombe Leicester made me 1611'.

33 (b)

INTERIOR OF ALL SAINTS' CHURCH

Step inside the church and follow the route via the letters of the alphabet on the church plan. [A] blocked entrance to former upper storey quarters of the incumbent. [B] 15th century font. [C] 1675 tablet to Christopher Turnor of East Manor Farm. [D] 1866 stained glass window memorial to Lucy Starey of Milton Ernest Hall. [E] 1615 tablet probably to an Oakley Gent named Bartewe. [F] List of the vicars of All Saints' Church from 1215 to the present day. [G] Brass chandelier gifted by Thomas Rolt of Milton Ernest Hall in 1729. [H] 1717 tablet to Samuel Rolt of Milton Ernest Hall, MP for Bedford.

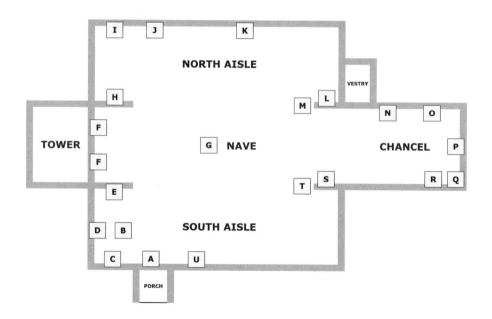

[I] 1726 memorial to Susanna Rolt, wife of Samuel. [J] dole board (bread cupboard) bequeathed by Susanna Rolt in her will to provide "...little loaves to 12 poor persons every Sunday for ever...". [K] worn marble grave slab circa 1340. [L] 1738 wall tablet dedicated to the vicar, Stephen Rolt. [M] Victorian pulpit. [N] stained glass window dedicated to the choir. [O] St Matthew and St Mark window provided by the children of the vicar, Charles Colyear Beaty-Pownall. [P] 'Peace on Earth' stained glass, designed by William Butterfield, in honour of the aforementioned vicar and his wife, Catherine. [Q] 14th century piscina recess used for the washing of the communion vessels. [R] St. Luke and St. John window, provided by George Hurst, a Gent from Bedford. [S] 1902 wall memorial to Alfred and Madeline Chapman of Milton Ernest Hall. [T] Victorian lectern. [U] Milton Ernest Roll of Honour, which lists all those involved in WWI. *Exit All Saints' via the porch door.*

WAR MEMORIAL

Straight in front of you is the war memorial. Please spare a thought for the 13 men of Milton Ernest who lost their lives in the line of duty. WWI: John (shown as Joseph) Farrar (27, Aubers Ridge, 1915); Harry Taylor (28, Somme, 1917); Alfred Bonham (19, Arras, 1917); Edmund Heritage (details unknown); Thomas Horne (25, Somme, 1918); William Jacquest (19, Sheffield Military Hospital, 1917); John Purser (38, Heuvelland, 1917); Cyril Solesbury (30, Berlin, 1918); Frank Solesbury (27, Calais, 1917); James Bailey (details unknown). WWII: John Michael Bryan (22, Calvados, 1944); Christopher Jack Haycock (19, plane crash in Scotland, 1943); John Hunt (24, 1940).

35

EAST MANOR FARM OUTBUILDINGS

As you walk down the churchyard path you'll pass through the graveyard which includes the graves of William Butterfield (1866, father of William Butterfield, the Victorian architect) and Underhill Robinson (1719, Bedfordshire's first printer). Look to the left and you'll see two old stone private dwellings. These were a threshing barn, a stable block and a thatched barn belonging to East Manor Farm. In 1979 they were converted into homes. Exit through the lychgate, which derives its name from the Anglo-Saxon name lich, which means corpse. This is because a lychgate is the roofed gateway to the churchyard through which the coffin is carried.

36

SITE OF

VILLAGE POUND

Immediately ahead of you is the Village Green. The area to the right, in front of the churchyard, used to be the village pound. It was used to hold stray animals and a fine had to be paid to retrieve them. How long the pound was sited here is unknown but it is shown on a map dated 1884. Also, a document dated 1741, states "Indictment of Thomas Serjeant for rescuing certain sheep found doing damage in a field called Lynch Furlong, ... in the occupation of John Sturges and which were being driven to the pound".

37

VILLAGE GREEN

Turn left and walk along Church Green. On your right hand side is the Village Green. There is no evidence of any houses between the Thurleigh Road Cottages and the Almshouses, so it can be assumed that this open space has been here since at least the 17th century. This land belonged to East Manor Farm before being bought by the Starey family and gifted to the village. In 1963 the Village Green was conveyed to Milton Ernest Parish Council. Village Green is the site of the annual Milton Ernest Village Fete and is used primarily by the Lower School. Their Sports Day is held here each year.

38

SITE OF
TURNOR'S ALMSHOUSES

Continue along Church Green. On your left are the Almshouses. These were erected in 1965 by Bedford Rural District Council. They are replacements for the original red brick almshouses which were built in 1695 and funded by Sir Edmund Turnor of East Manor Farm. Turnor felt impelled to help the less fortunate people of Milton Ernest and provided the 6 almshouses with 31 acres of land as a refuge for the aged of the village. During WWII two air raid shelters were dug into the Village Green at this spot. The almshouses were known as 'Scotland Yard' as you couldn't do anything without the inhabitants watching!

39

THE OLD SCHOOL

Next door to the almshouses is the Old School. An 1846 inquiry found that Milton Ernest only had a Sunday School and a daily school was badly needed. Five years later the Reverend Beaty-Pownall gifted a National School to Milton Ernest. On 2nd January 1851 there was a procession and festival, attended by 140 people, to celebrate the opening of the school. The new master was Mr D. Hanlon from Westminster Training School. There were 45 pupils in 1854. After the Lower School opened this Dame School (elementary education at 3d per week) was converted into a cottage.

40

THE MALTINGS

Turn left at the end of Church Green and walk along Bedford Road until you come to Fairbrother's who sell office furniture. This old brewery building is a 19th century red brick malthouse on stone footings. The Gibbins family were brewers in the village from 1839 and it's likely that they were based here. What is definite is that Henry Staff ran the Steam Brewery from these premises between 1881 and at least 1900. During WWII the building was used as a factory where many of the village women worked. Later a sewing business was based here with 100 sewing machines on the top floor.

41

STABLE COTTAGE

Carefully cross over Bedford Road and continue walking away from Milton Ernest. On your right is the Milton Ernest Hall estate wall. This took 10 years to build in the 1920s/1930s and has Grade II listed status. *Walk through the entrance and bear in mind: 'Permissive Path. The landowner has agreed to allow the public to use this path for the time being. There is no intention to dedicate this path as a right of way'. Follow the road.* On your left are some metal gates which used to be the location of Milton Ernest Garden Centre. *Continue and at the junction look left.* Stable Cottage was built in the 17th Century as a stable block for a previous manor house on the Hall site.

42 (a)

MILTON ERNEST HALL

Milton Ernest Hall is built on the site which was known as the manor of Bassets in the Domesday Book. The Basset family were resident here until 1372. By 1573 Thomas Rolt owned Bassets Manor. It was to stay in his family until circa 1740. One member of the Rolt dynasty, also named Thomas, married the daughter of Dr Thomas Coxe, the physician to Charles II. Their son, Samuel Rolt, was elected MP for Bedford in both 1700 and 1713. By 1841, Philip Booth owned the house. He employed 7 servants. In 1853, Benjamin Helps Starey bought the 590 acre estate for £22,000.

42 (b)

He knocked down the house and had his brother-in-law, the eminent architect, William Butterfield, design and build the gothic Milton Ernest Hall. This was completed by 1858 at a cost of £12,167. However, a series of disasters on the stock market meant that the Starey family had to sell the property in 1872. During WWI, Lord and Lady Ampthill owned the Hall and even had two children of King George V stay with them. Incredibly, in 1919, the Starey family, who had made a new fortune in the Ceylon tea planting business, bought back the Hall. During WWII Milton Ernest Hall was the base of the United States Eighth Air Force Service Command. It is believed that important activities were undertaken here, but their exact nature remains classified. What is known is that Glenn Miller, the famous American bandleader, stayed at Milton Ernest Hall. On 16th July 1944, Miller and his band played a concert in the grounds of the Hall to 1,600 people. The next month Bing Crosby was a guest at the Hall.

42 (c)

The Starey family owned Milton Ernest Hall until 1968 after which it became a hotel and restaurant. In 1984 the property was converted into a 29 bed nursing home. *Now leave the grounds of the Hall via the old entrance to the estate.* Glenn Miller passed through these gates on 15th December 1944 on his way to catch the flight on which he was to disappear. Local legend speaks of a phantom coach driven through these gates by a headless horseman, which turns into Bedford Road. *Now turn left into Bedford Road yourself and follow the path back to the Queen's Head.* You have now completed the Importance of Milton Ernest Heritage Trail. Hopefully you have enjoyed your walk and learnt something about the history of the village at the same time. Why not now go and enjoy a drink in the Queen's Head just as thousands of people from Milton Ernest have done over the last three hundred years! It is interesting to think that many of the characters who have lived throughout time, in the buildings that you have seen today, are more than likely to have spent some time in this very establishment!

The Importan[c]
Heritag[e]

Rushden Road (A6)

Butterfield Court

(21)

Huntsmans Way

(22)

Arkwright Road

(18)

Radwell Road

(17) (16)

Riverside View

(20)

(15)

(14)
(13)

(12)

(23)

(10)

(7)

(9) (8) (6)

London End

River Lane

(19)

River Great Ouse

Track

(11)

(41)

(42)